Presumptive Design

Design Provocations for Innovation

Leo **Frishberg**
Charles **Lambdin**

ELSEVIER

AMSTERDAM • BOSTON • HEIDELBERG • LONDON
NEW YORK • OXFORD • PARIS • SAN DIEGO
SAN FRANCISCO • SINGAPORE • SYDNEY • TOKYO

Morgan Kaufmann is an imprint of Elsevier

MORGAN KAUFMANN

Acquiring Editor: Todd Green
Editorial Project Manager: Lindsay Lawrence
Project Manager: Punithavathy Govindaradjane
Layout and Design: Kimberly Buckley Hill and Leo Frishberg

Morgan Kaufmann is an imprint of Elsevier
225 Wyman Street, Waltham, MA 02451, USA

Notices
Knowledge and best practice in this field are constantly changing. As new research and experience broaden our understanding, changes in research methods, professional practices, or medical treatment may become necessary.

Practitioners and researchers must always rely on their own experience and knowledge in evaluating and using any information, methods, compounds, or experiments described herein. In using such information or methods they should be mindful of their own safety and the safety of others, including parties for whom they have a professional responsibility.

To the fullest extent of the law, neither the Publisher nor the authors, contributors, or editors, assume any liability for any injury and/or damage to persons or property as a matter of products liability, negligence or otherwise, or from any use or operation of any methods, products, instructions, or ideas contained in the material herein.

ISBN: 978-0-12-803086-8

British Library Cataloguing-in-Publication Data
A catalogue record for this book is available from the British Library

Library of Congress Cataloging-in-Publication Data
A catalog record for this book is available from the Library of Congress

For information on all Morgan Kaufmann publications
visit our website at www.mkp.com

Working together
to grow libraries in
developing countries

www.elsevier.com • www.bookaid.org

To my parents, Mort and Sue,
who would have been proud beyond words.

—Leo

To Candace, Tatum, Henry, and Jack.
I love you guys.

—Charles

Table of Contents

Presumptive Design
DESIGN PROVOCATIONS FOR INNOVATION

Table of Contents

Presumptive Design
DESIGN PROVOCATIONS FOR INNOVATION

Presumptive Design
Design Provocations for Innovation

Presumptive Design
DESIGN PROVOCATIONS FOR INNOVATION

Presumptive Design
DESIGN PROVOCATIONS FOR INNOVATION

Table of Contents

Presumptive Design
DESIGN PROVOCATIONS FOR INNOVATION

Table of Contents

xviii

Foreword

What a joyful cornucopia of a book! What a delight to find a fresh and practical approach to involving stakeholders in rethinking the design of "products." The practical usefulness is broad, going beyond products *per se* to an expansive range of designed experiences. It is full of refreshing ideas and real-world examples, rich with images, visuals, and charts, all very helpful in articulating the practicality of the Presumptive Design (PrD) approach. This book offers a much needed balance to the well-documented and oversubscribed traditional usability and user-centered approaches. Historically, user experience design (UXD) professionals have focused on refining details of an artifact instead of considering what the product space *might* be. Frequently, too little is known about the problem space and domain, which can hinder more open-ended meaningful and participatory conversations. In this book, we learn how eliciting such conversations can ultimately lead to better product design solutions.

For example, during years of experience in teaching students, urging them to take a user-centered approach to product design, I'm used to their reluctance to start with rough prototypes. Rather, they push back, suggesting they cannot build artifacts unless they have access to specialized tooling. I asked one student to find something he could use to make a physical artifact. He struggled and eventually said he liked baking bread. So I said he should bake a bread artifact, which he did as his first handheld artifact. What a difference this book would have made (and will make going forward) in helping teach! Now, with PrD in hand, students can increase their understanding of how best and effectively to achieve a successful design; the approach legitimizes being rough, fast, and iterative. Thankfully this book will help focus students' time and attention on a critical part of the product design process: the very early ideation design stages—when they are just starting to grapple with the problem.

Presumptive Design
DESIGN PROVOCATIONS FOR INNOVATION

This book explains clearly how to use open-ended, almost humorous artifacts as key tools to begin conversations with stakeholders. The many examples in this book highlight the ease with which team members can participate in creating such working "tools." More than just a cookbook on rapidly producing rough prototypes, this book offers details on how to help when things go wrong. Our authors offer detailed examples of "engagements gone wrong," suggesting clear ways to change the discourse and improve the outcomes of stakeholder conversations. These insights and examples are realistic and immensely helpful; they effectively let us learn from these two masters.

I could have used this book so many years ago! In 1999 while designing a portable audio device for a music museum, my team "accidentally" designed a feature-rich device. We started to develop the prototype way too late into the product development cycle, believing we understood what was needed based on our (misguided) ideas of who was the typical visitor. We started our process by refining those perceived needs. But as this book clearly states, we should have started our thought process by ideating early and often with very rough notions of what visitors might want from the experience, *and then try those assumptions out with real users*. PrD would have also given us the tools to illustratively support and defend the process of how we got to where we landed, how we derived our solutions, and how our interdisciplinary team pruned our thought processes. Sadly our resulting product suited few visitors, functionally doing way too much! PrD would have been very helpful at defending a much simpler, useful product following a team-based, fast, and defensible process.

PrD requires the designer to take on unusual practices such as failing fast, throwing away ideas, and feeling safe about feeling foolish! It is often hard to "design rough," or to "design for failure," to "actively listen" to receive truly open input about "any" loosely defined artifact. But as these authors successfully defend, it is far better to try "something" out than wait and refine later "draft" product artifacts. This book makes a compelling case that throwing away these artifacts is far less costly than merely refining something already in place—less costly, as long as the designers offer the artifacts directly to end-users and are prepared to throw them away. And, if they are willing to quickly go through many iterations to get closer to what is really needed. The whole approach sounds so much like common sense I'm surprised it has taken so long for it to be legitimized! I wonder why we have not had such a book before; it makes so much sense—really!

On a personal note I know how much more I've learned from my failures as opposed to successes. The authors embrace notions of failure as an alternate way to move designs forward, to view failure as a positive opportunity to experiment and explore new territory. When we are pursuing disruptive innovation, the authors suggest that the fastest way to reduce wasted effort is to rapidly and iteratively fail. "Management is rewarded for efficiency not effectiveness," so they quote. The authors challenge the tenets of industry by their celebration of failure; they triumph lack of success in multiple small ways as the least expensive way to ultimately succeed big. This book shows ways we can legitimize the need for failure to make the resultant designs more effective. This book begins to challenge the *status quo* within our corporations, which is always a valued provocation.

The authors liberally sprinkle memorable phrases and images throughout this book to help readers easily remember the PrD approach. "Roughly right is better than precisely wrong" (from Keynes), "Messy artifacts are ambiguous to encourage engagement," and SMART: specific, measurable, achievable, relevant, and time-bound (from Doran's seminal paper). The photos of real people practicing PrD techniques alongside humorous vintage touches are lovely and enjoyable. This book is carefully crafted and an easy read. I hope it becomes required reading for design and business students; most critically it is a must-read for business and UXD *professionals*. With its quick lists, reminders, easy recipes, and tips, it can be used "just-in-time" as a go-to reference, even as it makes compelling arguments for improving UXD's impact on the bottom line.

This book offers UXD professionals a palette of work products to accelerate return on investment (ROI) when exploring new product territories. By incorporating PrD into their work processes, companies will reduce the risks of innovation. The authors position PrD within agile product/engineering management: Managers and business leaders will learn how best to fit PrD into their current business operations to improve their innovation processes and team productivity.

Thank you for putting the time in to create this fun and excellent resource for us all. I believe this book will have a place in our vocabulary for a long time.

Joy Mountford
Senior Director, Akamai Technologies

Preface

Extraordinary begins with discomfort.
—Sally Hogshead

This book is fundamentally about being wrong.

That isn't what I (Leo) thought this book was going to be about when we set out to write it. What better example could I wish for of how easily we get things wrong?

In fact, everything we know is wrong.

Humor me for a moment and reflect on that sentence. Even after re-reading it hundreds of times, I still feel a twinge of ... anger? Self-righteousness? I hear a little voice saying: "Well that may be true for *you* buddy, but not for *me*." And I wrote the sentence!

According to the research, that's a completely normal reaction; it has its roots so deeply buried in our evolution that there is nothing we can do about it. Every day we operate in the world based on a set of well-worn beliefs, and mostly we are successful, or so it would seem. So, surely my statement that "*everything* we know is wrong" is hyperbole. Or not, if you look at the world through Plato's eyes. In brief, all we know about the world comes in through our senses and is processed by our brains before being committed to memory. The whole system is fraught with potential error. In short, how well can we trust our senses, cognition, and memory?

Still, I'm more interested in the emotion around the reaction to the statement than engaging in a philosophical argument. My point is, when we read the statement "*everything* we know is wrong," we resist agreeing with it. And, now, humor me one more time for a moment: Read the statement again and let yourself accept it as true. It might take a few tries and a couple of deep breaths, but give it a shot.

Presumptive Design
DESIGN PROVOCATIONS FOR INNOVATION

Figure Pr.1 "Maison tournante aérienne" by Albert Robida, a nineteenth-century conception of life in the twentieth century

How does *that* feel? If you're really engaging here, it should feel uncomfortable. Disorienting. Rudderless. (Of course, if the statement were really true, you wouldn't be able to read these sentences because you're wrong about your ability to read along with everything else. But stick with me for a second.)

To summarize: We don't like to think we're wrong, and we feel uncomfortable when we learn we're wrong.

Irrespective of how frequently we think we are wrong (maybe not about everything, but at least once in our lives—and let's hope *you* weren't wrong about picking up this book), the real question for us is, "What are we going to do about it?" Our focus is on applying our errors to our best advantage, use them to positive effect, and ultimately make our teams and organizations successful, not in spite of our errors, but because of them.

Let's restate the hyperbole: Everything you know *about the future* is wrong. That feels a little easier to admit, right? This book is written for people who are "inventing" the future: building products, services, companies, strategies, policies, or whatever, in service of a future state.

Presumptive Design (PrD) begins with the following operating assumptions:

- We are wrong (at least about the future).

- We are in denial of being wrong (except perhaps about the future).

- We generally don't like learning that we are wrong. (Where are those flying cars, or aerial houses (Figure Pr.1)?)

After reading this book, you will see how PrD eliminates the third assumption. (You'll look forward to learning from your errors and experience the surprise and joy of your discoveries.) The process helps you accept the second assumption. (Face it, we can't eliminate our denial—it really is baked into our brains—but we can at least recognize our denial.) And with respect to the first assumption, it's irrelevant. PrD works whether you believe you are wrong (about the future) or not. The process asks only one small thing of you: that you at least *pretend to believe you are wrong* (about the future).

Why We're Excited About Presumptive Design

Let's just put it out there: PrD is the fastest way to converge on a future state your stakeholders really "want." The approach isn't all that novel, and it's not really all that different from a bunch of other techniques user experience researchers and designers already use. Parts of it have been around for well over 30 years while other parts have been around for thousands.

As you'll learn, we're not positioning PrD as the magic solution to every problem. It has its place in the toolbox of research techniques. *It is a research technique*, in spite of its name. It is peculiar because it leads with design and with the crafting of artifacts. It depends on individuals who have mastered facilitation with a modest talent in improvisation. It requires designers as well as other disciplines in your organization.

Although it is easy to describe (in spite of the length of this book, the steps are fairly simple), PrD isn't necessarily easy to apply. It is filled with risks (one of the reasons this book is so long) and is just as likely to generate garbage results as any other research technique if it isn't applied with care.

With all that said, PrD's many proven advantages over other research methods (in the contexts of innovation, agile software development, and business strategy, to name a few) far outstrip the risks and challenges of the process.

Who Is This Book For?

In the early decades of the twenty-first century, businesses are recognizing the competitive advantage of designing user and customer experiences. This book has a distinctly business tone to it: The business value of PrD will be discussed throughout, because it is fundamentally about improving time to market and customer satisfaction and reducing risk. With that said, we offer case studies and stories of applying PrD in a variety of contexts, not just business.

Specifically, with its relationship to Participatory Design, PrD is an equally effective tool for social innovation, for at-risk populations and situations in which you design *with*, not for. Its primary audience is the practitioner "on the ground" trying to build better experiences for her organizations' stakeholders. Properly designed experiences drive better business, so at its heart, this book is written to help practitioners improve the competitive value of experiences they are designing and building. And by "practitioner" we mean any member of the team: business leader, manager, analyst, engineer, designer, and researcher.

If you are a business leader who is trying to position your company for top-line growth, this book offers insights into expanding your current market research efforts. As you'll see in Chapter 3, PrD is about improving *the competitiveness* of the end-user experiences you are bringing to market, specifically by identifying market whitespaces where users are currently underserved. To get a deeper understanding of how to apply PrD, you'll likely want to read Chapters 1–3, as well as skimming Chapters 4–13.

Similarly, if you are team, program, project, or product manager, trying to increase your share of market through relevant features and rapid adoption, PrD is an effective risk reduction tool. It raises confidence in your offering at the very start of the program. Further, if you are trying to maximize the productivity of your staff and/or reduce the cost of development, you will see how PrD reduces development risk by removing waste, increasing opportunities for alignment, and establishing a shared vision. For you, Chapters 1–13 will be paramount. You will also benefit from skimming Chapters 14–16 so that you have a deeper understanding of the skills required of your team.

If you are a designer, interested in expanding your research insights with users, the entire book will be of immediate use to you. And, of course, we expect researchers of all stripes will benefit from reading the entire book.

Most of PrD's principles will be very familiar to designers, because it is based on the way designers approach problem solving. With that said, if you are an experienced designer, aspects of PrD may be challenging to you. PrD uses principles from Participatory Design and rapid prototyping, but it isn't either. If you are a user experience researcher, market researcher, or social scientist, many of PrD's principles will be familiar to you because it identifies underlying needs. It is both a "generative" research tool (in which informants cocreate ideas with you) and an evaluative research tool (e.g., usability testing). The approach requires subtle facilitation with quick wits and a design partner working with you. PrD is a powerful way to tie research results into actionable designs in a matter of minutes and hours, rather than weeks, months, or not at all.

One final note of caution to designers: If you are an experienced designer, you will both recognize pieces of the process and possibly be flummoxed by them. Over the past several years we have introduced designers of all stripes and background to the process, thinking they would immediately understand it. What we've found is that designers, even those familiar with Participatory Design, have been challenged to use it appropriately. Pay special attention to Chapter 2 and all of Part 3 in which we highlight key differences between PrD and typical design activities.

How to Use This Book

This book is split into three main parts: context, principles/risks, and a how-to manual with recipes. As mentioned above, based on who you are, you may wish to skip directly to the chapters in the part that best addresses your interests.

Part 1: Context (the Why)

While we would hope everyone reads the three chapters in this part, business leaders and managers unfamiliar with design research and design thinking may find this the most useful material in this book. Further, because software has radically changed the way business is being conducted, in Chapter 3 we shine a light on using PrD in your strategy toolkit.

Part 2: Principles and Risks (the What)

The 10 chapters in this section describe the 5 principles of PrD and its hazards. We expect managers will want to skim these chapters (at a minimum) to get a lay of the land and understand the process and its risks. Practitioners (researchers, designers, engineers, and project managers) will want to read these chapters in detail as they provide the bulk of how PrD differs from other forms of research and user-centered design.

Part 3: How-To Manual and Recipes (the How)

We offer detailed prescriptions for executing PrD in your organization in the three chapters of this part. For practitioners already well versed in other techniques of user-centered design, we invite you to skip straight to these chapters to get details about how to field this process. With that said, much of what we discuss in these chapters relies on information we've provided earlier in this book, so you may need to skip around to get clarifications on vocabulary and concepts.

Appendices

This book wouldn't be possible without the contributions of practitioners who have successfully used PrD in a wide variety of contexts. Throughout this book we refer to lessons learned from the cases as they relate to specific topics. You may wish to read those cases (in Appendix A) in their entirety *before* reading this book, as they offer overviews of PrD in the context of real-world problems. We provide additional supporting material in the appendices we believe is useful but geekier than was appropriate in the main body of this book.

On a Personal Note

I (Leo) coined the term "Presumptive Design" in 2004 for the CHI2004|ICSID mini-conference. I chose the name as more palatable than other candidates, including "the Barf method of design" or "ruminative design," both of which were too colorful or earthy. But that event was just the moment of naming the process. My initial attempt at documenting the idea was in 1979, when I authored a paper (unpublished) I had titled *The Barf Method of Design*.

That was when I started writing about it, but the story goes back just a little further, to 1975, in my first year of undergraduate architecture school. I was facing a personal crisis: I was failing my design studio class. Sometime after I'd been called into the professors' office to reflect on my past semester's failings, and my return to school after winter break, I'd had an epiphany: To be successful in design, I had to make a *decision*.

It's not that I hadn't made decisions before, but the types of decisions I was being asked to make fell into a completely different class from the sorts of decisions I was used to. These types of decisions had to be made based on limited information, limited experience, and an enormous amount of risk. Risk, for this first-year college student, meant making the *wrong* decision. Unbeknownst to me, I had tripped over what David Snowden has called the Cynefin framework.

I realized no matter what I did I would be wrong in some way, so delaying action would not prevent error. I would be better off getting the idea into the open and letting others reflect on it, than to hold on to it. It required I take a stand and a position.

I had discovered "design thinking" in its purest form (a topic we'll cover in greater depth).

Roll the clock forward several years and I'm working with electronic engineers in high-tech manufacturing environments. One of the characteristics of these environments is how quickly teams converge on a specific solution. Engineering is about constraints; design is about possibilities. Enlisting engineers to relax constraints, to imagine wild and crazy possibilities, and to not jump to the first solution is challenging.

Enter PrD.

Rather than fight my engineering partners, I welcomed them to offer their solution. In many cases team members already "knew" the answer (they'd been thinking about it for years), but they had a much harder time telling me what the problem was! It's so much easier to let my partners presumptuously offer their solution than question their good judgment. It's so much easier to have users provide unequivocally devastating feedback on a proposal than to prevent it from being expressed.

My approach to "getting the idea out there as quickly as possible" dovetailed beautifully with the desires of my coworkers. With a twist: I presumed we were wrong and relished the opportunity to discover by how much and in what ways.

The more I've used the process, the more I've realized how few people are familiar with it. Over the past several years I've made it a standard practice in my design studios. As a result Charles and I concluded it was time to share it more broadly and with greater precision and discipline.

Acknowledgments

By all accounts, this book came together in record time. That was possible only by the heroic efforts of our contributors, reviewers, friends, and family.

A huge shout out to Todd Green, our publisher at Morgan Kaufmann, for his tenacity and perseverance in getting our proposal the air time it needed. This book doesn't fit into neat categories and we credit Todd's possibility thinking in finding a place for it in MK's catalog.

To Nancy Frishberg, for her ongoing backboarding, immense optimism, and unparalleled social networks. Nancy has both witnessed the emergence of PrD from its very beginnings as well as nurtured many of the ideas we formalize in this book.

To our contributors of the case studies: Steve Sato, Steve Portigal, Evan Hanover, Anne Schorr, Janna Kimmel, David McKenzie, Chris Stapleton, Alisa Weinstein, Maggee Bond, Diego Bernardo, Amanda Geppert, Helen Wills, Janice Wong and Jaime Rivera. The time spent with us capturing their use of PrD and the subsequent reviews of our interpretation has been invaluable. These contributors have added color, dimension, and depth to what might have been just another dreary process book.

To our reviewers, Steve Sato and Tim Piwonka-Corle; your willingness to dive in when our concepts were still primordial showed great courage. That our sentences were incomprehensible couldn't have made your jobs any easier. We want to acknowledge several other individuals who offered us important feedback and willingly volunteered to read this book in advance: Lynn Boyden, Steve Portigal, Dave Gray, Leah Buley and Jim Kalbach. In particular we want to recognize Joy Mountford for her enthusiastic support and her gracious contributions. Joy was the keynote speaker at Nancy and Leo's 2004 conference in which PrD made its first public appearance.

Presumptive Design
DESIGN PROVOCATIONS FOR INNOVATION

Acknowledgments

To the production staff at MK, specifically Punithavathy "Punitha" Govindaradjane and Lindsay Lawrence, working with a group of professionals made our job so much easier. Your patience with two newbies to the publishing business was much appreciated.

This book's graphic treatments were curated and influenced by our esteemed associate, Kimberly Buckley Hill, an artist, designer, and enormously talented professional we are honored to call our friend.

Last, and certainly not least, thank you to our families who at minimum tolerated our absence from movie nights, chores, and the acts of daily living. From Leo: Sue, I love you. Your support for my obsession is a true definition of love. To Ariella and Melina—I love you both. Hopefully it won't take years before you crack this thing open. And lastly to brother Michael—you helped introduce me to customer-focused research over 20 years ago. With your enthusiastic embrace of Haiku poetry, I hope you will appreciate this one:

> *Vision the future*
> *imagining you are wrong*
> *Presumptive Design*

From Charles: Candace, I love you! Tatum, Henry and Jack, I love you! You guys are my world.

Naturally, none of these people are responsible for the errors, misstatements, wild assertions, and indefensible positions we promote in the pages that follow. All such egregious violations are ours and ours alone. We let this book go fearlessly into the world, knowing we are wrong.

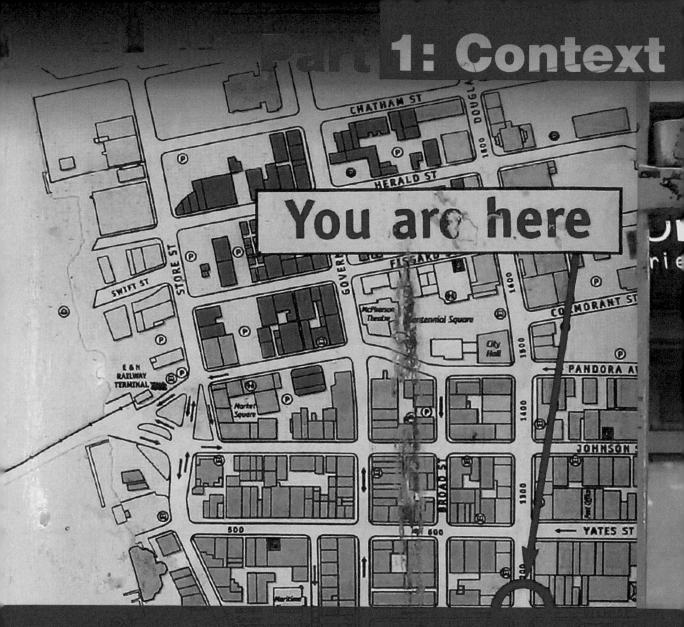

The three chapters in this part address *why* you should consider using PrD as a part of your practice, whether as a part of business strategy, innovation pipeline management or in service of product and service development.

We begin in Chapter 1 positioning PrD within the broader context of design research as well as offering a quick flyover of PrD's five principles.

In Chapter 2 we introduce the design thinking model underpinning PrD. We differentiate PrD from more traditional forms of user-centered design approaches.

In Chapter 3 we argue business strategy, innovation management and product development have been irrevocably changed by notions of *agility*. We illustrate PrD's advantages to reduce risk within these contexts.

Chapter 1: Introducing Presumptive Design

Presumptive Design
DESIGN PROVOCATIONS FOR INNOVATION

The future does not just happen. Except for natural events like earthquakes, it comes about through the efforts of people ....
—Jacque Fresco

Overview

PrD is a *design research* technique. Organizations, large and small, use PrD to quickly identify their target audiences' needs and goals. It is fast. It is cheap. And it is definitely good enough. If you are looking for ways to rapidly and inexpensively reduce risk to your project, PrD is the best technique we've found in our 30 years of experience.

PrD differs from (and is complementary to) traditional market research methods. It provides intimate insights into the desires of end-users (for products and services), communities (for social innovation), and internal stakeholders (for strategy). The method reduces risk to our projects by capturing our target audience's reactions to a future we have envisioned. As we describe in detail throughout the book, the devil is in the details: How we envision that future and how we capture those reactions is what sets PrD apart from other research methods.

Consider a typical example from industry: A firm has technology with competitive advantage (it's faster, more robust, smaller or requires less power than the competition). In traditional market research, the research team identifies target audiences, crafts a quantitative instrument (a survey, typically), and performs a conjoin or other multifactor analysis. The team discovers the technology's competitive advantage to address current customers' needs as well as those in adjacent markets. This is absolutely necessary when placing big bets—necessary, but insufficient.

Quantitative research takes time and money; to do a conjoin correctly takes months and many tens of thousands of dollars. In contrast, PrD takes a week or two with the cost of a few days of travel. The insights gleaned from these rapid, inexpensive sessions are fundamentally different from the results of a quantitative approach, but they are no less valuable in reducing the risk of the venture. PrD's qualitative results inform the design of a quantitative instrument, and vice versa. Although both can be done at the same time, we've found greater advantage in using one to inform the other. PrD costs less to execute than a quantitative instrument; its results are much broader.

Here's how a typical PrD approach would play out: We invite key *internal* stakeholders (product marketing, technology leads or architects, sales leads, UX design, and the key organization leader) to a "Creation Session" (a "visioning" workshop). The outcome of the Creation Session is an "artifact" encapsulating the team's presumptions about the new venture. The artifact is something an *external* stakeholder (a user or customer external to the team) will interact with. Depending on the size of the venture, the Creation Session could take a few hours, or perhaps as long as a few days. Subsequently, a small research team goes on the road with the artifact and works with external stakeholders in "Engagement Sessions."

During these sessions, stakeholders are tasked with using the artifact to accomplish a goal. Each session may take as little as 30 minutes, and there only needs to be a few of them (again, depending on the size of the venture). Within a couple of weeks, the team will have captured hundreds of data points, reactions, and, most important, clear indications of how the internal team's assumptions resonate with external stakeholders' needs (Figure 1.1).

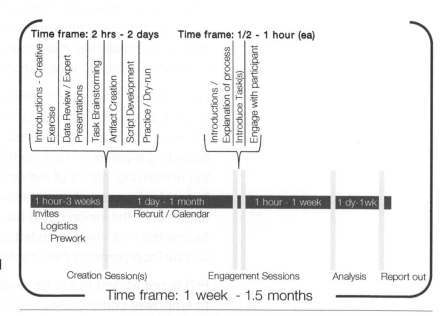

Figure 1.1 A typical Presumptive Design timeline

PrD isn't limited to a product or service. When we use the word "project," we mean any endeavor with material impact or risk. PrD is an inexpensive and easy tool to inform a strategy. It is a powerful means of identifying disruptive innovation. Disruptive innovation, by definition, is high risk: Discovering latent customer needs may expose an organization to gaps it can't bridge. For companies facing emerging competitors, PrD illuminates threats early letting teams address these gaps strategically.

This Book's Value Proposition

PrD will be familiar to any designer because it involves the creation of artifacts for the purpose of engaging with stakeholders. It will be familiar to any UX researcher because it involves understanding end-user needs through a form of interviewing. With that said, PrD shifts traditional ways of working in ways that may be disorienting to both designers and researchers.

For product managers and market researchers, PrD provides a rapid, qualitative-based research method. It supplements large-scale aggregate statistical investigations. PrD is an inexpensive way to explore the customer/user landscape, identifying "white spaces" that would otherwise be hidden or unavailable through quantitative methods. It is a customer-centric approach relying on small numbers to reveal important data.

For business leaders, PrD enables frank and open discussion about pain points in the organization. When rolling out a new strategy, changing the organization's culture, or providing a vision for moving forward, PrD rapidly identifies the underlying values of the group. PrD, because it is a "codesign" approach, establishes a two-way conversation about what the vision could be. It engages constituents *before* the final vision is rolled out, starting their investment in it by incorporating their contributions as a part of it.

PrD is not limited to the for-profit world. It is an easy tool to empower communities seeking to improve services, representation, access, and civic engagement. In the world of social innovation, in which communities make their voices heard, PrD rapidly uncovers issues that matter to community stakeholders.

Although one of us (Leo) discovered the process independently, PrD has been around for many years, in a variety of contexts and with a variety of names: Suzanne Howard of IDEO calls it "Sacrificial Concepts,"[1] Koskinen et al.[2] call it "Constructive Design Research," and Anijo Matthews of the Institute of Design at the Illinois Institute of Technology (ID-IIT) calls it "provotyping" (short for "provocative prototypes"). In spite of it being used by design firms, academics, and applied researchers for over 30 years, we could find no book providing a step-by-step way of doing it. As we dug into the process and teased out its steps, we engaged with other practitioners who had used it. Throughout the book, their stories and case studies help illustrate PrD's breadth and effectiveness.

A Twist to the Familiar

PrD relies on an approach to problem solving peculiar to the ways in which designers approach their work. The "design thinking" model we use throughout the book is based on a long-standing framework originating from Chuck Owen at the ID-IIT.[3] We go into details of this problem-solving approach in Chapter 2 because design thinking is fundamental to PrD execution and success.

Agile Culture

Because it fits within the context of design thinking, PrD is part of a larger set of tools and techniques emerging in the early twenty-first century. Titles such as *The Lean Startup*, *Lean UX*, and *Business Model Generation* are indications of how the discipline of design is moving from the studio to the factory floor and ultimately to the boardroom. Inspired by Tim Brown's seminal article in *Harvard Business Review*[4] (and by the introduction of revolutionary devices by Apple) organizations of all stripes recognize the need for design, designers, and design thinking. PrD and design thinking are inseparable. Design thinking is fundamental to the method's success.

PrD also aligns with shifts in business thinking and approaches to leadership. Business leaders are being bombarded with messaging about changing the culture, changing thought processes and behaviors. Robert Schaffer's article on "basic behavior traps" managers often fall in is an example.

> To escape the [behavior] traps, managers have to do battle with their own resistance, as they would in trying to change any well-entrenched habit. Each person needs to experience viscerally the dramatic improvement that is possible, which is why individuals should start with their own modest, low-risk experiments.[5]

The attraction and benefit of PrD is its immediacy—an antidote to what Schaffer identifies as the fourth of four behavior traps: waiting.[6] With PrD there is no reason to wait.

Another benefit of PrD is its inherent *agility*. Agile (originally a means of delivering software solutions) is spreading into the boardroom. Its low investment, along with its speed, positions PrD as a research technique well suited to agile cultures—whether in the product development context or in the boardroom.

In their *Harvard Business Review* article, business consultants Marin Reeves and Mike Deimler list four tenets of contemporary strategy: reading and acting on signals, experimentation, managing complex systems, and enabling people to act,[7] in brief, *rapid adaptation*. If the context wasn't managing large corporations, the article might as well have been discussing the culture of agile software development.

Participatory

Building consensus through a process of *inquiry*, as opposed to top-down *advocacy*, has become a standard part of business leadership.[8] This inversion of attitude is fundamental to PrD, leading to PrD's *political* implications. This inversion also forms the basis of Participatory Design, of which PrD is a part. Participatory Design is an approach to designing *with* constituents as opposed to designing *for* them. In brief, Participatory Design sprang from populist resurgences in the 1960s to provide a voice to labor and to reestablish its influence on the design of national policy. In a similar way, agile software development mirrors that populist ethic. Engaging with your targeted population, in fact, having *you* as the target of *them*, is a key transposition of roles and orientation. This mind shift is an essential part of PrD, as you'll read throughout this book.

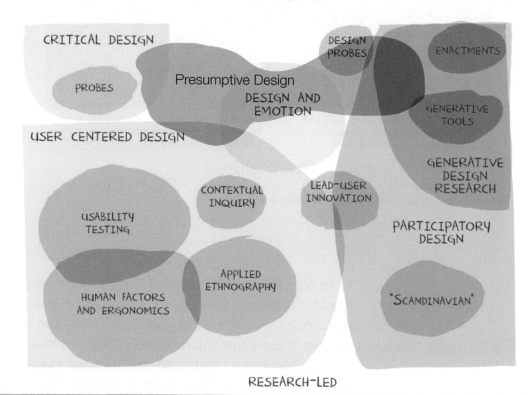

DESIGN-LED

CRITICAL DESIGN

DESIGN PROBES

ENACTMENTS

PROBES

Presumptive Design
DESIGN AND EMOTION

GENERATIVE TOOLS

USER CENTERED DESIGN

GENERATIVE DESIGN RESEARCH

CONTEXTUAL INQUIRY

LEAD-USER INNOVATION

USABILITY TESTING

PARTICIPATORY DESIGN

APPLIED ETHNOGRAPHY

HUMAN FACTORS AND ERGONOMICS

"SCANDINAVIAN"

RESEARCH-LED

EXPERT MINDSET "USERS SEEN AS SUBJECTS (REACTIVE INFORMERS)

PARTICIPATORY MINDSET "USERS" SEEN AS PARTNERS (ACTIVE CO-CREATORS)

Figure 1.2 The emerging landscape of design research approaches

In Liz Sanders and Pieter Jan Stappers' map of research approaches,[9] PrD is bimodal: It has one foot in Critical Design[10] (in which objects are used to provoke reactions to stakeholders) and the other in a generative tool (in which constituents design *with* researchers) (Figure 1.2).

Presumptive Design
Design Provocations for Innovation

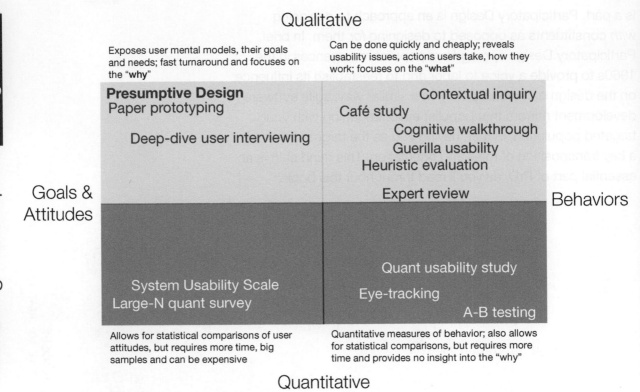

Qualitative

Exposes user mental models, their goals and needs; fast turnaround and focuses on the "**why**"

Can be done quickly and cheaply; reveals usability issues, actions users take, how they work; focuses on the "**what**"

Presumptive Design
Paper prototyping

Contextual inquiry
Café study
Cognitive walkthrough
Guerilla usability
Heuristic evaluation

Deep-dive user interviewing

Expert review

Goals & Attitudes

Behaviors

System Usability Scale
Large-N quant survey

Quant usability study
Eye-tracking
A-B testing

Allows for statistical comparisons of user attitudes, but requires more time, big samples and can be expensive

Quantitative measures of behavior; also allows for statistical comparisons, but requires more time and provides no insight into the "why"

Quantitative

Figure 1.3 A map of research approaches adapted from Konno and Fong

In an adaptation of Konno and Fong's map[11] (shown in Figure 1.3) we position PrD as a qualitative research technique focusing on the goals, attitudes, and mental models of user/customers/stakeholders. To minimize risk to our projects we must learn which of our ideas resonate with these constituents and which don't. More important, we need to know *why* those ideas fail.

Looking through the lens of "user intimacy" and time, PrD is quick and intimate as illustrated in the constellation map given in Figure 1.4.

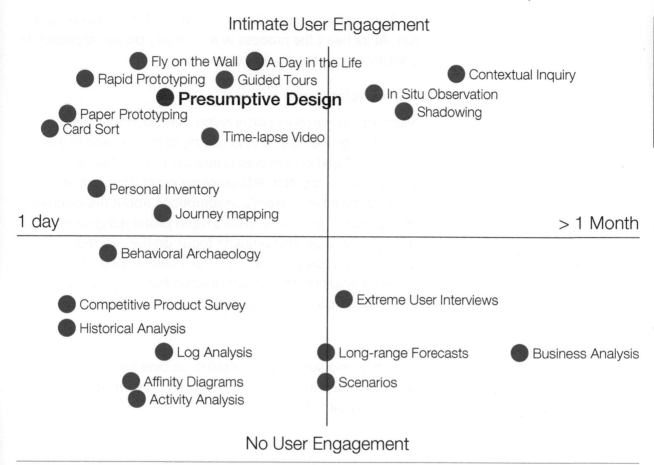

Intimate User Engagement

Fly on the Wall   A Day in the Life   Contextual Inquiry
Rapid Prototyping   Guided Tours
Presumptive Design   In Situ Observation
Paper Prototyping   Shadowing
Card Sort
Time-lapse Video

Personal Inventory

Journey mapping

1 day   > 1 Month

Behavioral Archaeology

Competitive Product Survey   Extreme User Interviews

Historical Analysis

Log Analysis   Long-range Forecasts   Business Analysis

Affinity Diagrams   Scenarios
Activity Analysis

No User Engagement

Figure 1.4 Constellation map of user research approaches

A High-Wire Act

In the hands of masters, PrD is a fluid, exciting, and
extraordinarily fast method to identify stakeholders' needs.
But, as with any high-wire act, it requires practice to master.
Understanding customer and user needs is challenging.
Doing it quickly requires nuance, subtlety, and quick wits.
With that said, the skills to do PrD effectively are easy to
learn and are likely in your team just waiting to be released.

And, as with any masterful performance, PrD is immensely fun. At its heart the process is a seriously playful approach to capturing your stakeholders' needs.

Rapid Prototyping

Much of the preceding discussion may sound familiar, especially to individuals who use rapid prototyping in their practice. Rapid prototyping is integral to PrD, but, once again, there is a catch. PrD employs rapid prototyping to capture the internal team's assumptions about the external stakeholders' problems. Where rapid prototyping refines a design *solution*, PrD artifacts focus on the external stakeholders' *problem* space. PrD artifacts are designed to be disposable: The artifact is important only insofar as it drives good conversations and illuminates insights.

The Five Principles of Presumptive Design

The following subsections provide an overview of PrD's fundamental principles. Each is covered in depth in the chapters that follow.

Design to Fail

Consider the following scenario: You are about to engage with a group of people who don't know you very well, who may harbor reservations about doing business with your organization or aren't completely bought into your mission. Even if they are not outright hostile, they may not be forthcoming about their needs, concerns, or fears. (In fact, they may not be able to articulate these things.) People rarely have accurate insights into their own needs, let alone their constituents' needs, and so, if you simply ask them, their answers are likely to mislead.[12,13] At the same time, you know a change must be made—whether it's to the operations of the group, the strategy for the company, or a new product or service. It may be as basic as getting access to fresh water. You can't afford to be wrong; you rarely get a second chance.

This first principle of PrD gives us permission to be wrong. In fact, it outright requires us to *assume* we are wrong and assumes we will fail. Consider that shift: If we *know* we are wrong and we *know* our audience will chop to pieces whatever we're about to offer them, how might we feel going into the engagement?

Foolish.

And that is exactly the frame of mind PrD requires. We must accept as *fact* any proposal, whether it's a new vision or new product, is always *wrong*, even after it is fielded. Brooks wrote in 1975, "The management question, therefore, is not *whether* to build a pilot system and throw it away. You will do that. [...] Hence *plan to throw one away; you will, anyhow.*"[14] Let's face this fact: Nothing we do is ever perfect; we simply need to be "right enough." Our goal is to raise our confidence we've crafted an experience crossing a threshold of "fitness." PrD *requires* us to engage with our constituents so they will chop our offering to pieces as early as possible. In engaging our constituents in the process of *critique*, we engender intimacy and buy-in, not only with the end result but with the process itself, and this in turn helps improve the likelihood of the effort's success.

As we describe in the detailed chapters, keeping Design to Fail in mind at all times is one of the key benefits and differentiators of PrD.

Create

Create, Discover, Analyze

PrD, being a *design* research activity, rooted in theories of design thinking, starts with the creation of artifacts. It is distinctly different from other forms of research in which we spend time researching our audience before offering them artifacts, presumably designed based on those discoveries.

Discover

PrD proceeds by offering artifacts as provocations, purely in service of making discoveries. Because we know the artifacts we've created are wrong, we are assured our audience will have something to say about their fitness to their worldview, values, and latent needs.

PrD relies on the design process of critique, but it uses critique very differently from traditional design:

- Whereas design critiques are focused on the offering itself, PrD critiques focus on the assumptions behind the offering.

- The objective of design critique is to improve the design; PrD critiques are to improve the internal stakeholders' (your team's) understanding of the external stakeholders' (customers'/users') problem space.

- Design critiques are performed by other designers (in design reviews); PrD critiques are performed by external stakeholders (the users/constituents not on your team).

To be clear, design critiques are not the same as design *presentations*. Presentations are a form of sales and knowledge *sharing*, from the team to the audience. Design presentations gather feedback from the audience around the desirability of a solution. In contrast, PrD requires audience engagement with the artifact—they are asked to use it to perform a task.

In PrD, the critique reveals elements of the problem space, not the solution space.

Analyze

Only after the design/research team has had the right conversations with external stakeholders (through offering presumptive artifacts) does it proceed to analysis. But even in the analysis phase the process differs from many social science research approaches. In many traditional research approaches, the team is asked to hold off drawing conclusions or finding patterns until enough information is available. But In PrD, commonalities emerge after only a small number of engagements with external stakeholders. Almost immediately, because the artifacts offered to stakeholders are likely wrong, the team discovers misalignments between its own worldview and those of its constituents.

PrD's analysis is similar to codifying the stories and conversations ethnographic researchers collect. In PrD, analysis is in service of two outcomes: identifying underlying values, needs, and mental models of the target audience (similar to ethnography) *and* identifying ways in which the artifact and subsequent interviews can be changed to test these new presumptions (as opposed to simply refining the artifact). As The Case of the Black-Magic Batman illustrates (see Appendix A for all of the cases), Evan and his team were surprised by their users' reaction to the artifact. Rather than changing the artifact, they changed their protocol.

> Read how Evan's team was so surprised by an Engagement Session they ended up changing their whole approach.
> See Appendix A: The Case of the Black-Magic Batman

> Requiring internal stakeholders to explicitly state their assumptions up front forces team alignment going in.
> See Appendix A: The Case of the Business Case

In The Case of the Business Case, the team set out to test a key assumption: whether external stakeholders would comprehend the concept of an "app store" (à la iTunes) in the context of their work. The idea had already been demonstrated in a marketing deck but had never been tested with its intended stakeholders, i.e., key users who would recommend the solution.

> Make Assumptions Explicit

A remarkable thing happened during a debrief session after working with the users. The technical lead suggested an app store like iTunes wasn't at all what he'd had in mind when he first proposed the idea earlier in the year. This came as a surprise to the product manager (and to the UX team who were relative newcomers) since we had been talking about it as part of the PrD for the prior month. How much longer would that misalignment have continued before the team realized they weren't all talking about the same thing?

We all operate with assumptions about how the world works, how our employees think about us, our organization, our organization's mission, how our customers think about our brand, products, and services, how our users think about the features and attributes of our offerings, or how our services can improve the lives of our constituents.

As we embark on something new (whether a new feature, a new service, or a new strategy) we harbor beliefs and assumptions about the right thing to do. One of the greatest risks of starting a new venture is beginning with firmly held—and completely incorrect—operating assumptions. Failing to align on operating assumptions leads to disastrous results.

But in many organizations it is those very assumptions driving discussions, plans, and, ultimately, work products. In the worst cases, the teams discover only after they've released their offering how wrong their assumptions were. PrD forces the issue by surfacing the team's assumptions *at the outset* of the project, when it's least expensive to learn the most. By surfacing the team's assumptions to both itself (and other internal stakeholders) and, more critically, the external stakeholders for whom the experience is being designed, the organization quickly learns the value of those assumptions.

Iterate, Iterate, Iterate Here's a thought experiment: It's the kickoff of a new project. Team members are excited to start something new. The early optimistic glow of doing something big, bold, and impactful is in the air. You decide you're going to try this new approach to delivering value to your customer: PrD. Within a few days of the kickoff your team is in front of real customers with your first artifacts. Hooray! You're on your way to getting to the heart of their concerns, values, and needs.

What are the chances you will have learned everything you need to know in that first round?

Slim.

In that first round, you've probably uncovered more questions than answers.

PrD depends on multiple iterations for your team to raise its confidence in its findings or, put another way, for you to reduce the risk of proceeding down a specific path. As you'll learn in Chapter 7, doing multiple iterations with a handful of people (perhaps the same people, perhaps different) will reveal far more insights, far more quickly, than doing fewer iterations with more people.

As with agile software development, Lean Six Sigma, and Transient Advantage,[15] the key here is to experiment, iterate, and *learn*. You know you're done when one or more of the following conditions are met:

- You've not learned enough different in the most recent iteration to warrant doing another.

- You've run out of time.

- You've run out of resources.

Getting the most out of PrD requires finding the least expensive ways to iterate (addressing the final bullet) and to find ways to iterate quickly (discussed in the next section). The process requires team members who can quickly identify what is being learned and whether it is novel. This last point may seem odd, but as we discuss in detail later on, teams may not immediately see stakeholders' disruptive and awesome revelations without some professional interpretation.

IT shops across the world are grappling with rapidly changing technical environments—increased demand by employees for consumer-grade experiences (the "consumerization" of IT), increased security threats, greater expectations for immediate bug fixes and updates, just to name a few. The Cloud (Software as a Service (SaaS)) provides an extremely compelling alternative to building "on-premise" applications.

Imagine being able to outsource all of the employee applications to service providers whose businesses are dedicated to building the best possible solution in their application market! But there are significant experience challenges with that model, even if the financial aspects are compelling. What happens when employees are offered a dozen separate applications, from a dozen different service providers, none of which have the same look and feel, none of which use common vocabulary for similar terms, and few of which *connect* to one another? How can we *presumptively design* a solution to this problem to test employee reactions to such an environment, well in advance of actually constructing it?

Before you see our suggestion a little further along in this sidebar, take a moment and consider how you might "prototype" such an environment. What *hypothesis* are you testing (to put it in Lean UX terms)?[16] What problem space are you trying to survey? What sort of artifacts would you craft to help drive the right conversations? How much time would it take to get in front of customers to have these conversations?

17

Presumptive Design
DESIGN PROVOCATIONS FOR INNOVATION

The Faster You Go, the Sooner You'll Know

One way to test this hypothesis is given in Figure 1.5.

It's sitting in our pockets. A PrD session to answer the question of what might be problematic with a multi-SaaS employee experience is as simple as asking fellow employees to try and complete a collaborative task using the elements on their smartphone home page.

Have them *demonstrate* how they would complete a task (perhaps filling out an expense report) using the apps available on the phone.

Design to Fail: Clearly this can't be a proper solution to the problem—the phone was never designed to solve this problem.

Create, Discover, and Analyze: Offer the phone; listen to the reactions. Collect enough to understand the patterns.

Make Assumptions Explicit: The primary assumption in this case is the notion separate vendors can offer a coherent solution—somehow.

Iterate, Iterate, Iterate: After the first couple of conversations, you might need to switch it up a little, or you may need to use a different artifact.

The Faster You Go …: Total time to set up the test: less than 5 minutes. Total time to complete the interviews: 1 hour. Total time to review the results: less than one day. How much faster does it need to get?

In his oft-cited article "What Is Strategy?" Michael Porter laid out the principles of strategy for a generation of business leaders.[17] More recent thought leadership from Harvard[18] has argued against Porter's notion of "strategic positioning through sustainable competitive advantage."

The world is changing. Fast. Strategies, once thought to last years, are crafted on a yearly or even quarterly basis. Product features are continuously being updated, uploaded, and swapped. Amazon, Google, Netflix, and other giants change their offerings every few *minutes*.

Even companies and organizations that must move more slowly (companies requiring years of lead time, such as hardware manufacturers or pharmaceuticals) are under extraordinary pressure to find strategic advantages as quickly as possible.

No matter the product life cycle or its timing, every organization faces shorter and shorter cycles to identify desired end results with greater pressures for their success. How do we know an initiative is going to return on its investment? How do we know what the customer and user reaction is really going to be? In brief, how can we reduce risk as quickly as possible?

PrD, as a research method, is fast. Really fast. In a matter of days the team crafts an artifact suitable for testing with external stakeholders. In a matter of weeks the leadership can learn what, if any, value there is in pursuing further investment. As new competitive threats arise, the team goes back out quickly and tests their assumptions against the market.

Have Fun!

As the next chapter describes in detail, PrD depends on *design thinking* and, for designers, designing is *fun*. Think back to times when you had the time to think, and play and simply get silly. For most designers, that was likely just a few minutes ago. The design process requires a relaxed frame of mind.

For designers, the act of creation is massively fun. For others, maybe not so much. As you'll see in the next chapter, design thinking requires switching "sides of the brain"[19] from left to right and back again. For individuals who have spent their lives on the left side of the brain, the right side can be uncomfortable, disorienting, and in some cases painful. That doesn't sound like fun! Yet, the design process in general, and PrD specifically, succeeds when teams enjoy the work and explore wild possibilities.

Later on in the book we've provided example exercises to increase the fun factor of your team and of your work.

Figure 1.5 Smartphone home page as componentized experience

PrD is a powerful means of discovering information leading to strategic advantage through a rapid series of engagements with our constituents. The lessons learned from these engagements inform everyone on the project, from the product managers to the technologists and the UX team. One of the greatest benefits of PrD, and, ironically, its greatest risk, is how easily teams identify disruptive innovations. Because we offer our constituents views into the future, we learn where our predictions don't align with our constituents' reactions to them. More often than not, their reactions don't negate our predictions; instead they *adjust* them in ways we cannot anticipate. Those insights are the source of game-changing opportunities.

So, Why Bother?

Chapter 2: PrD and Design Thinking

"Oh, Kitty, how nice it would be if we could only get through into Looking-glass House!"

In another moment Alice was through the glass, and had jumped lightly down into the Looking-glass room.

Presumptive Design
DESIGN PROVOCATIONS FOR INNOVATION

Good design is good business.
—Thomas J. Watson

Overview
For leaders and managers, this section describes what teams do when running projects using PrD. Because design thinking is a way of solving problems, it applies to any part of the organization's engagement, from early strategy definition to go-to-market planning and service/product development. In turn, PrD applies in these contexts as well.

PrD turns classic research on its head. For researchers, accustomed to a particular way of proceeding in a project, PrD can be disorienting: It expects the internal team to craft a solution *before* interviewing prospects. For designers, accustomed to offering artifacts to prospects for purposes of review, PrD can be disorienting because the conversations aren't about the artifacts at all. For these two practitioner audiences (researchers and designers), this section provides design thinking frameworks supporting PrD's approach to design research.

Design Thinking
As of this writing, design thinking is all the rage; it appears to be the answer to many troubling challenges:

- How can we improve our possibility thinking?

- How can we think "outside the box?"

- What can we do to accelerate the "innovation pipeline?"

and on and on.

As designers, do we think differently from other people?[1] Alternatively (if we allow everyone is a designer because it is an inherent trait of being human), do we think differently when we're "designing" versus performing other activities?

For purposes of this book, and, more critically, for the purposes of PrD, we believe people behave, think, and solve problems in specific ways when designing. This thinking process distinguishes design from other activities and ways of approaching problem solving. Much of the discussion about "design thinking" is about problem solving through a designerly lens. The difference is subtle but important: There are people whose careers and lives are dedicated to the act of design. We will assume these people "think like designers," by definition. But hundreds of times a day each of us faces opportunities to approach a problem using various modes of thinking. We don't have to declare ourselves "designers" to solve problems using a designer's toolkit.

PrD requires us to be comfortable with the designer's way of thinking, because it relies on a cycle of reflecting and making, one of the fundamental themes of all design thinking models.

Design thinking is so fundamental to PrD we spend much of the chapter looking at its key attributes. These include:

- A flipping back and forth between "reflecting" and "making"

- A flipping back and forth between real and symbolic objects

- A flipping back and forth between divergent and convergent thinking

- A reliance on abductive reasoning (guessing and playing pretend)

- The creation of multiple putative solutions versus refining a single solution

If you are already familiar with design thinking, you may wish to skim this chapter.

A Brief Review of Design Thinking Models

Presumptive Design
DESIGN PROVOCATIONS FOR INNOVATION

The IIT School of Thought

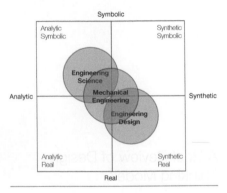

Figure 2.1 Charles Owen's Design Thinking model distinguishing among professions

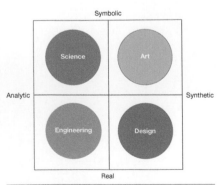

Figure 2.2 Owen's model illustrating decomposition of specific disciplines

Figure 2.3 Owen's model applied to four related disciplines

Charles Owen

Owen, from the Institute of Design at the Illinois Institute of Technology (ID-IIT), provides an excellent foundation for this discussion.[2] Owen proposes a 2 × 2 graph in which the x-axis represents a scale ranging from "analytic" to "synthetic" and the y-axis a scale ranging from "symbolic" to "real." He goes on to suggest we can position various disciplines within each of these quadrants, based on their "center of gravity." Owen proposes a few ideas about how to position these disciplines (Figures 2.1 and 2.2).

Owen emphasizes there are no hard and fast rules here. We propose the distinctions given in Figure 2.3 among four disciplines.

Engineering is "applied" Science, just as Design is "applied" Art. Similarly, artists and scientists endeavor to understand the world: to "know." The artist pursues knowledge through expression, whether the pursuit is self-expression or expressing knowledge of culture or society. Science is more obvious: Scientists pursue "Knowledge" and truths about the world.

Owen distinguishes the left and right sides of Figure 2.4 in terms of how work is done.

The top and bottom of Figure 2.4 could also be distinguished by the purpose of the activity (Figure 2.5).

Owen is quick to suggest a discipline isn't limited to a specific quadrant; rather, the types of activities and ways of approaching problems draw disciplines into different quadrants.

Design thinking applies to PrD in two ways: how we approach our research effort and how we *reason* about the problem space itself. On the left side of Figure 2.6, we

24

approach problem discovery using *deductive* reasoning (going from the general to the specific) or *inductive* reasoning (going from specific instances to some generalized rule). These are the forms of reasoning in finance, engineering, and science.

On the right side of Figure 2.6 is *abductive* reasoning, in which a rule is presumed against which data are fit. This is the realm of "playing pretend" where we take a leap of faith and make guesses. In Appendix B we go into details about abductive reasoning; abductive reasoning is both a key part of design thinking and an essential part of the PrD process.

Vijay Kumar/Steve Sato Model

Vijay Kumar,[3,4] also from ID-IIT, builds on Owen's model in several key ways. First, he changes the names of the axes slightly. "Symbolic" becomes "abstract" and "analytic/synthetic" becomes "know/make." The left side remains about finding, the right about making, the top about knowing, and the bottom about executing.

The second key change is Kumar's overlay of a *journey* through the quadrants, beginning with a question, or hypothesis, and concluding with the delivery of an artifact. Where Owen's focus was on understanding how knowledge is acquired, its context, and the nature of thought, Kumar applies these different modes of thinking to accomplishing a goal.

Steve Sato, also from ID-ITT, takes Kumar's model and modifies it once again, this time in service of differentiating designers' approaches to solving problems from others in the business ecosystem. Sato relies on this model to identify the value of design activities in the context of business operations (Figure 2.7).[5]

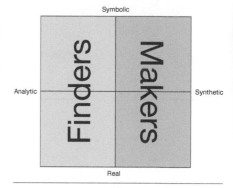

Figure 2.4 Finders and makers in Owen's model

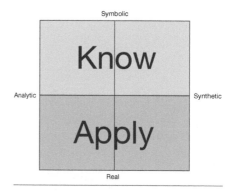

Figure 2.5 Knowing versus applying in Owen's model

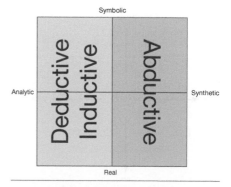

Figure 2.6 Types of reasoning overlaid on Owen's model

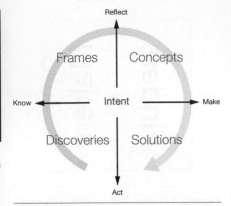

Figure 2.7 Steve Sato's Design Thinking model

Sato modifies the axes labels, helping clarify the intention of the graph in service of activities ("abstract" becomes "reflect" and "real" becomes "act") and places "intent" in the center. Sato reinforces Kumar's notion of a journey, emphasizing it is *iterative*. Design thinking doesn't stop with one cycle.

Using Sato's map, we can begin to discuss different approaches to *problem solving* based on different ways of approaching problems, one of Owen's original intentions. For example, Sato proposes a distinction between "straight-line" thinking and "design thinking" (Figure 2.8).

On the left of Figure 2.8 is just one form of straight-line thinking; staying on just the left, right, or top of Figure 2.8 are other ways of straight-line thinking, each producing different results from design thinking.

Sato suggests teams traveling through all four quadrants are more likely to discover broader solution spaces because they discover broader *problem* spaces before they converge on a result.

Both Kumar and Sato suggest our movement through the quadrants is not as simple as Figure 2.7 suggests. Individuals may leap from one quadrant to the other, diagonally, backwards, and so on, depending on the nature of the problem. As we'll point out a little further on, we distinguish PrD from other research activities by virtue of its starting position. For the types of problems PrD is best suited to solve, our journey begins on the right side of Figure 2.7.

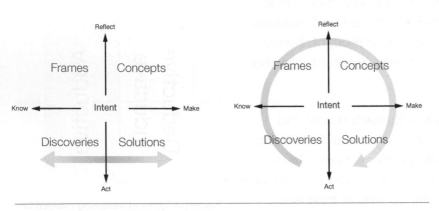

Figure 2.8 "Straight-line" thinking and "design thinking" in Sato's model

Bill Buxton and Paul Laseau's Models

Bill Buxton's discussion of design thinking[6] rests on two design activities: critique and sketching. In sketching, designers craft artifacts to express knowledge in their heads. In critique, designers receive feedback from other designers on those artifacts.

Buxton's activities look much like Owen's earlier notions of finding/making (Figure 2.9). As with Kumar and Sato, Buxton also proposes iteration and moving frequently back and forth between the two activities.

Buxton references earlier work by Paul Laseau who proposed two funnels, one illustrating the elaboration of ideas and the other illustrating idea reduction (Figure 2.10).

Buxton also echoes Sato's notions of straight-line versus design thinking to distinguish between creating *multiples* versus refining a single solution. This attribute distinguishes engineering approaches to problem solving from design approaches. Engineering's charter is to maximize outcomes using the minimum of resources, summed up nicely by the adage, "Anyone can design a bridge that stands up, but only engineers design bridges that *barely* stand up." Design's charter is to maximize the possibility or solution space by exploring radical alternatives within the problem space (Figure 2.11).

What is common to all of these models of design thinking are notions of trial

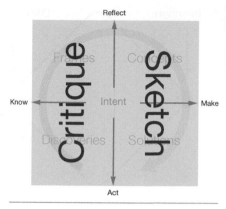

Figure 2.9 Buxton's Design Thinking model overlaid on Sato's model

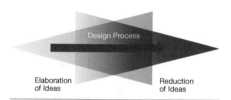

Figure 2.10 Laseau's Design Thinking model

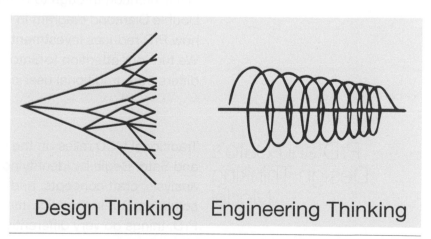

Figure 2.11 Design thinking as branching multiples; engineering thinking as refining optimization

Presumptive Design
DESIGN PROVOCATIONS FOR INNOVATION

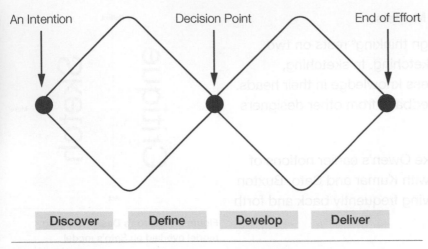

An Intention   Decision Point   End of Effort

| Discover | Define | Develop | Deliver |

Figure 2.12 UK Design Council's Double Diamond diagram

and error, guessing, and iterative approximations to best fit, meaning a combination of deductive/inductive *and* abductive reasoning.

The UK Design Council Double Diamond Diagram

We finish this survey course with an important contribution from the UK Design Council: the Double Diamond diagram (Figure 2.12).[7]

The diagram echoes Laseau's funnel across four phases. Divergent thinking occurs in the Discover and Develop phases, whereas convergent thinking occurs in the Define and Deliver phases. The diagram offers a succinct view of how design thinking applies to both strategy development (activities prior to the decision point) and execution. We use this diagram as a road map illustrating our progress from initial intention through to completion. We'll return to the Double Diamond diagram in later chapters when we discuss how PrD reduces investment in reaching the decision point. We turn our attention to Sato's model to illustrate how PrD differs from traditional user-centered design (UCD).

PrD and Sato's Design Thinking Model

Traditional UCD relies on the same cycle proposed by Kumar and Sato: Begin by identifying the problem, frame it through analysis, craft concepts, and ultimately craft prototypes and solutions. But in the Alice-through-the-looking-glass world of PrD, things go very differently: PrD relies on exactly the same steps, but starts the process 180° away in the upper right quadrant.

As the image on the right-hand side of Figure 2.13 suggests, PrD *starts* in the "concepts" quadrant, moving quickly through "solutions," and *then* into the "discoveries" quadrant, ultimately proceeding from there around the circle.

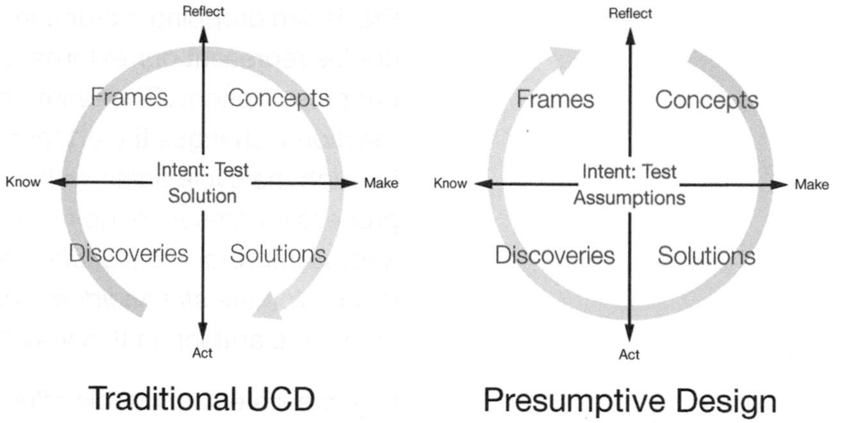

Figure 2.13 Traditional UCD versus PrD in Sato's Design Thinking model

This simple rotation addresses two key challenges facing researchers in today's rapidly changing environments:

- It "gets to the point" right off the starting line. Time spent in research is directed and focused on the things that matter most to the organization.

- It forces the internal team to put their assumptions on the table *immediately*, and then *immediately* puts those assumptions in front of customers and users.

When performed correctly, PrD quickly moves the entire team through the cycle, enabling them to view their assumptions through their external stakeholders' eyes. As David McKenzie notes in The Case of the Balking Bicyclists, nothing changes a team's mind more quickly than having a customer trash its great ideas!

When the internal team witnesses external stakeholders trashing its ideas, it will not spend time debating. It will pivot and quickly.

See Appendix A: The Case of the Balking Bicyclists

This rotation of the starting point within the design thinking cycle accelerates the team's understanding and learning about their stakeholders' needs. The challenge facing any UX research effort is to uncover stakeholder mental models, desired ways of working, definitions of delight, and the like. Imagine the information we are looking for is locked up in our stakeholders' heads, like the still surface of a pond.

How PrD Accelerates Learning

PrD is like dropping a stone into that still surface; the ripples represent our external stakeholders' reactions to our presumptions. The team captures and reflects on those reactions, changes the artifact as necessary, and returns through the cycle again with stakeholders. This iterative process creates an ongoing dialogue and conversation about *what is important to stakeholders*. The ripples of thinking and discussion are *stakeholders'* responses to the team's dropped stone, the artifact. In this way the artifact acts as provocation.

Designers are comfortable offering artifacts to their stakeholders; it's a fundamental part of the design process. But PrD asks designers to shift their orientation. Rather than *presenting* the artifact, PrD asks designers to let it go. In our experience, this has been a difficult shift for designers to make, but it is key to PrD's success. Similarly, designers are comfortable with the process of critique: reflections on the artifact for purposes of refining it. Here again, PrD asks designers to shift their understanding. PrD requires designers to accept critique, not of the *artifact* but of the *assumptions* behind it.

A compare and contrast of the two ways of proceeding through the design thinking cycle underscores how PrD accelerates learning. We'll use a hypothetical situation to illustrate PrD's increase in velocity over traditional UCD.

How PrD Differs from Traditional UCD

Your team has the opportunity to develop a control interface for an industrial process. You've been given only a handful of requirements: The environment is noisy, potentially contains hazardous materials, and meets ISO 3 (Class 1) cleanroom standards.

The Traditional (Waterfall) UCD Cycle

Using the waterfall approach to design thinking, the research team begins by performing a literature search, identifying competitive solutions, conducting field trips to similar facilities, interviewing potential users, participating in observations of existing control systems, and so forth.

After collecting the information, the team sifts through all of the data, and identifies several issues and insights suggesting opportunities for improvement, innovation, pain points, and the like. The research team completes its portion of the cycle by offering the architecture and design (A/D) team the insights they've gathered, moving from the left to the right side of Figure 2.14.

The A/D team then shifts into conceptualizing how those insights might take form, exploring a wide variety of possible solutions, some outlandish, some incremental.

Finally, the A/D team develops artifacts, which (in the most enlightened of product design/development environments) the research team brings in front of users for their reaction and feedback.

At this point, if the group's process is mature, they return through the cycle at least one more time to incorporate the fresh lessons learned from the prior step.

There's nothing wrong with this approach; in fact, many organizations would be overjoyed to develop products using this approach. On the surface it appears to reduce overall effort by informing the group early on about key requirements, context, environmental factors, and so on.

This process takes time—a lot of time in some cases. Sometimes it takes so much time the stakeholder environment may have changed before the process completes. We have participated in cycles which took *nearly a year* to complete due to the complexity of the engagements, the number of teams contributing, and other constraints within the organization.

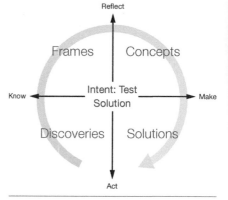

Figure 2.14 Traditional UCD and Sato's Design Thinking model

A second and perhaps more critical risk from this tollgate approach is the barriers it creates to executing on insights. Months may pass from the time data are captured to the time A/D teams receive it. Additional weeks or months may pass before the information is converted into something executable. Information evaporates from people's memory; it is expensive to capture completely or, alternatively, re-represent it in its original richness. The waterfall approach suffers from what Lean practitioners call "waste:" when artifacts are "thrown over the wall" from team to team or phase to phase.

Consider the common method of communicating research results: a white paper with accompanying slide presentation. Even when these are executed flawlessly, they are no substitute for the design team's direct observation of the data. This loss of information can be fatal to a project; all too often, late in the design cycle the design team learns of (or finally internalizes) a critical insight (that had been captured during discovery but lost along the way) requiring a complete restructuring of the product.

The PrD (Agile) Approach

Using the PrD approach, the team starts by brainstorming and ideating, based on the limited information they've been provided, their own experience with applications and environments of this nature, and minimal competitive research—whatever they've got—*as long as it doesn't delay the creation of a testable artifact* (Figure 2.15).

They immediately schedule engagements with the targeted user population to do a quick walkthrough of the external stakeholder's work (similar to the classic approach described in the previous section, but usually abbreviated), and spend some time *looking at a possible solution*.

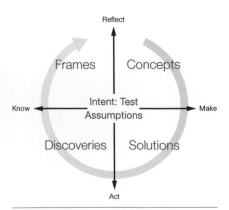

Figure 2.15 PrD and Sato's Design Thinking model

During the stakeholder's walk-through, team members make notes about language, task flows, artifacts, and pain points, just as they would during a waterfall-style session.

And then they invite the stakeholder to participate in the PrD session itself, offering the artifact the team has created as a potential solution to the stakeholder's needs.

Here is where magic happens.

How can the team possibly have anticipated the stakeholder's needs if they'd never done the upfront research? The PrD sessions use the artifact to focus on the stakeholder's needs, *not on the artifact itself*.

So, for example, the stakeholder may have mentioned during the walk-through her need to wear special gear. She may have pointed out where several of the controls on some of the interfaces are especially difficult to set accurately. The team's artifact hasn't accounted for that problem—perhaps it was proposed to be a mobile app, operable on a tablet. The touch interface wouldn't work with a gloved hand.

Clearly, the artifact will fail to meet a key need, but that won't prevent it from being useful in exploring the stakeholder's mental model with respect to that problem. Simply pretending the mocked-up tablet would work, with her gloves on, permits the team to continue to explore their assumptions, even as they make note of this major failure.

So, let's stop and step back a moment. We can hear many of you saying, "Well, if you'd done even a little amount of research you'd have known there was a problem in your approach and you could have avoided this situation before it came up." Or, "If you had a subject matter expert on your team, this would have been an obvious approach to avoid."

True on both counts, but they miss the point. If it wasn't the gloved hand problem, it would have been something else even the experts would have missed, or that no amount of prior research could have discovered. As we discuss in detail in Chapter 3, the environments we are exploring are, by definition, unknowable in advance, even by experts. We must perform some set of experiments, what agile practitioners call "spikes." The PrD spike puts someone into a situation and asks him to perform a task. The result is all sorts of fantastic information even experts couldn't have anticipated. It is as if we are watching stakeholders work in the future.

This one major error in the team's assumptions (needing to account for a gloved hand) has opened an opportunity to consider radical changes to its approach. And that opportunity opens the door to disruptive innovation. Maybe it isn't a tablet application at all. Maybe it is an add-on hardware device permitting gloved hand operation of any tablet, which opens multiple markets beyond the cleanroom application.

Whether the organization is poised to address these opportunities is a separate discussion, but this single mistaken assumption revealed useful and potentially game-changing opportunities.

Ignoring the disruptive innovation potential, and considering only the original assumptions of a tablet-based application, the team has still learned a considerable amount. Within minutes of the discussion, and after only a day or two of initiating the project, team members will have discovered dozens, if not tens of dozens, of bits of information *having immediate impact on their thinking going forward*. Note: Most of these bits have nothing to do with improving the design, but rather have to do with improving their understanding of the problem space.

In other words, the insights gained from the research and framing quadrants are achieved *and communicated to the team* almost immediately after engaging with stakeholders, simply by presenting a completely inadequate and inappropriate artifact. All in one coherent step, the team is exposed to the problem space, vets its assumptions, uncovers possible design paths, and facilitates innovation.

As we detail throughout the book, PrD's velocity has far more to do with the speed of communicating insights than with the crafting of artifacts. It is the transformative way the team thinks *about the problem* where PrD has its greatest impact.

Summary

- PrD rests on design thinking: the shifting back and forth between "knowing" and "making," critique/reflection, and sketching.

- PrD differs from traditional UCD approaches in how it enters the design thinking cycle: In PrD, teams begin by making rather than researching.

- Because PrD involves the entire team from the start, the time to insights is shortened, and, equally important, insights are enriched.

Chapter 3: PrD and an Agile Way of Business

"I declare it's marked out just like a large chess-board!" Alice said at last.
"it's a huge game of chess that's being played—all over the world..."

Presumptive Design
DESIGN PROVOCATIONS FOR INNOVATION

Innovation is creativity with a job to do.
—John Emmerling

Overview   In 2011, Marc Andreessen, cofounder of Netscape, coauthor of Mosaic (one of the first widely used browsers), and founding partner of the eponymous VC firm Andreessen Horowitz, proclaimed in the *Wall Street Journal*, "Software is eating the world."[1] Andreessen's article illuminated a trend growing for over a decade: massive fortunes being made by companies delivering software-only solutions, companies becoming completely dependent on software for their operations, and the very fabric of entire industries shredded by the disruption of software-based solutions.

For "old-school" business leaders and managers, the changing business landscape presents a difficult challenge. The disruption to the economy, markets, and industries has been likened to the Industrial Revolution, and for good reason. Workers are being displaced by automation; established companies face existential threats from tiny upstarts. The very foundations of business operations and management theories are being shaken up by a completely different approach to business.

But recognizing we are in a highly disruptive era (and few question the assertion) is only half the solution: We must find ways to thrive in the turbulence. While the rate of change will eventually subside, companies can't wait. In this chapter we outline how PrD provides an actionable approach to three key business concerns: strategy, innovation, and product/service development. Because PrD is an "action-first" approach to research, it is the tool of choice for leaders facing an unknown landscape with few mileposts to guide them.

Software-centric organizations are likely familiar with agile practices and culture. The "Agile Manifesto," written in 2001, declared four principles (Figure 3.1).

The fundamentals of business and management theory are also being overtaken by the agile ethic. Andreessen's statement extends beyond software as a structural part of business operations.

The Changing Nature of Business Strategy

An Agile Notion of Strategy

With the increasing rate of change in technology and market landscapes, leaders can no longer rely on static strategy statements intended to drive five- or even three-year planning horizons. In large and small enterprises, whether for-profit or nonprofit, across industry segments, leadership faces a constantly shifting landscape. In a matter of months, competitors who weren't on the radar become an existential threat. Customers drive harder bargains with each deal, based on emergent product and service offerings coming seemingly from nowhere. Suppliers apply ever-increasing pressure on an organization's strategy as they seek better pricing, easier terms, and friction-free relationships.

In the nonprofit world, the needs of constituents seem to increase every year, even as sources of funding become more challenging. Emerging technologies are both disrupting and enhancing service delivery, requiring leadership to constantly review their strategies. Of equal concern is how new technologies affect the populations these organizations serve.

The Manifesto for Agile Software Development

We are uncovering better ways of developing software by doing it and helping others do it.

Through this work we have come to value:

- **Individuals and interactions** over processes and tools
- **Working software** over comprehensive documentation
- **Customer collaboration** over contract negotiation
- **Responding to change** over following a plan

That is, while there is value in the items on the right, we value the items on the left more.

Figure 3.1 Agile Manifesto

Leaders must adopt a more rule-based approach to strategy, what Ruth McGrath calls "Transient Advantage."[2] Her Transient Advantage "playbook" consists of eight parts (six of which, italicized below, sound very similar to the Agile Manifesto):

1. Think about arenas, not industries.
2. *Set broad themes, and then let people experiment.*
3. *Adopt metrics that support entrepreneurial growth.*
4. *Focus on experiences and solutions to problems.*
5. Build strong relationships and networks.
6. *Avoid brutal restructuring; learn healthy disengagement.*
7. *Get systematic about early stage innovation.*
8. *Experiment, iterate, and learn.*

How can we rapidly pursue a new direction? How can we continually update our strategy? McGrath suggests a complete cultural overhaul (consistent with agile notions of culture). McGrath's Transient Advantage shifts business strategy from an act of *planning* to one of *constant experimentation*. This shift requires business leaders to reframe their decision environment.

Knowledge and Decision Frameworks

Consider the relatively well-known framework for dividing up knowledge of the world (Figure 3.2).

In the lower right quadrant of Figure 3.2, a strategist uses best known methods to devise a strategy. In the upper right quadrant, a strategist brings smart folks in to get data, analyze the results, and devise the next steps. As soon as we move to the left side we enter a realm in which collecting data, deep analysis, or reliance on best practices will fail us. In these situations, the only way to discover what is "unknown" is to perform an experiment, review the data, analyze the results, and try something else. Through a series of these experiments, the strategist identifies the key issues from the unknowns, moving the decision back to the right side. In the lower left quadrant we're faced with even greater lack of certainty. We must actually *try* something, perhaps a limited test, perhaps an experiment, but we must take action to understand how unstable the situation is.

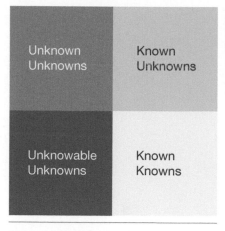

Figure 3.2 Decision matrix

David J. Snowden adds to this 2 × 2 in his Cynefin framework (Figure 3.3).[3] According to Snowden, leaders run the risk of micromanaging if they spend much time in the lower right quadrant. There, well-oiled processes operate without the need for or fear of disruption. On the other hand, he cautions, those situations that he labels "simple" come with the risk of complacency: If leaders depend on best practices even when externalities demand a different approach, the situation can quickly collapse into "chaotic." While leaders should operate in the other three quadrants (leaving the "simple" quadrant to operationally excellent managers), Snowden warns they must keep the simple quadrant in mind at all times, lest the company become irrelevant. In the upper right quadrant, leaders depend on subject matter experts to review the data and offer a solution. Experts have seen situations like this before—they recognize the unknowns.

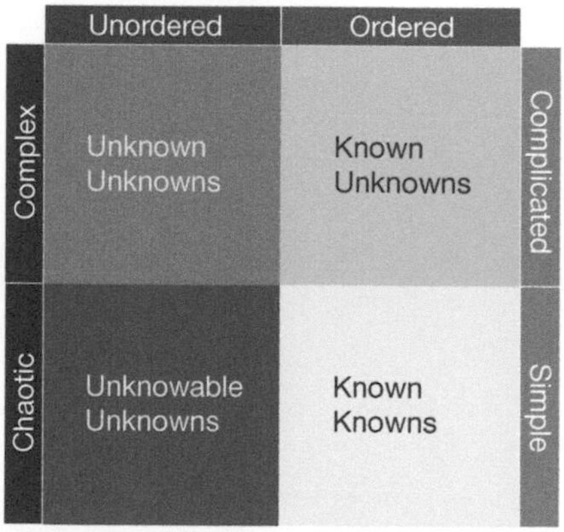

Snowden's Cynefin Framework

Snowden suggests the only way to understand situations falling in the upper left quadrant is to take action. Because we don't know what we don't know, we need to take a stab at something, measure it, and regroup, often to try something else. This is the quadrant in which many companies find themselves when it comes to innovation and market threats.

Figure 3.3 Snowden's Cynefin framework on decision matrix

PrD *can* be used effectively in all four quadrants, but it is least effective in the lower right. In the lower right quadrant a known best practice will suffice to resolve the situation.

PrD in the Context of Unknowns

41

Presumptive Design
Design Provocations for Innovation

Experimentation isn't necessary when the outcome can be reliably predicted in advance. In the upper right quadrant, PrD offers an antidote to "groupthink," one of the risks of bringing in experts to figure out next steps. We discuss how PrD disrupts groupthink and other in-crowd mentalities affecting decision making in Chapter 10.

Although PrD is suitable for situations defined by the left quadrants, it is most effective in the upper left quadrant. In both cases, the organization must act to determine what it doesn't know. For the upper left quadrant, those actions take the form of experiments. PrD's experiments rely on artifacts to provoke conversations. In the lower left quadrant, the organization must take an immediate action before it can determine what the right experiment is. In general, these are emergent situations, requiring leadership to go with their gut. The organization must capture the results of their actions and quickly re-act again. Depending on the nature of the crisis, PrD can be helpful, in that it is designed to move quickly, captures actionable information, and reduces handoffs among team members; but, in general, situations falling into the lower left quadrant are emergent, requiring immediate action.

PrD's action-first, lightweight approach is perfectly suited for dynamically shifting situations in the upper left quadrant. In The Case of the Business Case, for example, the business had a strong idea about an emerging market, ripe for disruption. Based on market research and initial customer contacts, the investment team thought they had a good handle on the business case, but they didn't understand the details of the ecosystem. Who were the decision makers within the customer organizations, who influenced decisions, and what risks would the team face when introducing their presumed disruption? By offering key customer stakeholders an artifact from their presumed future, the team provoked conversations about its proposed business model. These

> PrD helps internal stakeholders frame the problem they'll set out to solve. This informs not just design but all assumptions, such as the underlying business model.
>
> See Appendix A: The Case of the Business Case

42

led in turn to the team reconsidering several of its short-term plans and longer-term strategies.

The Cynefin Framework provides a theoretical context for McGrath's Transient Advantage: Organizations are situated in the "unknown unknowns" quadrant far more frequently today than ever before. Looked at through this lens, PrD offers strategists opportunities to experiment with "strategies from the future."

PrD increases the value of the business's innovation pipeline. It is most suitable for *disruptive* innovation as opposed to *sustaining* innovation, since disruptive innovation by definition involves unknown unknowns. Still, the process is lightweight enough to be used on an ongoing basis to drive incremental innovation efforts.

Disruptive Innovation and PrD

Disruptive Innovation

"A disruptive technology or disruptive innovation is an innovation that helps create a new market and value network, and eventually goes on to disrupt an existing market and value network."[4] So the entry in Wikipedia describes Clayton Christensen's basic notion as outlined in his seminal book, *The Innovator's Dilemma.*[5]

For leaders to take advantage of disruptive innovation they must shift their thinking as McGrath suggests, specifically focusing on a systematic approach to innovation. Innovation is likened to a funnel: lots of ideas up front, ultimately winnowed down by numerous factors until a few emerge. In the "open innovation" model, companies partner with outsiders to improve the likelihood of an idea making it to market—whether by insourcing ideas from other firms or licensing ideas that don't address the company's core market.[6] In "outcome-driven innovation," leaders are urged to look at customers' needs first to identify whitespace in the market. In doing so, early stage ideas are quickly evaluated against market needs, improving their chances of survival.[7]

Because few ideas make it through the funnel, innovation managers increase the number of ideas at the front of the funnel. One technique is to run "harvest days," intellectual property workshops to capture ideas based on technologies currently in the company's labs. Another common approach is to incent employees to file invention disclosures and pursue patent applications, even if the idea has no known application or business case.

PrD marries the inside-out approach of business development ("what problems can we solve with the technology in the lab?") with the outside-in approach of market research ("what problems are extant in the world our technology could best address?"). PrD depends on the company's technology leadership directly interacting with external customers. When technical leaders (intimately familiar with technical possibilities) directly interact with end-users (the individuals who are most in need of a change), amazing invention emerges.

Invention, but not necessarily innovation. We don't suggest this approach alone reduces the risk of moving inventions to market. But we do suggest the inventions that emerge are far more likely to succeed because they are vetted with customers *before* they begin their tortuous journey through the pipeline. Conversely, we've seen PrD reduce the risk of innovation by identifying those early stage ideas that have no likely benefit and do not deserve further investment.

As we suggest throughout the book, the devil remains in the details: Who are the technical leaders? (*Hint*: It isn't top management.) Who are customers? (*Hint*: It isn't customers' top management or the folks paying for the product.) What do we mean by "interact?" (It is a carefully considered and orchestrated form of interaction, not merely relying on a few magic questions or interviews.)

PrD offers technical and marketing leaders a glimpse of the future, perhaps as far as five or 10 years out. Because the artifacts are ambiguous by design, customer stakeholders fill in the gaps and rationalize the object. Through stakeholder rationalization, the team learns what is inherently desirable, what is confusing, and ultimately what issues the marketing team, product team, and leadership team will need to address to move their ideas into the market or establish an entirely new market.

Design thinking has been heralded as one method of reducing the cost of generating inventions. Phil Gilbert at IBM, for instance, stresses design thinking reduces cost by eliminating wasted effort, reducing developer hours sunk into work that doesn't matter.[8] But the true cost of innovation isn't during the ideation stage—ideas are cheap. The most expensive innovations are those that make it through the pipeline and fail to fulfill their promise: whether that's breaking into a new market, extending the organization's offerings into adjacent ponds, or going head-to-head against an incumbent. *Effectiveness* (building the right pipeline) matters more than *efficiencies* (building the pipeline right).[9] It doesn't matter how efficient your innovation pipeline is if you're not creating products that matter to your customers.

Michael Schrage's position on prototyping and innovation rings true for PrD:[10]

Increasing the Value of Ideas in the Innovation Funnel

> The conventional wisdom that "innovation processes" drive prototype development is misleading. Empirical observation of organizations with effective innovation cultures confirms just the opposite: changes in prototypes and simulations drive the innovation process. Leaders from the CEO on down must step back and ask: Will we get more value from better managing our innovation process to get a prototype, or from better using the prototype to manage our innovation process?

45

Looking through McGrath's Transient Advantage lens, organizations need to maintain a large pool of opportunities in the event the external environment changes dramatically. To put it in Darwinian terms, individuals within a species have widely and sometimes weirdly different attributes from the "norm." When environmental change forces many individuals to die off, some individuals will have just what it takes to thrive in the new environment.

In this instance, early stage innovations represent the individuals with weird attributes, lying in wait for just the right business conditions to appear and allow the company to take a 90-degree turn. These mutations[11] represent proto-innovations in Snowden's "complex" quadrant; that is, we don't know by inspection whether they will fit or not. We have to test them in the right environment to understand their likelihood of survival. How best to know what mutations to pursue and which to let go? At a minimum, an organization may need to broaden its definition of "best fit." Highly uncertain environments and radically shifting market conditions demand it.[12]

As Schrage, Ulwick, and others suggest, the key is to efficiently identify survival candidates for the desired markets. This is where PrD comes in: It not only identifies the right product (effective) but also does it in as efficient a manner as possible. PrD focuses on the right problems (as defined by customers and markets) with a minimum of expense and effort.

A Hypothetical Example

PrD provides a rapid way of evaluating potential innovations, without major investment, by starting with action.

Consider the following scenario: In your organization, an engineer working on a leading-edge product is frustrated—she can't find any single tool to help her move her design forward. She needs several different applications from different vendors, none of which provide a common standard, forcing her to constantly translate between the different interfaces, data formats, and workflows. The cost of moving forward on her work is significant, not to mention the cost of the different tools. This appears to be a problem in efficiency. If she had a single tool, or even a common standard by which her multiple tools worked together, she could move forward on her design much quicker, reducing time-to-market. This single tool is a potential mutant.

But there's more going on here. This engineer's problem may be more widespread in the industry at large. If so, this single problem becomes the company's opportunity. How many of the company's own customers are facing a similar problem with their own engineering efforts? Might this problem be an opportunity to disrupt the market? Is this engineer a "canary in a coal mine?"

Assume your organization has a team chartered to keep its eye on just such opportunities. Their first questions include:

- Is this a one-off, peculiar to this engineer?

- How many customers might have this problem? (What is the total addressable market [TAM]?)

- What are the existing solutions?

- Does the potential solution take advantage of the company's core competencies?

- What external partnerships could the company forge to broaden its footprint in the market (or extend its core)?

- What is the desired customer or UX?

Many of these questions can (and should) be answered through traditional market research: identifying the competition, the TAM, and the key product differentiators. But when it comes to understanding how the desired customers' experience impacts the decision, nothing beats PrD in terms of speed, depth of insight, or potential for differentiated innovation. To what extent would such a solution *resonate* with end-users? What, specifically, is the desired set of capabilities distinguishing the proposed solution from the current available solutions? Product managers may be stumped by mutants: There may not be good data available to help determine a potential innovation's fit in the market.

Product managers typically use surveys such as conjoint analyses to determine the right set of product attributes. These are highly accurate tools, but they can take months to execute, are costly to design and implement, and fail to identify breakthrough ideas; they can test only what the team believes are the key attributes for the solution. Not only is the opportunity difficult to compare with existing solutions, its optimal market might also differ dramatically from those served by current solutions. It's too early for quantitative research; there are just too many unknowns.

In contrast, the team can field PrD in less than a week (the greatest delay is getting on your customer's calendar) and the only cost is travel. Because PrD expects us to be wrong, we won't have spent much time creating a working prototype (or even a fancy marketing deck). Further, PrD isn't limited to the organization's current market or customers; it's just as effective testing ideas against unfamiliar or unknown markets. Remember, as a process, it excels in the upper left quadrant: unknown unknowns.

- Does the proposed solution resonate with prospects?
- Do they lean forward and engage or do they dismiss it out of hand?
- Do they begin to cocreate[13] a solution by offering their ideas about how it should work?
- Do they reveal internal mental models by pointing out where the idea won't work, adding to your understanding of their problem space?

- In the course of the Engagement Sessions, does the team begin to notice common themes either validating the engineer's proposal or shifting it into something more compelling?

- Is a business case emerging?

If the answers are "No," the team has spent a minimal amount of resources to quickly dispense with an idea that has no clear benefit. But if the answers are generally "Yes," it has raised its confidence there is merit to proceeding. Either way, this small investment greatly reduces risk. The team has identified (or eliminated) a potential opportunity, making their innovation process not only more efficient but also more effective.

In fact, the most likely outcome is not a yes/no result, but a much deeper understanding of prospective customers' pain points. Assuming the engineer who proposed the idea in the first place isn't completely idiosyncratic, *something* about the original idea will have merit. It's just not clear before the PrD sessions what that something is.

Organizations using McGrath's Transient Advantage playbook are likely using a form of PrD. Even as they are staying on track with last quarter's strategy, they are continually identifying customer needs and their reaction to potential future strategies, the essence of Transient Advantage. In this context, PrD is a means of looking "over the time horizon" to see where the organization needs to steer the ship, next quarter or next year.

PrD in a Culture of Agility

PrD is an agile approach: Get assumptions in front of users as soon as possible, experiment, iterate, and refactor. PrD, as a design research tool rather than a software engineering approach, differs dramatically from agile.

- PrD requires relatively little effort compared with agile development. All told, most PrD engagements are completed with a few people within a few weeks.

- PrD reliably reduces risk to the project by identifying what users want and need, not just what they say, without relying on working code.

- PrD reduces risk at the earliest stages of the project, impacting strategy, architecture, and infrastructure.

A Culture of Agility

Whether we discuss the latest theories about crafting strategy, PrD, or agile development, we have to look below the superficial techniques at the "culture" and underlying principles:

- Engaging with key customers and users

- Rapid iterative "closed loops"

- Focusing on *actions*, *behaviors*, and *context*

PrD invites all members of the team (business, technology, and UX) to contribute to both the strategic vision and the day-to-day development effort. In addition to helping craft and validate winning concepts for products and services, PrD helps define and refine the offerings as they emerge.

Using PrD's rapid, iterative user-focused approach, UX professionals design and deliver highly satisfying experiences quickly, in a predictable time frame with reduced risk overall.

PrD, Design Thinking, and Business Value

Let's recap some of the points we've made in this chapter:

- Agile is a means of developing software, an approach to construction. It is not a means to conceptualize, strategize, or do UX design. Agile's primary tenet is to maximize business value early.

- Transient Advantage has taken agile sensibilities into the boardroom by eliminating a static strategy planning process. In its place, strategy is defined as ongoing and dynamic, responding to rapid cycles of competitive advantage.

- PrD is an agile approach to design research, whether in service of strategy, product definition, or product execution.

- The only way to work within an environment of "unknown unknowns" is to take action. PrD is an "action first" approach.

Summary

In the traditional view, strategy (or "What game are we playing and how are we going to win?") focuses an organization on three key elements: measurable objectives, scope, and differentiators. McGrath's Transient Advantage suggests such a static definition of strategy no longer serves organizations facing highly turbulent market dynamics.

In the 21st century, software is eating the world. Not only have companies made their fortunes based on software, but software also is now ingrained in operations throughout an organization. With the adoption of agile development practices, agile culture has moved into the boardroom. Transient Advantage's playbook reads like a 21st century Agile Manifesto for the C-suite.

But agile development practices and culture focus on execution: delivering highest business value outcomes as efficiently as possible. Other, agile-like processes such as Lean or Six Sigma also focus on reducing waste and improving operational efficiencies. None of these methods help execute on McGrath's Transient Advantage. None of them identify:

- New market opportunities

- Innovative product offerings

- Desirable value propositions

- Differentiated products or services

PrD does. PrD provides business stakeholders with insights into new markets, new problem spaces, new applications of technology, and new business opportunities. As you'll learn in the remainder of the book, PrD's focus is on delivering a usable *artifact*, not as a design solution, but as a means of illuminating a customer problem. The outcomes from PrD influence a wide variety of business elements: strategy, supplier and partner engagements, go-to-market definition, messaging, training, and road maps.

During strategy development, PrD reduces risk: Which opportunities show greater promise, what key customer pain points are not being addressed, how can core technologies deliver desirable UXs to improve market position, and where are "whitespaces" or adjacent ponds in the marketplace?

Businesses are under pressure to innovate—to bring differentiated products and services to market. Moving from ideation to monetization (i.e., managing the innovation pipeline) requires constant attention, not only to inventions coming from within but also to the changing market dynamics without. PrD is a cost-effective tool for identifying "good-fit" inventions in the context of target markets and customers. It helps improve the value of the innovation pipeline by eliminating low-value inventions early, and, conversely, identifying hidden opportunities in "mutants" that might otherwise die off.

PrD, agile, and UX share many similar attributes, namely, their focus on end-users, their rapid iterative approach, and their expectation of being wrong. But perhaps their greatest commonality is where they reside in the Cynefin framework: complex situations with unknown unknowns. As a UX design research tool, PrD is an agile method of approaching unknown unknowns.

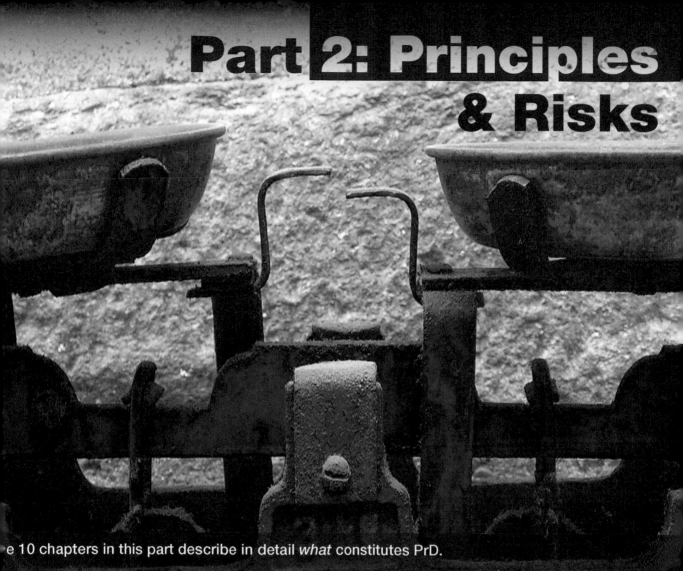

Part 2: Principles & Risks

The 10 chapters in this part describe in detail *what* constitutes PrD.

The first five chapters focus on PrD's five principles: Design to Fail; Create Discover, Analyze; Make Assumptions Explicit; Iterate, Iterate, Iterate; and The Faster We Go the Sooner We Know.

The second five chapters address the risks and hazards of using this power tool.

Chapter 9, The Perils of PrD, offers reasons *not* to use the approach. Chapter 10 illuminates the need for diversity on the team. Chapters 11-13 focus on the hazards of poor objectives, distracting artifacts and inappropriate attitudes.

Presumptive Design
DESIGN PROVOCATIONS FOR INNOVATION

Try again. Fail again. Fail better.
—Samuel Beckett

Overview

In this chapter we focus on the first principle of PrD: Design to Fail. As we introduced in Part 1, PrD rests on a fundamental shift in thinking and process: beginning with an artifact to drive research. Here, we explain in detail why at this stage failing is absolutely the right thing to do. But we're not after just any type of failure: We're seeking "intelligent" failures.

We're Going to Fail—It's a Question of When and by How Much

David McKenzie took an "artifact-first" approach, but he quickly realized he'd overinvested in it.

See Appendix A: The Case of the Balking Bicyclists

In The Case of the Balking Bicyclists, David McKenzie quickly realized how counterproductive it can be to overinvest in an idea. He could have started with up-front research and conducted a series of interviews before creating something and testing a proposed solution—but he didn't. He and a small team built a physical artifact, got it in front of external stakeholders, and proceeded to swallow their pride. In David's words, "They completely trashed it."

Familiar with PrD and sacrificial concepts,[1] David saw this as a win. It had taken less than a week to disprove his team's assumptions. After reflection, however, he realized his team's investment in a 3D-printed artifact was still too much. A simple foam core model would have enabled them to fail even faster. This is the first principle of PrD: Design to Fail. David and his team built an artifact to represent their assumptions, got it in front of external stakeholders, and, by focusing on reactions to their assumptions (and not the artifact), blew the problem space wide open.[2]

Designing the Right Thing

"What's the right thing to build?" We determine the fate of all the work that follows by how well we answer this question. Yet not a lot of attention is always given to it. Agile methods assume we already know we're building the right thing.[3] Historically, user-centered design (UCD) spends considerable effort on answering this question up front. UCD starts with (often lots of) research before anything at all is built. After investing time and money learning about the population to be served, the research team's findings are baked into a proposed solution. Then the development team sets about refining *that* design (see Chapter 2), investing even more than was required for the original research. Except if the product fails spectacularly in the marketplace, the problem space will not be revisited again. Even under those extreme circumstances, management will be unlikely to revisit the project. Opportunity costs, sunk costs, and additional development costs (along with lost time and potential loss of customer faith) are tough conditions to make a case.

Neither UCD nor Agile stresses the importance of dwelling in the problem space, of generating, rejecting, exploring, and vetting multiple *possible* design solutions even as the team struggles with the design problem itself. Other "discovery" methods, such as in-depth market research techniques, don't provide high resolution of the problem space. This desire to exit the problem space and jump to execution isn't limited to product development: Teams working within innovation pipelines frequently begin investing in solutions without fully understanding the nuances or landscape of the problem space (Figure 4.1).

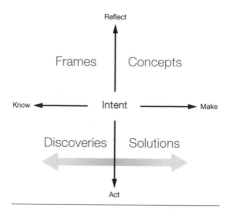

Figure 4.1 Sato's design thinking model showing "straight-line" thinking from requirement to solution

As a result, once a solution is proposed based on up-front research, the remainder of the project is typically spent climbing the same hill, refining the same solution, fixing bugs, identifying usability problems, etc.—and woe to the team member who, late in the process, asks if it was even the right solution to pursue. And "late" may not be very far into the execution phase, even using an Agile approach. Once an architecture has been established (or worse a solution has been ratified), teams are typically unwilling to revisit it. By the time a "structure" is in place, teams have invested too much to casually refactor it. If that structure doesn't address the problem space, the team faces an expensive problem: Either they must restructure the solution or they incrementally move toward the desired solution over many release cycles.

The good news is this type of problem can be easily avoided without compromising schedules or throwing away a lot of work. The team will achieve several goals if it spends a little more time exploring the problem space by offering proto-solutions (that are likely wrong), which depend on *a sketch of an architecture*:

1. Testing assumptions about a structure without building it out.

2. Exploring a variety of design directions, inexpensively.

3. Surveying a broad swath of the problem space.

Regardless of whether an initial design idea is used for research purposes or is intended for market, rarely is it the optimal solution.[4] Our operating principle is it's better (and more cost-efficient) to realize our design ideas are wrong on the first day of the project than waiting any amount of time. We discuss when "enough is enough" in Chapter 12.

There's Nothing Wrong About Being Wrong

One of the best and most time-efficient ways to understand a design problem is to offer up solutions to it. It's important for the team to agree these "solutions" are not taken seriously. If the team forgets this, if they latch onto and defend an idea, they blind themselves to other, better paths. At this early problem exploration stage, any proposed solutions are canards —fabrications or fever dreams based on unaired assumptions and limited understanding. Rather than being prideful of its ideas, the team should build them into artifacts,[5,6] get those artifacts in front of external stakeholders, and let them react.

Only after an idea has been vetted by stakeholders will it have served its best purpose. If we want to save time and money, we should start with this mind-set of sacrificing ideas.

In designing to fail, the key is to get over any guardedness, any protectiveness of ideas. We should want them to fail as quickly as possible. We must go in assuming we're wrong. The solution, after all, *will* be a failure—to some *n*th degree. Instead of worrying we're *going to* fail, we must realize we already have. We must accept it. And let it go. It's liberating, isn't it? Now fail quickly and cheaply and *learn*.

Whether an organization is averse to error (the pessimistic view of being wrong) or embraces it (the optimistic view) may have much to do with its values and origins. Most manufacturing and engineering-based firms fall into the pessimistic camp, making them averse to failure. They strive to avoid it. When failure does happen, they try not to acknowledge it, denying it's inevitable, or, worse, denying it's *valuable*.

Because of the pervasive pessimistic view of failure, the mere whiff of it can damage reputations, whether at an individual or an organizational level. Failure remains stigmatizing, even in organizations verbally touting the value of "risk taking." What these organizations need is a shift to an optimistic view of failure: To understand risk taking is to appreciate the *benefits* of failure. Sim Sitkin, in his classic article on the strategy of small losses,[7] argues we all too often ignore both the benefits of failure and the liabilities of success. His thinking at first blush feels counterintuitive.

Sitkin argues teams with unending strings of successes may not be "high performing"—they may actually be stagnant, operating with unchallenging goals and failing to truly innovate. Innovation requires failure. Where is this team's "scrap pile?" How big is it? Without a sufficiently large distribution of outcomes, how is the team really *learning*? Such a team has effectively chosen to focus on reliability in

Optimistic Versus Pessimistic View of Being Wrong

Let's stop for a moment though and forgive ourselves for our extreme aversion to being wrong: No doubt aversion to error has been an effective survival strategy for millions of years. In the wild, we rarely get a second chance (and the gene pool is adjusted accordingly). Over time we've come to accept error as dangerous, humiliating, and distasteful, a "pessimistic" view. The problem with the pessimistic view is that it focuses solely on the damages associated with a specific failure, and, in so doing, fails to look at the damages associated with erring in general. That is, for the adherents to the pessimistic view of being wrong, it is crucial to avoid being wrong at all costs, which drives behaviors that may actually increase large-scale errors.

Accompanying the rise of industrialization were sibling disciplines associated with reducing errors in manufacturing. Engineering in general concerns itself with limiting errors to within acceptable tolerances. Human Factors, Six Sigma, Lean, and Industrial Engineering all begin with the pessimistic view of error: Errors must be identified and reduced, if not eliminated entirely.

If there is a pessimistic view of error, then there must be an optimistic view as well, and here we enter the world of art and design. In both of these contexts, "the experience of being wrong is hardly limited at all. Surprise, bafflement, fascination, excitement, hilarity, delight: All these and more are a part of the optimistic understanding of error."[8]

lieu of adaptability and innovation (and in some contexts, this is fine). But consider the typical Agile project: The team thinks it "knows" what the best solution is and sets about time boxing its work, running sprints, and iteratively producing a solution that gets little negative feedback. Success will most certainly be declared—but the solution may in fact be far less optimal than if the team's thinking had first been honed through a process of informative or "intelligent" failures. In brief, "succeeding" early is a risky strategy.

We Seek Intelligent Failures

Our end goal, it should be noted, is not to fail. Failure is a means to an end. If we're going to fail along the way, then we should do so in a way that maximizes its benefits—in a way that minimizes the costs of failing while maximizing the learnings to be gained. Whenever we need experimentation, we have to fail along the way, since we don't know answers in advance. Calling this approach "trial and error" is misleading.[9] *Error* implies there could be a *right* outcome, when at this stage there isn't one! There's no error, only *trial*. The answer is *not* knowable without failure (trial); therefore, to get closer to right, we must fail.

As we introduced in Chapter 3, in simple contexts with clear cause-and-effect relationships, such experimentation is unnecessary. In such an environment, outcomes are predictable and the best course of action can be known in advance. Even in more complicated contexts, when there are still clear cause-and-effect relationships, the best course of action can be identified up front by those with expertise in the area. In this context of innovation, however, we're talking about complex, unpredictable environments. Here we've moved from the "known known" and the "known unknown" to the true "unknown unknowns."[10] Trial will always be the best course of action in complex contexts where we can really only understand why things happen in retrospect. In such a decision environment, the best thing to do is to set up experiments in which it is safe to fail. Further, by conducting them, these experiments, or probes, reveal the optimal path forward, much like the sonar of a submarine.[11]

Failure, however, can be expensive, harm morale, damage reputations, and anger customers.[12] Furthermore, not all failure produces such learnings. How, then, do we ensure our failures are informative? If they're not informative, then they waste time and money. We want our failures to act like echo location, teasing useful information from the landscape. The results of our trials shouldn't be ambiguous (Figure 4.2).

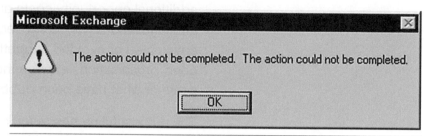

Figure 4.2 A useless, information-free signal

The trick lies in engineering "intelligent failures," which vet our assumptions and reveal where future investment would be wasted. Intelligent failures contain or minimize the downside of failing by manufacturing failures as fast and cheap as possible. Returning to Sitkin, he discusses five criteria of intelligent failures:[13]

- They result from *planned* actions designed to yield valuable information—regardless of whether the outcome is deemed a success or a failure.

- They have *uncertain outcomes*. They are probes deployed when the outcome cannot be known in advance. (Predictable failures do not provide new information about how things should be done differently in the future.)

- They are *modest* in scale. The failure must be large enough to be noticed as failures and small enough to allow for a productive, exploratory response.

- They are executed and responded to with *alacrity*. The goal is to obtain information, and the more we do this the more we learn, so we should want to generate information, evaluate, and adjust to it quickly.

- They take place in a domain familiar enough to permit effective learning. In other words, the failure must be recognized as relevant to existing assumptions. In PrD, this is the context of the external stakeholders' goals/tasks/work/needs/frustrations.

Organizations fail a lot more than they succeed, and yet they typically don't take advantage of their potentially valuable failures.[14] By failing to capitalize on failure, they create additional opportunity costs and surrender possible insights and innovations. Since subsequent failures could have been anticipated or avoided altogether by learning from previous ones, organizations expose themselves to the risks and costs of what have been dubbed "predictable surprises."[15]

The purposeful orchestration of "intelligent failures" is foreign to our normal way of thinking and behaving. Our typical organizational culture is not entirely to blame, however. There are also cognitive biases to contend with, such as loss aversion[16] and the confirmation bias.[17] We tend to give more weight to a loss than to a gain of the same amount. We would rather accept smaller, sure gains than gamble over larger gains, whereas we would rather try to gamble out of larger losses (and thereby risking even greater losses) *than accept smaller, sure losses*. But accepting small, sure losses is exactly what we're being asked to do here! We just need to move past seeing them as "losses." They're not. *They're sacrifices.* What is gained by these small, sure (and as we have suggested, *planned*) losses far outweighs their cost. (The confirmation bias will be discussed in detail in Chapter 11.)

The artifact itself doesn't have to be a physical object. It could be a message or announcement. What matters is how it fails and why.

See Appendix A: The Case of the PowerPoint Play

In The Case of the PowerPoint Play, Steve Sato worked with a team at a Fortune 50 tech company to help a VP craft presentations to other executives. Their goal was to strategically position design within the company. Their VP was supportive, but the team wasn't certain how their vision and aspiration for design would resonate with his peers. They had weekly sessions with the VP, which they leveraged as an opportunity to do some PrD. "We purposefully placed really far-reaching provocations in the presentations. When execs reacted, we always asked 'Why?'"

This is a great illustration of Design to Fail. Sato was intentionally pushing the presentations to the point where they would fail. The ensuing conversations exposed unstated positions and opinions. In his words, "We wanted to learn about things like the role designers could and should play in business-to-business sales. This enabled us to find the VP's comfort level. It helped us uncover how the executives viewed design, exposed their mental models about design and designers and their role in the org."

To produce a culture more comfortable with the concept of strategically failing, Sitkin suggests the following. This also, incidentally, keys us into ways in which PrD can be used as a catalyst for discovery and innovation.

1. *Increase the focus on process.* Outcomes are not as important as the process. Remove constraints on experimentation. The smaller scale the actions, the quicker we can generate outcome distributions with a variety of failures.

2. *Legitimize intelligent failure.* Intelligent failure must be accepted and supported, and by more than lip service. The aim should be a culture where "failure can be a badge honor." Publicly recognizing individuals who intelligently fail will show commitment to strategic failure, experimentation, and innovation.

3. *Engender and sustain commitment to intelligent failure.* If an organization is serious about risk taking and stra-tegic failure, then intelligent failures must be viewed as an asset. This leads to a seemingly ironic result: Teams might be penalized for not failing enough, as they might not be sufficiently taking risks, dealing with and learning from their failures, or bringing their experi-ments to resolution.

4. *Emphasize failure management systems rather than individual failure.* Strategic failure must be implemented at the organizational level. Individuals will tend to produce safe successes or predictable failures, neither of which are all that informative. Organizations should then spotlight and encourage experimentation and intelligent failure. The number of successful innovations can be increased only by purposefully increasing both the number and the diversity of failures.

Part 3 of the book describes how to implement PrD, and, in the process, how to take actionable steps, at an individual level to practice intelligent failure.

Risk Factors

Designing to fail, and PrD in general, requires the right team makeup, as discussed in Chapter 10. Without a good facilitator, the internal team easily falls into the trap of presenting or defending its concepts. The core idea is to craft futuristic artifacts suitable for assessing the internal team's assumptions. Crafting such artifacts requires teams with design thinking skills. Engineers and analysts may be uncomfortable with PrD until they've seen its benefits. Designers may be too attached to their own ideas to permit them to fail. The facilitator, then, should ideally be a researcher, someone familiar with social science research and qualitative techniques.

We've worked with folks who, after being exposed to this technique repeatedly, still don't get it. They look at it like it's all unicorns and pixie dust; in a way, they're right! By insisting "Reality can't bat last,"* these individuals fail to realize the business value of intelligent failures. They don't appreciate how PrD reduces risk through early elimination of bad ideas and assumptions. In PrD, the only genuine failure would be failing to fail. Stakeholders still firmly stuck in older, industrial age

---

*"Reality bats last" is the battle cry of many brainstorming exercises and design thinking approaches

ROI concepts have a hard time reconciling failure as a benefit. Their position hijacks true ROI by ignoring the presence of opportunity costs and by refusing to consider risk reduction as a legitimate and important source of true business value.

It's often not the "You're going to fail, so fail quickly" part they object to, but rather *what* exactly is failing. Some, such as agilists, insist real value comes from having built functioning code that fails, so it can be iterated and refined. To this we like to say, "We can sketch a stupid idea faster than you can code it." If there is business value in failing fast, the faster you fail, the greater the value (assuming an equal effort and equal amount of learning). If PrD increases our velocity of failure with less effort and without sacrificing learning, then it must generate greater business value. Some engineers and agilists focus on failing fast solely in service of a solution. We want our ideas to fail fast *so we can reject them altogether*. We're trying, as Sitkin argued, to increase our overall distribution of ideas, to arrive at a solution delivering greater business value. We're not trying to squeeze the most business value from a suboptimal solution.

Conclusion

PrD's first principle, Design to Fail, rests on the notion failure is not a negative state, but a necessary step to improving. Rather than leaving it up to the market, users, or other external forces, Design to Fail requires us to take control of our failures, to literally induce them as part of a conscious strategy of innovation. It requires the organization to shift from a pessimistic to an optimistic view of failure.

Design to Fail is inherently an optimistic view of error: Innovation and discovery often occurs in the margins where we trip and stumble over mistakes, when something doesn't quite fit, and we're puzzled as to why. Rather than trying to eliminate those errors by modifying our solution, we eliminate the error *state* by modifying *our understanding of the problem*. It's we who have it all wrong, not our stakeholders. By embracing the notion of intelligent failure we can rapidly explore problem spaces and identify opportunities in record time with minimal effort.

Summary

- We're going to fail. The real questions are how quickly and to what degree are we going to fail? PrD stresses the importance of using failure as a catalyst for insight.

- In PrD, the internal team builds its assumptions into physical artifacts and gets them in front of external stakeholders (users) as quickly as possible. By revealing its ideas immediately, the team airs and vets its assumptions about the external stakeholders and their real needs, goals, frustrations, and requirements.

- The goal is not to refine the idea or design or artifact, but to sacrificially offer it up to learn about the real problem space at hand. The more ideas the internal team cycles through, the more failure will be minimized.

- Failure is not something we should be averse to—not if we fail intelligently. Though it might seem counterintuitive, succeeding early is actually a risky strategy. It robs us of the wealth of information only intelligent failures can provide.

Chapter 5: Create, Discover, Analyze

"I don't understand you," said Alice. "It's dreadfully confusing!"
"That's the effect of living backwards," the Queen said kindly: "it always makes one a little giddy at first--"

Presumptive Design
DESIGN PROVOCATIONS FOR INNOVATION

Follow effective action with quiet reflection. From the quiet reflection will come even more effective action.
—Peter Drucker

Overview As we described in Chapter 2, traditional user-centered design (UCD) treats user research as an up-front activity occurring separately from design. (We say "traditional" to emphasize that PrD is also a form of UCD.) Following Sato's iteration of the Owens/Kumar model, traditional UCD starts in the lower left quadrant of the matrix, whereas PrD starts in the upper right (Figure 5.1).

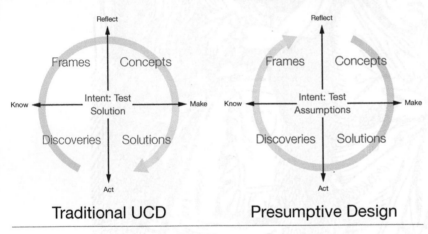

Traditional UCD   Presumptive Design

Figure 5.1 Traditional UCD versus PrD in Sato's Design Thinking model

Traditional UCD starts with research, with discoveries, and moves through frames and concepts and then decides upon a solution. In most traditional UCD projects, once a team has landed on a solution, it spends the remainder of the project exploring, refining, and improving on *that* solution. PrD starts with concepts, moves to conceiving solutions based on them, and then through discoveries and frames. Early on, these discoveries refine our concepts, causing us to craft *new* solutions based on the new frame of reference. Typically, several cycles through the four quadrants are required before the team lands on a desired solution. This approach reduces the likelihood of landing on a solution too early because it starts with a divergent thinking process (conceptualization).

In PrD, teams are required to begin with what could be called "iterative debunking sessions." The team exposes its

68

assumptions by crafting an artifact representative of them (see Chapter 15 for more). What is being created is the *provocation*, not necessarily a mock-up of a specific solution or product. This is a crucial point: The PrD artifact—what is *created*—does not have to be a representation of the solution *per se*. The artifact might be:

- A series of vision statements
- A rough business plan
- A representation of a product or interface.

The variety of possible artifacts is reflected in the cases:

- In The Case of Constricted Collective Conversation, the artifact was a chalkboard on a public sidewalk.
- In The Case of the PowerPoint Play, the artifact consisted of provocative statements about design.
- In The Case of the Black-Magic Batman, the artifacts were second-hand action figures.
- In The Case of the Hard-Boiled Eggs, the artifact was a carton of plastic eggs.
- In The Case of the Pushy Pillboxes and The Case of the Rx Reminder, the artifacts were in fact representations of possible solutions.

Artifacts need not be a rendering of the expected solution at all. Sometimes the artifact is just an object. What matters is rendering the team's assumptions.

See Appendix A

No matter the form it takes, the artifact is used to represent the internal stakeholders' assumptions and provoke a reaction from external stakeholders (users, customers, etc.). Once we've created it, we get the artifact in front of external stakeholders so the internal stakeholders can see, firsthand, how their assumptions were wrong. Leo has long compared this technique with a scene in *Through the Looking Glass*. In the story, the Unicorn comments on how Alice goes about serving cake, saying, "You don't know how to manage Looking-glass cakes. Hand it round first, and cut it afterwards"[1] (Figure 5.2).

Begin at the End

Presumptive Design
DESIGN PROVOCATIONS FOR INNOVATION

Figure 5.2 "You don't know how to manage Looking-glass cakes. Hand it round first, and cut it afterwards"

PrD shifts the UCD cycle by following the Unicorn's advice. So, in the PrD cycle, things are done "backwards." Building stuff does not wait for anything. We start by *creating* something (a representation of an assumption). As we learned in the last chapter, we *know* what we've created is going to fail. That's fine. We're failing on purpose to iteratively reveal valuable insights about our stakeholders' problems. This is especially important when trying to innovate, when neither the problem nor the domain is understood. How well the problem is defined goes a long way to shape what happens once the team enters the solution space. The result of this work might not be a specified solution but a clear, crisp product vision. When Apple set out to build the iPod, for example, Jobs framed the problem to be solved with a single sentence: "1,000 songs in my pocket."[2]

The Artifact Provokes Discovery

As soon as the artifact is built it is handed over to external stakeholders, without reservation, protectiveness, or defensiveness. We place the artifact in front of a stakeholder and give him some tasks to perform with it. Then, without leading, we prompt him to explore, play pretend, and tell stories. This moves us to *discovery*. Here, as the internal team engages with external stakeholders, they together co-explore ideas, propose solutions, and, in some instances, rework the artifact together. This means PrD is not only empathic, like traditional UCD, but also participatory. This broader focus lends itself extremely well to generating stakeholder "buy-in," as the external stakeholders themselves become active participants in the vetting and development of ideas from Day One. To paraphrase the adage: It's much easier to edit than to start from a blank slate. In this case, external stakeholders are invited to edit the team's assumptions about the problem space by engaging with the artifact.

As long as the team is in problem space the emphasis is on the left side of Laseau's funnel (Figure 5.3).[3]

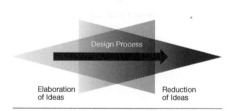

Figure 5.3 While the team is in the problem space, they remain on the left side of Laseau's funnel

The focus is on *generating* ideas about the problem space, not refining potential solutions (what we call "hill climbing"). Similar to Activity-Centered Design,[4] PrD focuses on gaining a deep understanding of the goals and tasks of the stakeholder, not on usability and not on testing the interface to see what stakeholders' preferences are. This comes later, in solution space, after the decision regarding what will be built has been made.

Analyze What They Mean, Not Just What We Heard

Once we've captured external stakeholder reactions to our assumptions, we move to *analysis*, in which we hope to uncover stakeholder goals and true needs. The analysis we use in PrD is similar to other qualitative social science research techniques: We review the actual words used by our external stakeholders, paying close and particular attention to their emotional reactions to our provocations and the common themes that emerge among the different Engagement Sessions (Figure 5.4). We are searching for *meaning* in the data. What are stakeholders actually saying? What is the true need they are expressing?

As we discuss in Chapter 16, the sessions may be recorded to capture stakeholder reactions

Figure 5.4 Note not just what the stakeholder says, but how she feels

verbatim, but even if they are not recorded, Observers in the sessions should strive to capture exact utterances.

It's not about tweaking designs. Does the very concept make sense to external stakeholders? Is it the right overall direction?

See Appendix A: The Case of the Business Case

In The Case of the Business Case, for example, it was clear from several Engagement Sessions the user interface itself was not familiar to many of the targeted users. For some teams, that finding would be enough to analyze and dig into. What needs to change? What preemptive marketing needs to be done to help prepare users for this novel interface?

But the case shined a light on a more profound issue: The stakeholders were completely baffled by the business proposition itself. They expressed their confusion in terms of the interface, but a deeper examination of their concerns revealed apprehension about the business offering. We can't rely on the superficial reactions stakeholders offer us; we must step back, preferably during the Engagement Session itself (see Chapters 14 and 16), to understand the meaning behind those reactions. We consider their comments in the context of our assumptions and our objectives. And, we very likely begin a new *concept* phase as a result.

We'll scrap our idea and come up with a better one, a natural consequence of the process of reflecting, critiquing, and reworking. PrD has far greater impact while the team is exploring the problem space than after it has landed on a solution. Without this "surveying of the land" we won't know what other hills there are that could have been climbed (Figure 5.5).

Figure 5.5 Analysis and framing during the problem space investigation lets the team identify the problems of interest

Let's talk about what we're actually creating at this point. This whole process, the process of creating, discovering, and analyzing, of cycling through the quadrants of concepts, solutions, discoveries, and frames, is best done using low-investment, low-fidelity artifacts.

Taking the Low Road

First, low-fidelity artifacts or sketches that look, well, "sketchy," communicate exploration and send the signal there are still a lot of degrees of freedom left in the design process. Buxton[5] discusses how sketches (and we would add low-fidelity artifacts) let stakeholders know the conversation is about a tentative proposal; at this point the

High-Fidelity Artifacts Look and Feel Like Finished Products

team is noncommittal. This approach invites stakeholders to be more vocal: to suggest, explore, question, and propose. Low-fidelity artifacts therefore are more appropriate while in the problem space of a project.

High fidelity, Buxton argues, sends the message the team is already in solution space. The process is now more about resolving specific issues and refining the solution. This, he insists, is a very different exercise, more about usability improvement than idea vetting. With high-fidelity artifacts, the team telegraphs its goal is to make the best of the decided-upon direction and solution. If the team isn't at a refinement stage, this is the wrong signal to send. External stakeholders will feel the design is already fixed, regardless of their feedback or input.

Low-Fidelity Artifacts Cost Less Low-fidelity artifacts have another advantage: They're often faster and cheaper to produce. (This is not, however, always the case. See Chapter 8.) In PrD, after all, speed is of the essence. In addition, since we know we're wrong going in, we want to reduce our investment in crafting artifacts.

Risk Factors

Create, Discover, Analyze is fraught with risks, many of which we cover in detail in later chapters, but here are a few worth mentioning.

Effort Hands down, the most frequent risk cited by newcomers to PrD is the idea of wasted effort. "How can you just embark on some wild set of ideas, knowing it'll likely be a waste?" Depending on the speaker, the waste being alluded to varies: Researchers express concern about building stuff before we know who we're talking to; developers express concern we're building stuff before we know we can even deliver it.

Figure 5.6 Craft an artifact with the least investment to drive the most insight

As stated earlier, the real concern is about how much effort the team puts into these exercises. PrD works best when the team expends the least effort expressing its assumptions. Bottom line: If it feels like the team is taking too long to get in front of stakeholders, it probably is. The solution is to "just do it"; stop the hand wringing, the analysis paralysis, and the fussing over design details. Just. Get. Out. There. The goal is to get to insights with the minimum investment of time, money, and energy. The earlier and cheaper we can validly vet an idea, the better (Figure 5.6, left). As they ask in Lean UX, what's the smallest experiment we can conduct to test our hypothesis?[6]

For many teams, the true risk in the Create, Discover, Analyze principle is a failure to get outrageous. We hear it all the time from sponsors: How do we get a group of people to really "break out of the box?" How can we get the really wild ideas on the table so teams can explore the stupid, the unfeasible, the nonviable approaches with stakeholders?

We see it in nearly every Creation Session we've run: Some member of a team resists the principle and focuses the team's

Reality, Timidity, and Incrementalism

effort on an incremental shift in a current approach, "because it's what can be built." To be clear, even this timid approach will produce results from our stakeholders, but it likely just delays the inevitable and, more importantly, delays the project.

By "incrementalism," we mean starting with the status quo and changing only one aspect of it in some way that is easily envisioned. If it is a product, as in The Case of the New Case, the team may simply move pieces of the front panel around to the side. If it is a strategy, it may mean increasing gross revenue. In any case, incrementalism begins with what the team knows can be accomplished and never ventures outside that envelope.

> When the team uses early Engagement Sessions to refine a single idea, it misses broad insights.
>
> See Appendix A: The Case of the New Case

Consider the following scenario: The team decides to go with an incremental approach and sets up interviews with stakeholders. Assuming the team has internalized the real purpose of these interviews (not to test its idea but to test its assumptions), the likely outcome of the first couple of interviews will be stakeholders declaring the idea indistinguishable from what they have today. If the sessions go well, these external stakeholders will not only denounce the approach as a waste of time but also offer up their rationales.

Incremental or Disruptive Innovation?

PrD, as discussed in the introductory chapters and in Chapter 9, is best suited for complex or chaotic situations: those which existing processes or experts cannot resolve. For example, a business faces an existential threat, primarily because its approaches are ill-suited to new market conditions. Or an emergent situation requires action first, any action, as a way of discovering the underlying problem. Tweaking an existing approach in these circumstances is a form of denial and in the most dire of circumstances may lead to an organization's demise.

In these complex and chaotic areas PrD provides a long-term vision or road map to help internal stakeholders rationally move into a future state.

The sessions can be viewed as a success in only one key way: They have forced a reluctant team to face the real problem, a problem no amount of incrementalism will address. For some organizations, this alone is a major breakthrough, but we believe that gulf can be crossed during the initial Creation Session itself, accelerating the process by days or weeks.

The antidote to this risk is strong facilitation during the Creation Session. Force the teams to get wild, set up some kind of competition, and offer awards for outrageousness. In Appendix B we offer a few ways to encourage "box breaking" and get past this risk.

A third risk is when teams fail to view insights through an appropriate critical lens. This happens for several reasons:

- The data don't get collected correctly. (The chapters in Part 3 address this risk.)

- The analysis focuses on the small, not the big-picture issues.

- The "answer" is sitting right in front of us but we can't see it.[7]

Focusing on the Small

In The Case of the Business Case, the team (new to PrD) was writing up its results as if they were usability tests. Although it's true the *framework* for the report is very much like a usability test, the *content* is very different. After reading through the rough draft, we pointed out where they were focusing on the "small," rather than profound insights. For example, in the original report, the team pointed out where users failed to understand a particular interaction with the screen, or pointed out the need for additional data. While those were certainly true, they missed the more important point: The proposal was light years ahead of stakeholders' understandings. This single insight was worth the entire effort—the business leaders needed to know how far ahead of the curve they really were so they could adjust their road maps, marketing, and of course the experience design itself.

Regardless, after going through all of the effort to get assumptions in front of stakeholders, the risk is the team fails to hear the profound results coming back. And there are almost always profound discoveries in this process. In fact, *knowing* there are likely profound results in the data is one of the ways we keep ourselves on the hunt for them. If we haven't had a profound breakthrough, either we weren't listening or the data didn't get captured correctly.

When the team focuses on details instead of big assumptions and meaning, it risks missing the forest for the trees.
See Appendix A: The Case of the Business Case

Presumptive Design

DESIGN PROVOCATIONS FOR INNOVATION

Create, Discover, Analyze

Hiding in Plain Sight

Often the results are obvious, so obvious the team races past them in search of a hidden jewel. Leo recalls a Participatory Design (not PrD) session he led to redesign a website for key stakeholders. After collecting pages and pages of input from the participants, he returned to the office. Taking over a conference room, he pasted up all of the sheets, grabbed a cup of coffee, and just sat back looking at what the stakeholders had done. The sheets were covered with scribbles and sticky notes—a riot of noise and color. But after several minutes of squinting his eyes, of letting his laser-beam attention go out of focus, a solution appeared out of the noise.

That one "aha!" established the conceptual design for the solution, satisfying two competing stakeholders. Prior attempts to reconcile these competing needs had failed. The solution was staring him in the face, hidden in plain sight. By paying attention to the overarching patterns, not the details, Leo was able to see the real problem (and ultimately the solution) emerge.

Diminished Value One risk, while unlikely, has potentially high impact *on the team's credibility* with its sponsors: The team "discovers" an already well-known problem. Here's how this plays out: The team goes through the artifact creation process, sets up stakeholder engagements, and returns a major discovery of "the problem." Sadly, when it reports out its discovery, other members of the organization discount the discovery as something that's been well known for a long time. The only saving grace here is at least the team didn't spend a lot of effort retreading old ground.

There are a couple of antidotes to this risk. The first is to make sure the Creation Session is populated with the right folks—those folks who "already know what the problem is" should be in those sessions, if possible. This reduces

78

the likelihood of viewing the problem as novel. The second antidote is to place the obvious discovery in the context of all the others. PrD Engagement Sessions usually don't return a "single" problem statement. In most cases, the team returns with too many critical issues, not just one. Reporting out a "top three" set of issues, of which the "well-known" problem is just one, lends credibility to the process in that it too found a known problem, perhaps without the team being previously aware of it.

Finally, if a particular problem (in this case a "known" problem) resonates more strongly than others, across multiple sessions, then this is a major point of validation—and validating a known problem using a different method is an important data point. Essentially, the response to the naysayers should be: "Yes, we too found this to be *the* key problem as well. Perhaps it's time to do something about it. Here's some additional information we gleaned from the stakeholders that might provide a path to a solution."

Summary

- Traditional UCD begins with research, followed by the team moving into solution space with a design based on what was learned. In contrast, PrD couples research with creating stuff—in PrD we *start* with design and use it as the vehicle of discovery, all the while staying in the problem space.

- As we cycle through ideas and analyze our failures we iterate closer and closer to an optimal solution.

- Time to insight and overall cost-benefit is typically best served by focusing on low-fidelity, quick-and-dirty artifacts.

- This approach is not without risks. Mitigate them by including the right people in the initial Creation Sessions, by expert facilitation, and by looking for deeper meaning in the captured data.

Chapter 6: Make Assumptions Explicit

Presumptive Design
Design Provocations for Innovation

Your assumptions are your windows on the world. Scrub them off every once in a while, or the light won't come in.
—Alan Alda

Overview

Our assumptions are like a building that confines us. We're trying to learn about the world around us. We're trying to survey the landscape, trying to map it, but we see outside only through the windows of the building in which we're standing. Moving from window to window won't help. To make matters more challenging, the building may be an eyesore in the landscape—a discovery we can't make from inside. We need to exit the building and look at it from a fresh perspective. But we can't do this by ourselves. Our assumptions confine us and they won't fall away on their own.

We imagine a future we believe is desirable, but we see it through the lens of our assumptions. Our assumptions, built from our past experiences, knowledge, and expertise, may not address the needs of a new situation—a new strategy, new market, new customer base, or new technology.

PrD is designed to make our assumptions obvious. To continue the analogy, we self-consciously craft a "building" (an artifact, during the Creation Session) explicitly rendering the team's assumptions, and then we plop that building into our external stakeholders' landscape to learn their perspective of it (during the Engagement Sessions). In PrD, once we've created an artifact, we quickly exit it to see it as our stakeholders do. Just as when we pass by an ugly building we are compelled to comment, external stakeholders can't help but point out where our assumptions don't make sense.

The approach resolves the dilemma of asking ourselves (or our stakeholders) what we should do next: We set up an environment to trigger conversation and provoke thoughtful engagement. When the team creates an appropriate artifact, the Engagement Sessions result in a series of discoveries. By design, PrD generates surprises.

Their value lies in generating novel insights. As The Case of the Black-Magic Batman illustrated, only after offering action heroes to the children of the village did the research team uncover the underlying framework of their society—a crucial (and surprising) understanding to support the client's goals. This discovery changed everything. It revealed an entire world of folk beliefs, traditional medicine, superstitions, and witchcraft, inherent to the village's culture and way of life. This surprising result was essential to the client's ultimate goals: Any new approach to medicine would have to accommodate an environment rife with competing folk beliefs concerning health and medicine.

Sometimes the team's assumptions are about the *protocol* for the research.

See Appendix A: The Case of the Black-Magic Batman

The parable of the Pharaoh, his architect, and the pyramid offers an excellent example of how difficult it can be to reveal our assumptions. In its original form, the story argues against traditional forms of programming.[1] Here we illustrate how the discipline of UX is best positioned to illuminate our assumptions.

Revealing Assumptions Isn't Easy

> A Pharaoh approaches his architect and says: "Build me a pyramid that will dwarf all others."
>
> The architect gathers his workers and begins to build the Pharaoh's dream.
>
> He starts with the bottom layer, and after 25 years it is finished (Figure 6.1).
>
> The architect proceeds to the next layer, and after 15 years, it too is finished (Figure 6.2).
>
> As the architect begins the next layer, the Pharaoh suffers a fatal illness and lies on his death bed.
>
> "You have failed," he whispers to the architect. "You have left me with a monstrosity."

Figure 6.1 The first layer of the Pharaoh's pyramid

Figure 6.2 The next layer of the Pharaoh's pyramid

Presumptive Design
DESIGN PROVOCATIONS FOR INNOVATION

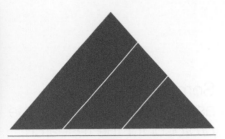

Figure 6.3 An agile approach to building the Pharaoh's pyramid

Figure 6.4 What the Pharaoh meant when he asked for a pyramid

The Pharaoh's son, looking at the architect's work, is struck with a brilliant insight.

"Look," he says, drawing on a tablet. "If you proceed this way, you will always complete a pyramid no matter what" (Figure 6.3).

In the story, Mayo-Smith argues for constructing incrementally, completing small components to build a larger system. The story is also an argument against detailed project planning:

> Because large software projects have many functional components, a good way to guarantee success is to finish the design, coding, and debugging of each component before you begin the next piece. This Complete Before Continuing process … starts with an overall model and a feature list, then proceeds with small development steps.

It's a powerful argument and speaks eloquently to the beauty of agile methods. But note the clause after the ellipsis: "starts with an overall model." And here is where many project teams are well served by their UX teammates.

Inherent in the parable is a big assumption: All parties actually know what each is talking about. We naturally assume we share a common language or, metaphorically, a common *architecture* of experience. Just exactly what is the "overall model" referred to by Mayo-Smith?

Consider an alternate (or extended) ending for the parable based on the UX perspective.

> The son and the architect ponder this revelation when the Pharaoh, agitated by the failure, musters his strength and interrupts them.
>
> "No, no," he whispers. "That is not at all what I wanted." In his trembling hand he draws a form on a slate tablet, illustrating what he meant (Figure 6.4).

How often do our customers "ask" for a pyramid, when what they want is an elephant?

This is the fundamental challenge of UX: What do our users actually *mean* when they say they need "a pyramid?" Of all the disciplines engaged in product development, UX is the one best trained and most experienced in getting the answer to that question. And PrD is one of the most powerful tools we can use.

Figure 6.5 HiPPs debating their opinions about what the solution should be

Imagine a cross-disciplinary team of developers, analysts, architects, program managers, and a product owner. It's very early in the product life cycle—Iteration 0, Gate 0, Pre-Explore, Charter. It should be the time for ideation and divergent thinking, to look at the problem space and really get wild about the possibilities. Instead, what typically happens? Several team members propose solutions to the

Discussing Solutions, not Assumptions

problem or the requirements *as perceived*. Instead of parking these ideas off to the side, tensions rise and, after lots of highly paid people sit around debating things in meetings, the team yields to a couple of team members who Know. What. The. Solution. Is. Maybe everyone just adopts the HiPPO (highest paid person's opinion; Figure 6.5).

In many instances, the team fails to set aside this early deep dive into solution space. Team members with other ideas are forced to "disagree and commit."[2] The team plows ahead based on what they imagine can be built. From the start, the outcome is crippled: The result isn't defined by what stakeholders can use or need, and, worse, the team hasn't committed to discover stakeholders' true concerns. If that isn't bad enough, many on the team won't see a problem—they achieved consensus on an outcome, they crafted a plan, and they're executing on it. The apologists in the group rationalize the approach. They suggest no one can really predict the future, so it's best to get something out there and adjust it later, if there's a problem. Unfortunately, all that follows is damage control (Figure 6.6).

Released Product is No Place to Learn What Stakeholders Need

Figure 6.6 When teams focus on solutions too early, all that follows is damage control

Damage control comes in many forms: marketing messaging, transition change management (market education), training to remedy poor UX, or "customer support." Each of these activities costs money—a lot of money—and none positions the organization to execute on its true strategy: improving its position in the market or delivering on its underlying charter.

PrD offers an alternative. In PrD everyone's ideas become

concrete immediately with little argument or infighting. A liberating aspect of PrD is how easily people get on to the same page. PrD *requires* internal team members to get their ideas and opinions out of their heads and into the artifact, even if those ideas conflict with one another. The artifact doesn't have to make sense; it does, however, have to represent the team's assumptions.

This idea has been controversial—that an "impossible" artifact generates useful results. It's more than some team members can accept. Once a team has experienced it, there's no going back, but getting them to believe it will work beforehand requires expert facilitation (which we cover in length in the chapters that follow). Even if a proposed idea seems foolish or ridiculous, the team must find a way to express it, to articulate the idea as faithfully and truthfully as possible.

Nonsensical Artifacts Generate Useful Results

Getting team members to even *recognize* their underlying assumptions is often a challenge. We don't think about our assumptions very often—we simply act on them.[3] Here again, an expert facilitator teases out the team's underlying assumptions, even as the team bakes those assumptions into an artifact. This process is not familiar, but it eliminates tensions. Rather than arguing about whose assumptions make most sense, the discussion shifts to making those assumptions manifest—how to articulate them in an artifact so stakeholders can react to them. The focus is no longer on which idea is better but on getting all ideas expressed appropriately.

Good Assumptions are Hard to Find

As described in The Case of the New Case, Leo urged a client's development team to question their assumptions about the very charter of their program. The product manager had assumed merely changing the envelope of the product, or rearranging some of its external components, would suffice to address long-standing customer complaints.

Early on, the internal team should be airing and vetting its big-picture assumptions. Nothing at this stage should be taken for granted.
See Appendix A: The Case of the New Case

87

But going into a test with an incremental change would likely not provoke the reactions the product manager was hoping for: His end-users wouldn't see much of a difference between his proposed changes and the current product. The team had gone in with the assumption the product's form factor would remain unchanged. Leo prompted them to call out and question this assumption. What would happen if they did change the form factor? Perhaps more importantly, what if changing the form factor *didn't* address the perceived customer pain points? Would a radical change in form factor provoke customers to reveal needs having nothing at all to do with form factors?

Chris used PrD to challenge an entire field's approach to therapy with People With Aphasia (PWA).

See Appendix A: The Case of the Transformed Treatment

In The Case of the Transformed Treatment, entertainment expert Chris Stapleton used his work in play testing and mixed reality technologies to challenge assumptions in therapies for aphasic patients. Working with therapists, patients, and their caregivers, Chris and his team identified a radically different way of approaching therapy: challenging traditional therapy's key operating assumption (getting language skills back) by demonstrating a different assumption (enabling storytelling). In this case, professional therapists were unable to step out of their frameworks to see how their operating assumptions might be counterproductive.

Ass.U.Me—Implicit Assumptions Make Us All Look Stupid

Make Assumptions Explicit forces the team to reflect on its own values and beliefs. It doesn't matter whether reflection occurs during the Creation Session or with external stakeholders during the Engagement Sessions. All that matters is the team truly understands its operating assumptions and has reduced the risks associated with them.

Most projects proceed from problem to solution space without such purposeful reflection (Figure 6.7). The organization's assumptions are baked into the outcomes without anyone realizing it. At minimum, these solutions are expensive because they fail or require significant rework.

In the worst cases, the results are dangerous, leading to potential harm.[4] In any event, implicit assumptions create hidden risk. Implicit assumptions include:

- What the internal team can deliver
- How the problem should be approached
- Who the external stakeholders are, including their needs, frustrations, and goals

Without surfacing assumptions, the team risks delivering a wholly inappropriate solution. Our assumptions shape and ground our response to the problem at hand.

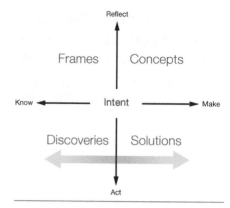

Figure 6.7 Straight-line thinking from discovery to solution within Sato's Design Thinking model

Returning to our opening analogy, what we want to do is exit the building we're in (and the quicker the better) to see if it's even the right building in the context of the larger landscape (the problem space). We want to avoid spending effort or money on a solution based on the wrong set of assumptions.

We naturally rationalize our work based on our underlying assumptions. But we rarely step back and question those assumptions before we get started. As The Case of the New Case shows, a team can be so enmeshed in its assumptions that either they don't realize those assumptions exist or they are surprised they should even be questioned.

In Three-card Monte, the "mark," or victim, goes in assuming he's about to play a game of chance (Figure 6.8). It's this assumption that allows him to get taken. Our external stakeholders are not trying to con us. That's not where the analogy lies; rather, by failing to vet our assumptions we risk conning ourselves.

We can't even assume we know our team members' assumptions. In the Creation Session we strive to get them all on the table, but we're not always successful. In The

We *Really* Want to Believe

Until the team was pushed to question its assumptions, they were unaware of them.
See Appendix A: The Case of the New Case

Figure 6.8 In Three-card Monte, the mark assumes he's playing a fair game of chance

We Don't Know Anybody Else's Assumptions Either

Presumptive Design
DESIGN PROVOCATIONS FOR INNOVATION

Sometimes the team's assumptions don't emerge until well into the process.

See Appendix A: The Case of the New Business Case

Case of the Business Case, only after going through a full PrD cycle of Creation and Engagement Sessions did the product manager and the lead technologist reveal they were operating under radically different assumptions. Here was an example of the whole team not just being unaware of its assumptions about the problem space but also not even agreeing on assumptions for the solution space! Sometimes our assumptions are way off. The earlier we identify and assess them, the better.

For any project intending to introduce innovation into the marketplace, the team must agree on its underlying assumptions. Without that alignment and shared vision, the project faces insurmountable risks.

Risk Factors

Making assumptions explicit is tricky. It requires a huge amount of trust among the team members. If the team doesn't start with mutual trust, the process is likely to fail (of course, many other processes are likely to fail as well). Because assumptions are often hard to detect, team members may be unaware of them. A spirit of play, an environment of trust, and excellent facilitation are necessary to tease out the team's assumptions.

Insincerity

Insincerity or lack of authenticity is never a good quality in our professional or personal lives. It also has no place in the PrD process. Our ethics and integrity are on the hook. PrD asks people to be vulnerable, to voice their heartfelt opinions. In some cases, years of pent-up frustration are released when people are finally given permission to air their beliefs.

When we are focusing on assumptions, we must be on our best behaviors. If we are facilitating, we must adjudicate among many competing opinions, finding a way for each to be expressed in the artifact. Crafting an artifact incorporating everyone's assumptions is an intense design problem. All the while we have to keep in mind the artifact itself is likely worthless. Designers have experience interpreting client requirements. Their job is to translate requirements into meaningful artifacts. But designers don't have the luxury of criticizing team members' assumptions or dismissing them as silly. The team will look to the designers to help articulate its assumptions, not be critical of them. Making assumptions explicit is an in-the-moment act, requiring complete sincerity and passionate advocacy for each team member's point of view.

We always assume good intentions: Attendees at the Creation Session are sincerely interested in having their point of view represented. While it's possible a team member could subvert the process by offering a completely insincere idea, PrD self-corrects: External stakeholders will react to it like anything else.

The second most likely risk is failure to get the team's agreement on the artifact—a failure of getting to "Yes." What are we supposed to do when three conflicting ideas are proposed by team members?

Not Getting to Yes

Again, expert facilitation and leaving our egos at the door mitigate the problem.

Rule Number 1: Everybody's assumptions must be addressed.

Consider the following ways to accomplish Rule Number 1:

- An individual eventually decides to take her idea off the table because she sees a better expression of it coming from someone else.

- The artifact is crafted to permit multiple pathways through it, each path expressing a different idea.

- The team crafts multiple artifacts.

- Most elegantly, the team crafts a single *ambiguous* artifact permitting an external stakeholder to interpret it in any number of ways, including the ways the internal team believes it should be interpreted.

This last resolution offers the team an emergency exit when there are multiple beliefs (with potentially opposing consequences).

Rule Number 2: (see Rule Number 1).

Summary

- PrD reduces risk to a project by having team members reveal their assumptions early on. The team puts its cards on the table on Day One. The challenge is for team members to overcome guardedness, reluctance (at revealing ideas "too soon"), or defensiveness.

- Make Assumptions Explicit also builds team cohesion—all with little debate or infighting.

- Revealing assumptions involves the entire team in the UX research process.

- When differing opinions result in conflicts, expert facilitation is required to permit everyone's assumptions a place in the artifact.

- Whether assumptions are truly tacit knowledge or merely fabricated rationales, the stakeholders ultimately adjudicate their value.

Chapter 7: Iterate, Iterate, Iterate!

Presumptive Design
Design Provocations for Innovation

The phoenix must burn to emerge.
—Janet Fitch
There is no harm in repeating a good thing.
—Plato

Overview

The principle of Iterate, Iterate, Iterate requires us to repeatedly expose our assumptions to our external stakeholders. Through each cycle, we:

- Vet and refine those assumptions.

- Build our knowledge about our stakeholders and their needs.

- Increase our knowledge about the problem space in which we're working.

With each subsequent iteration, our assumptions, artifacts, and ideas increasingly resonate with external stakeholders.

PrD is like a magic trick. We present our canard in all seriousness. We vanish it and then make it reappear as something slightly more on-point, useful, appealing, and compelling. But, unlike a magic trick, we repeat it over and over until, finally, the canard manifests as something beautiful.

Each iteration tests the internal team's assumptions, expressed as an artifact and task list. PrD is based on this axiom: Although our stakeholders cannot design the future, they can (and most certainly will) criticize it when it's shown to them. The external stakeholders *will* tear our design and ideas apart. When they see something that just isn't right, and we invite them to critique it, they will reveal their latent and inherent needs to us. When they do, we want as many team members as possible to observe it firsthand. There isn't a faster and more compelling way to disseminate "ahas" across a team (Figure 7.1).

375

5555

555

555

5555

55555

55555

In The Case of the Balking Bicyclists, the artifact used in the first iteration was thoroughly trashed by external stakeholders. By the third iteration, the team deeply understood their external stakeholders' problem space and had honed in on possible solutions. In The Case of the Preoccupied Passersby, the first iteration of the researchers' artifact was a low-fidelity game. The team used it to discover key requirements for the final installation, including how much time residents of the city of Chicago would take to explore ideas about the city's arts and culture.

Figure 7.1 Creation Session team members brainstorming on their assumptions

As the internal team progresses in its learnings, the artifacts evolve. In the first couple of Engagement Sessions, stakeholders may tear apart assumptions about what they do and how they do it. Maybe in the next few sessions they're tearing apart assumptions about their main goals. As the internal team produces ideas with greater resonance, the focus of critique shifts—from underlying assumptions to details of the designs. This is how teams iterate from problem to solution space. At first the internal team will have to swallow its pride as stakeholders tear apart its misconceptions and ignorance of the problem space. Soon they're tearing apart the details, until, eventually, the tearing apart becomes nitpicks. This is when we know PrD has served its purpose (Figure 7.2).

By throwing ideas out and rapidly reengaging with new ones, David and his team quickly evolved their understanding of the problem.
See Appendix A: The Case of the Balking Bicyclists

Jamie designed a set of low-fidelity games to quickly learn how Chicagoans would react to a public installation.
See Appendix A: The Case of the Preoccupied Passersby

95

Presumptive Design
DESIGN PROVOCATIONS FOR INNOVATION

Iterating Is Not Wasted Effort

Iterating entails throwing stuff in the garbage. From a waterfall (i.e., "fail-late development") perspective, throwing stuff out and starting over sounds like added cost. It sounds *expensive*, and it is expensive—if it happens late in the cycle. But, as we've said before, ideas are cheap. With PrD, we test the validity of these ideas economically (as we discuss in Chapter 8). More importantly, by engaging with stakeholders early, those tests have their greatest impact. The more ideas we vet (and the earlier we vet them), the more confident we can be in our final solution. The key is to test and iterate ideas *quickly*.

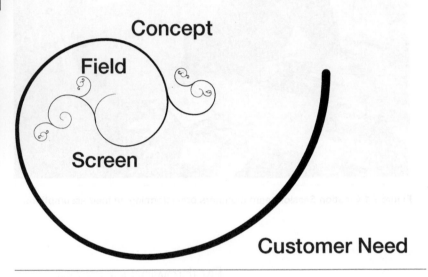

Figure 7.2 How PrD scales with project focus

Iteration reduces the real risk of downstream wasted effort. The iterative throwing out of ideas prevents early, small errors from having later, large impacts.[1] In highly structured, phase-gate development practices (such as waterfall), our initial plans become the measure of our success: How well did we achieve what we said we were going to do? But PrD (as in agile-type cultures) suggests our initial plans should be treated as irrelevant—since we don't know what the problem is, how can we trust a plan to solve it?

Iteration Begins Day One

A crucial difference between PrD and traditional user-centered design (UCD) is in PrD we iterate on Day One, before any important decisions have been made. In contrast, in traditional UCD, iteration typically occurs after many of the key decisions have long been made. A crucial moment in any development project is the point of decision: the point when the team decides what the final solution will be. (Recall from Chapter 2, the Double Diamond diagram. See Chapter 8 for more on this topic.) The time before that point is the "problem space" and the time after it the "solution space." PrD and traditional UCD differ the most in how each process approaches the problem space.

Of course, no project has a single, isolated decision where the team agrees on the final solution. In practice the "decision point" may be encountered several times. Nevertheless, at some point the team does shift from defining the problem to refining a solution to it.

We distinguish between predecision and postdecision project work. When designers speak of "iterative design" they're typically referring to the iterative testing and refining of prototypes past the point of decision. Iterative design normally refers to iteration in the solution space, not iteration in the project's problem space. In traditional UCD (even in projects considered "iterative" and "agile"), the problem space is handled in a waterfall-like or stepwise fashion. During the phases preparing for the decision point, product marketing managers conduct primary research. Finance and strategists determine pricing and impacts on production and operations. These activities culminate in a product definition, a fairly lengthy document with hundreds of requirements.

Implicit in those requirements are hundreds of unspoken assumptions about what the product will do. Those assumptions aren't tested predecision point because they aren't perceived as having an impact on strategic decisions. By design, phase-gate development delays investment in problem solving until after the decision point. This makes sense in the phase-gate world: Before the decision point we focus solely on the elements required to get to decision. Anything after that will be handled in the postdecision phase.

The challenge with that approach is many of the requirements going into the decision point are based on unstated (and unknown) assumptions about the stakeholders' needs (as we discussed in the prior chapter). Those assumptions have significant impact downstream as the development cycles bump into them and as external stakeholders ultimately review them.

PrD approaches both the problem and solution spaces iteratively. As a result, the team's confidence in the outcome of the project is raised *prior to* the decision point.

Iterating is a Risk Reduction Strategy

PrD's iteration of problem definition makes it an agile approach, distinguishes it from traditional UCD, and reduces risk. In such a risk-reduced project, teams are confident their offering will solve the right problems before setting out to build it the best they can. We've rarely experienced or heard of companies using this approach, even though it sounds logical. Those numbers are changing because market dynamics are forcing companies to change (as we discussed in Chapter 3).

Historically, management has been rewarded for efficiency (doing things right) and not effectiveness (doing the right thing).[2] Time and time again, organizations push solutions weighted toward what can be built, whether they are out of the box from third-party vendors or small incremental changes to existing offerings. Defenders of this approach put up a rational argument: Keeping development costs as low as possible reduces the risk of a bad ROI. This argument plays well with the agilists: Deliver the smallest increment of work returning the highest business value.

As the Pharaoh's story illuminated in Chapter 6, all of that is for naught if the team is focused on the wrong target.

If the team is only concerned about the cost of development, it misses a much larger potential ROI. For example, incremental cost of development pales in comparison to end-user loss of productivity, time on training, customer support, and other externalities.[3] And those costs only look at productivity losses. When we factor in higher adoption rates because users *want to use the product*, entire businesses flourish.[4,5]

In contrast, PrD starts by identifying the right thing to build. PrD iterates throughout the problem definition cycle beginning on Day One.

Moving fast is key. We not only start as soon as possible but also do only as many Engagement Sessions as necessary. We don't bog ourselves down by scheduling more than a few stakeholders per iteration. We learn more by running more iterations. More iterations with fewer external stakeholders are always better than fewer iterations with larger samples. Typically, three Engagement Sessions per iteration (each with one external stakeholder) are enough; five or six are plenty.

Here's the math (see Figure 7.3): Assume we have one hour each with 15 external stakeholders per month. The preferred approach is to complete five Engagement Sessions, create a new artifact, complete five more, rework the artifact (as needed), and then do five more. In this model

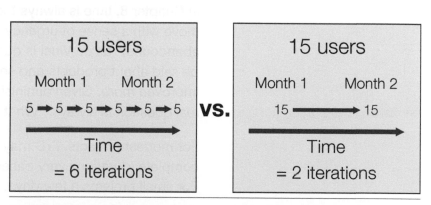

Figure 7.3 More iterations are better than few. Reduce the number of stakeholders per iteration

we complete six *iterations* in two months. If, instead, we engage all 15 stakeholders in a single iteration in the first month; rework the artifact and then do 15 more Engagement Sessions the following month, it's the same amount of time (two months), the same amount of stakeholder investment (one session per month), and the same number of stakeholders (15). But in the second approach we iterate only twice, one-third the number in the first approach.[6]

We iterate to learn. When we limit the number of iterations, we reduce the opportunity to discover how wrong we are and in what ways. Ultimately our goal is not to run bunches of Engagement Sessions; we're trying *to test our assumptions and throw lots of ideas away*. How many times should we turn the crank? We iterate until the team runs out of money or time or no longer learns anything new. These three resources act as operating constraints on the process.

Time   PrD, because of its reliance on immediate engagement with external stakeholders, is relatively quick as compared to other research approaches. Still, PrD requires some minimum amount of time to complete, below which it will fail to deliver value. As we'll discuss in greater detail in Chapter 8, time is always the enemy. The team must move with a sense of urgency. "Art is never finished, only abandoned," as da Vinci is quoted as saying. The same can be said about products and services. They can always be improved *more*. Given diminishing returns on investment, the real question is always, "What's good enough?"

For modest projects, PrD may take only a few weeks to complete (durations vary based on calendar and availability). For small projects a few days. PrD doesn't need a lot of time.

Every team complains about schedules and a lack of enough time. Assuming the team has enough time to do at least a minimum number of iterations, PrD's value (artifacts, interviews, and the process itself) doesn't necessarily increase with *more* time. The opposite is true: When the team faces time pressures, the process delivers extraordinary results. The challenge, then, is to ensure there is enough time to fit as many iterations as possible (as we'll see in the next chapter) and maximize learning in each engagement.

If time is a limiting factor, the team must identify the highest-value objectives they need to evaluate. These discussions occur with key internal stakeholders who help determine the value propositions for the project. In the interest of time, the team forgoes any objectives falling below the value line (we discuss objectives in detail in Chapter 11). In the event the team doesn't have enough time to accomplish key objectives, this constitutes a checkpoint on the project, requiring sponsors to make the call for next steps.

Money

With a few exceptions, PrD is most effective when teams work face-to-face, whether during Creation Sessions or Engagement Sessions. The key is to maximize the number of iterations the team can complete with the least cost. Given the bias toward face-to-face, merely relying on digital and remote collaboration technologies won't necessarily solve the problem. There are hidden costs of doing PrD digitally and remotely—costs that aren't immediately obvious.

We try to have at least a few face-to-face sessions with our target stakeholders, *in their context*, with the artifacts in hand. There is nothing more powerful than to have external stakeholders demonstrate how awful an artifact is, in person, in the real context of their work. Any detraction from this ideal scenario reduces insights. Not interacting with the stakeholder face-to-face, not handing her a physical artifact, or not conducting the session where she does her tasks negatively impacts the results. What if the artifact is so wrong that it inspires a stakeholder to pick up something in his environment and demonstrate it as an exemplar

Presumptive Design
DESIGN PROVOCATIONS FOR INNOVATION

When the residents of Vienna Haus didn't understand the teams' artifacts, they went to their medicine cabinets to offer their own pillboxes.

See Appendix A: The Case of the Pushy Pillboxes

Engaging with stakeholders in their environment generates insights impossible to glean in any other context.

See Appendix A: The Case of the Rx Reminder, The Case of the *Star Trek* Holodeck, and The Case of the Transformed Treatment

Learning Nothing New

addressing his needs (as the elderly women did in The Case of the Pushy Pillboxes)? Dramatic learnings increase when sessions are executed in person and on location.*

When we were working with sales teams in service of a large-scale PrD effort, a salesman demonstrated, in his cubicle, how he used business cards stacked in particular ways to manage his many contacts. In a separate instance, Charles observed a saleswoman leave her cubicle, go into the aisle, and describe an artifact she and her team used on a whiteboard. "Being there" has far greater ROI (in terms of capturing stakeholder needs or maximizing understanding) than snazzing up artifacts. When faced with crafting fancy artifacts versus traveling, we never flinch: Travel wins every time.

In The Case of the Rx Reminder, key learnings and observations were made by working with stakeholders in their own homes. Only by asking stakeholders to use the artifacts during their daily routine could the team have discovered the need for mobility in both the reminder and the pillbox. Similarly for The Case of the *Star Trek* Holodeck: Only by being present with stakeholders, in the moment, could Steve and his team have gleaned the key insights they uncovered. In The Case of the Transformed Treatment, only by being collocated with patients, therapists, and caregivers could Chris discover a key element to his innovative therapy.

As with many field research techniques, PrD starts to "discover" the same stories over and over again. In qualitative research this is called "saturation." Often, what was novel in the first couple of sessions becomes

---

*There's something deeply ironic in a process that requires moving atoms (i.e., meeting with people in person with a paper prototype), not bits, when the target of the investigation is almost certainly digital.

predictable by the third. Great facilitators learn to maintain freshness in their sessions, even if they could write the new stakeholder's story themselves. PrD requires us to stop inquiring about the stories we have heard more than a handful of times. If we don't, we're not increasing our learnings. If we've heard the same thing three times, that may be enough. A couple more for good measure if we can afford the time or money, otherwise it's not worth hearing again. But that is not to say we're done! There are many more stories likely waiting to be told—just not the ones we've already heard. The beauty of PrD is how flexible, fluid, and adjustable the process is.

Leo was visiting several customers in the same city to save on travel costs. After the first day of meetings, the team met that night in the hotel bar to go over what they'd heard. They quickly identified topics they'd heard enough about and adjusted the artifact and prompts accordingly. The artifact had left a particular interface very ambiguous, allowing the stakeholders to tell the team what it meant to them. In almost all cases, the external stakeholders offered similar interpretations. They suggested how the interface should operate and what their underlying needs were. The team altered the artifact that night to explicitly expose that interpretation. The script for the subsequent interviews *assumed* stakeholders would interpret the revised artifact as the prior stakeholders had. When new stakeholders interacted with the modified artifact, the team listened carefully. If these stakeholders moved through the interface without any conflict or questions, they would consider this interpretation valid. Instead of continuing to hear the same interpretation again, the team could focus on areas they hadn't had time to get to in prior interviews. Because the team iterated multiple times in the problem space, it increased its confidence and the quality of its product.

If the team truly isn't learning anything new, it's time to stop, even if they have the time and the money to keep going. Typically there is *something* new to learn; usually time or money comes up short before a lack of learning.

Risk Factors

Project Constraints

Anything constraining the team's ability to do multiple iterations is considered a risk to Iterate, Iterate, Iterate! We've already discussed the three constraints on iteration: Time, Money, and Learning Nothing New. Sometimes time and money are so constrained that there's not enough to do more than one iteration. This risk is serious enough to warrant a checkpoint on the program. If the program can't afford to do PrD, the least expensive process available, it is likely not prepared to sincerely engage with stakeholders in the first place.

So, if there are insufficient resources to do *any* PrD iterations, we recommend finding another program to apply your talents. But what if there is some time and money, perhaps enough to do just one iteration? Would doing one iteration be better than none? In companies where UX's value is still emerging, practitioners have learned to make excellent-tasting lemonade, so the answer is usually "Yes." Of course, doing something is far better than nothing, but in this case, the risk is around messaging. If our sponsors think we're going to get them the answers they need, reduce their program risk, and all of the other goodness we've sold them around PrD, we need to qualify those promises based on the actual budget.

Returning information from one iteration is only slightly less risky than none at all. One iteration is almost not worth doing if we're only talking to one stakeholder. At minimum, even if we can only do one iteration, we still need a handful of individuals—three to six at minimum depending on how broad or tight the investigation is.

PrD remains the least expensive, richest method of design research we've encountered, but it still costs *something*. If the project is so constrained that it's limited to one iteration, we will either pull the emergency stop cable and get off or lower our stakeholders' expectations.

As this chapter has said repeatedly, and as we'll discuss in greater depth in the next chapter, time is of the essence. The team can be its own worst enemy by failing to move with the speed and urgency PrD demands. Stalling can come from any quarter: Engineering can raise technical concerns, program managers can declare customers unavailable, designers can demand "one more day" to polish an idea, and so on. None of these, or the dozens of other examples of delays and hurdles, do anything to help PrD. Delaying does not improve the results. We start with the proposition we are wrong (as discussed in Chapter 4) and so, why wait?

One antidote to stalling is to set unreasonable deadlines. Working with the program manager, we set impossible due dates. This forces the conversations PrD demands, and it actually works. In The Case of the Hard-Boiled Egg, when the team appeared to be entering a multiday design session to figure out what the screens should look like, Leo demanded they get results within a day or two—long before they would have completed their design effort, let alone user engagements. Similarly, in The Case of the New Case, the team had only a few days to come up with alternatives to what they had already crafted. An hour of whiteboard sketching with key engineers was sufficient to establish enough technical confidence to proceed with refined Photoshop imagery.

Stalling

Insights can start today. All it takes is getting the right people together and offering up an artifact.
See Appendix A: The Case of the Hard-Boiled Egg and The Case of the New Case

Presumptive Design

Summary

- PrD differs from traditional UCD in how it approaches the problem space of a project, the portion of the project work prior to the "decision point."

- PrD distinguishes itself from iterative design by focusing on iterative problem definition. Where iterative design refers to the iterative refinement of a single solution, in PrD "iterating" refers to the iterative abandoning of ideas while still in problem space. (We're not iterating ideas if we pursue only a single solution.)

- Time to insight is improved by doing more iterations with fewer external stakeholders versus fewer iterations with more. Larger sample sizes here are a waste of time and money.

- PrD doesn't benefit from more time. Just the opposite is true: By creating a sense of urgency, the team is forced to offer its assumptions to external stakeholders as early as possible.

- Iterating continues until the team runs out of time, money, or new learning. If there is insufficient time or money to do more than one iteration, PrD (or any other research mechanism) will likely perform below expectations. Adjust accordingly.

Iterate, Iterate, Iterate!

Chapter 8: The Faster We Go The Sooner We Know

Presumptive Design
DESIGN PROVOCATIONS FOR INNOVATION

... enlightened trial and error beats the planning of flawless intellects.
... fail faster to succeed sooner.
—David Kelley

Overview

PrD requires us to get started, immediately. The faster we iterate our ideas, the more we learn and the more our guesses improve. Because the approach uses rapid iterations with external stakeholders, PrD is agile. But it differs from agile because it operates in the problem space, predecision. Similar to agile software development, PrD faces unknown unknowns, the upper left quadrant of the decision matrix discussed in Chapter 3. As we've discussed, in these situations the quickest thing to do is to take action.

Our first guesses about our external stakeholders' needs are wrong. Why polish and refine our errors? Getting more attached to them or investing more into them won't make them less wrong. Instead, we must fail intelligently, immediately. And then do it again and again, as quickly as possible. By each failure we learn; subsequently we fail *less*. Over time, we asymptotically approach the perfect solution. The faster we do this, the more money we save.

This chapter is ostensibly about speed, but we increase our velocity to save money:

- The faster we move, the better our time-to-market.

- The sooner we know, the higher our confidence in our next step (abandon the project or proceed).

- The less time spent crafting artifacts, the lower our investment in them.

Just Get Started

It's Day One. Ideally, we watch stakeholders use stuff on the first day. Calendars, schedules, and real-world constraints prevent such an ideal, but we keep it in mind at all times.

The more we delay engaging with stakeholders, the more we delay capturing insights. All team members may not share this sense of urgency. They offer several objections to getting started right away:

- *Intellectual property concerns*: They don't want to reveal too much too early.

- *Viability concerns*: The idea may violate laws of finance.

- *Feasibility concerns*: The ideas may violate laws of physics.

These are important concerns, but they start with the assumption the idea is remotely correct. Before the team begins financial or technical deep dives, we need to improve our confidence in the idea having a market at all.

Protecting Our Assets

In PrD we do not hold on to our ideas in service of protecting them. We don't hold on to them at all. We subscribe to the notion "information wants to be free" (as in liberty, not beer).[1] Ideas in the early stages of innovation are never half-baked; in fact, these ideas are more like an open container of alcohol: volatile, evaporating, and difficult to contain. It takes far more energy to keep them bottled up than to simply let them loose. It's far less expensive to reveal our cards, to lay them on the table (Figure 8.1).

Don't delay; do it today. The earlier we set ourselves straight about

Don't conceal your hand

Figure 8.1 There's no profit in hiding your cards

109

our assumptions, the bigger the impact we'll have on the outcome.

PrD doesn't expect a well-crafted design; it doesn't require us to know all of our assumptions to get started. Time wasted is money squandered. We start engaging with external stakeholders ASAP to rapidly accelerate our understanding of them.

Critics argue we'll compromise our intellectual property if we discuss ideas too soon. Ideas aren't protected. Execution on those ideas is. Without getting too wonky, we can agree the expression of an idea into an artifact could cross a line. Since PrD is most effective for disruptive or transformative sustaining innovation, we frequently find ourselves in this territory. We have not had trouble engaging stakeholders in discussions about our assumptions behind an idea. Nor have we had trouble finding ways to express our ideas without revealing the true intellectual property required to execute on them. Nor have we had to name any of our stakeholders as coauthors on any expression of the idea they may have discussed with us.

Critics argue the idea may not be financially viable, or it may not be possible to build today based on our current understanding of physics. They miss the point. The idea stems from our *assumptions about the stakeholders' needs*. If we propose a faster-than-light communication technology to illustrate our assumption about our stakeholders' need to be in the loop, what difference does it make? They'll tell us about their needs to be in the loop.

We don't waste time. We get started with what we know as soon as possible.

As The Case of the Hard-Boiled Eggs illustrates, the team struggled with this core principle of PrD. It was hung up on developing and accurately portraying ideas. They approached Leo, seeking a way to move more quickly. "Hard-boiled eggs! Just use hard-boiled eggs!" He threw

Speed is more important than fidelity. Internal stakeholders are often surprised by how much insight is gained by offering up even a seemingly irrelevant artifact.

See Appendix A: The Case of the Hard-Boiled Eggs

at them. They stepped back, concerned for his health. Still, one team member took up the charge. The outcome? "It worked!" they said, flabbergasted. "Stakeholders started playing with the eggs and envisioning different solutions, explaining their work and revealing their needs. We learned so much in one day!"

Addressing user issues up front is 10 times cheaper than fixing user issues during development and up to 100 times cheaper than after deployment.[2] These statistics focus solely on the cost of development, not opportunity costs of pursuing a suboptimal solution in the first place. Reducing risk early on benefits the solution in two ways: improving confidence in the decision to proceed (opportunity cost) and reducing the cost of execution.

An Early Start Reduces Cost

PrD's greatest impact is with that first risk reduction benefit: improving our confidence in the proposed direction. Teams using PrD in the earliest stages of the innovation pipeline maximize their understanding of stakeholder needs, contributing to market-based framing of early stage ideas.

Getting started is a conceptual hurdle the team must overcome. The next challenge is building the artifact as quickly as possible. PrD depends on crafting low-fidelity artifacts: physical objects designed to provoke. Several characteristics distinguish PrD artifacts from the more common notion of prototypes:

The Future Wasn't Built to Last

- Purpose
- Mutability
- Timing
- Level of fidelity
- Level of investment

We cover the first two bullets in later chapters. This section focuses on the others: timing, fidelity, and investment.

Predecision Versus Postdecision Timing

We return to the Double Diamond diagram (Figure 8.2). Before a decision is made, the project is in *problem space*. Postdecision, the project has entered *solution space*.

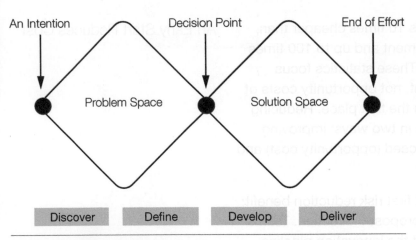

Figure 8.2 Double Diamond diagram illustrating the decision point separating problem and solution spaces

PrD's greatest impact occurs in the *problem space* of a project where iteration cycles vet team assumptions. Contrast that effort with iterating in the solution space, in which teams refine the proposed solution. The two regions are separated by the "decision point," sometimes referred to as the plan. PrD artifacts inform and impact the decision point, which in turn affects everything beyond.

Jared Spool classifies work products (prototypes, sketches, wireframes, journey maps, and so on) based on their timing, predecision or postdecision. An "artifact," he argues, is a predecision idea proposal; a "deliverable" is a postdecision representation of the "winning" idea. A prototype or wireframe, then, could be either an artifact or a deliverable *depending on when and why it was made*.[3]

How Faithful Is Our Artifact?

Generally speaking, teams operating in the problem space don't have enough resolution of the problem to express their ideas in high fidelity. Conversely, early on in the solution space, teams may still not have enough clarity to craft high-fidelity prototypes. Buxton is clear on the point: When exploring the problem space, sketch (use low fidelity). When iterating in the solution space, prototype (use high fidelity).[4]

In PrD, fidelity becomes a little tricky: What is the fidelity of a hard-boiled egg, after all? The artifact must be faithful to rendering the team's assumptions, at whatever level of fidelity that requires.

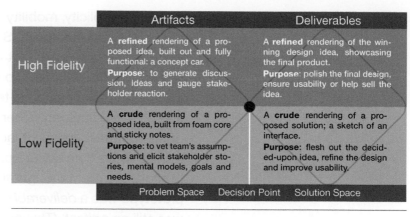

	Artifacts	Deliverables
High Fidelity	A **refined** rendering of a proposed idea, built out and fully functional: a concept car. **Purpose**: to generate discussion, ideas and gauge stakeholder reaction.	A **refined** rendering of the winning design idea, showcasing the final product. **Purpose**: polish the final design, ensure usability or help sell the idea.
Low Fidelity	A **crude** rendering of a proposed idea, built from foam core and sticky notes. **Purpose**: to vet team's assumptions and elicit stakeholder stories, mental models, goals and needs.	A **crude** rendering of a proposed solution; a sketch of an interface. **Purpose**: flesh out the decided-upon idea, refine the design and improve usability.
	Problem Space Decision Point Solution Space	

Figure 8.3 Timing versus fidelity

We've mapped both variables (timing and fidelity) over the Double Diamond in Figure 8.3.

PrD focuses on the left-side quadrants. Under what circumstances would a team be in the upper left? Rarely by choice. One bona fide example is the concept car and its research equivalents: high-fidelity artifacts in service of participatory innovation.[5] In those atypical instances, verisimilitude is required to achieve the desired provocation.

All other instances we encounter of upper left artifacts (and we encounter them all the time) occur by mistake. Any team (agile or waterfall) speedily building the wrong solution is at risk. Such projects operate under the illusion they are past the decision point, in the upper right quadrant. The day of reckoning occurs when their stakeholders review their work products and question the underlying assumptions. These teams discover, late in the game, their investment in high-fidelity prototypes was wasted. Two cases, The Case of the Rx Reminder and The Case of the *Star Trek* Holodeck, illustrate this point.

In The Case of the Rx Reminder, fully functioning products were built and used to engage with external stakeholders. None of the three finished products addressed key stakeholders'

Waiting to test assumptions with a finished product greatly increases the cost of the obtaining insights.

See Appendix A: The Case of the Rx Reminder and The Case of the *Star Trek* Holodeck

113

needs of simplicity, mobility, and discreetness. In The Case of the *Star Trek* Holodeck, Steve Portigal and his team were working with a smart TV. "It was like a futuristic smart TV on steroids," he told us. "To call it a smart TV doesn't do it justice." Initially he and his team were commissioned to rank and prioritize features. When consumers couldn't make sense of the system (because it lacked a coherent narrative), the team pivoted from feature prioritization to questions of *why*. In short, the client thought their high-fidelity, very expensive prototype was a *deliverable*; Steve's research suggested it was still an *artifact*. (This case also points to that rare bird we mentioned a few paragraphs back, the concept car. Steve suggests at least some of his team's findings wouldn't have been possible without such a highly refined prototype.)

How Little Do We Need?

Time is more important than fidelity, but that doesn't mean low fidelity is always *faster.*

See Appendix A: The Case of the New Case

PrD asks us to get artifacts in front of external stakeholders quickly. The key to speed is investment: Reducing our time investment in artifacts improves our velocity. Although low-fidelity artifacts generally take less time to create than high-fidelity artifacts, fidelity isn't a good measure of *investment*. As The Case of the New Case illuminates, high-fidelity Photoshop images required far less investment (in time or money) than building foam core mock-ups.

What is the minimum investment (of time, money, or expertise) required to get the most appropriate artifact in front of stakeholders? That's the business question.

Expanding the earlier matrix to include investment reveals additional insights (Figure 8.4). With the exceptions already noted, the top left of the matrix (high fidelity, high investment) occurs by accident or mistake. The next cell down (high fidelity, low investment) is more common, but problematic. Low investment is appropriate during the problem space investigations, but high fidelity usually isn't. As we discuss throughout, better conversations result from offering a sketchy artifact versus a highly refined one.

The bottom left (low fidelity, high investment) of the matrix is an obvious error, committed when teams spend too much time crafting a "beautiful" low-fidelity artifact. We've witnessed teams craft "sketchy-looking" drawings using software prototyping tools rather than quickly scribbling a drawing on paper.

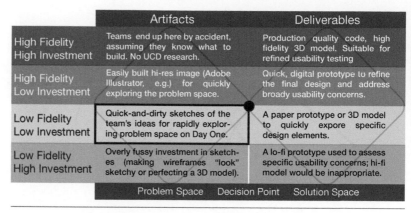

	Artifacts	Deliverables
High Fidelity High Investment	Teams end up here by accident, assuming they know what to build. No UCD research.	Production quality code, high fidelity 3D model. Suitable for refined usability testing
High Fidelity Low Investment	Easily built hi-res image (Adobe Illustrator, e.g.) for quickly exploring the problem space.	Quick, digital prototype to refine the final design and address broadly usability concerns.
Low Fidelity Low Investment	Quick-and-dirty sketches of the team's ideas for rapidly exploring problem space on Day One.	A paper prototype or 3D model to quickly expore specific design elements.
Low Fidelity High Investment	Overly fussy investment in sketches (making wireframes "look" sketchy or perfecting a 3D model).	A lo-fi prototype used to assess specific usability concerns; hi-fi model would be inappropriate.
	Problem Space Decision Point Solution Space	

Figure 8.4 Timing versus fidelity versus investment

PrD sits in the left cell second from the bottom (low fidelity, low investment). When we craft a low-fidelity artifact, with minimal investment, we are poised to quickly engage with stakeholders and investigate the problem space.

$$\text{Insight Overhead} = \frac{\text{Level of Investment}}{\text{Amount of Insight}}$$

Figure 8.5 Insight overhead—overhead decreases with increasing insight or decreasing investment

Our intention working in the problem space is to gain insight. The same amount of insight gained at a lower investment of time and money is worth more. It has a lower "insight overhead." In plain English, the quicker and cheaper we gain the same amount of insight, the less our overhead will be. Formally we express insight overhead as illustrated in Figure 8.5.

We minimize insight overhead when we work in the low-fidelity, low-investment cell. Landing in the upper left by accident, as in The Case of the *Star Trek* Holodeck, makes insight overhead skyrocket.

PrD's agile approach to problem exploration also lowers insight overhead by reducing hand-offs from one team to another. Recall from Chapter 2 the compare and contrast example of the cleanroom industrial control interface. In

Maximize Insight, Minimize Investment

As Steve emphasized, waiting until the end of a project to test assumptions is simply overspending on the test.

See Appendix A: The Case of the *Star Trek* Holodeck

Discovery Through Agility

115

Presumptive Design
DESIGN PROVOCATIONS FOR INNOVATION

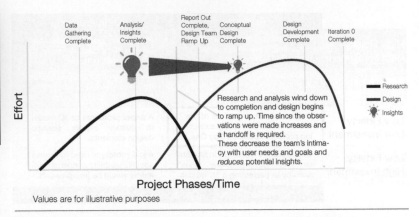

Figure 8.6 Research and design effort and insights (waterfall/traditional UCD)

the waterfall-like traditional UCD approach, the research and design teams operate separately from each other and the development teams. Each moves through the design thinking cycle sequentially, handing information off as it crosses boundaries. Eventually the development team receives a requirements document along with technical specifications, wireframes, and other deliverables. The process takes months, sometimes years, before the development team creates a working version of the idea. This investment of time increases insight overhead (Figure 8.6).

Investment overhead goes up for a second reason: Insights diminish from the start of the process until the end. By the time the research has been written up and communicated to the design team, insights have decreased due to:

- Layers of abstraction between the observation and the report out

- Distance in both intimacy and time from the original observation

- Recasting of the information for each group's needs

Contrast this with PrD's agile-like approach to design research (Figure 8.7).

Because teams are working together from the start of the engagement, few hand-offs are required. This *increases* the number and value of insights. Likewise, the time investment plummets. These two factors—increased insight and lowered investment—significantly reduce investment overhead.

PrD shortens discovery activities to a matter of weeks (or months for extraordinary projects). It simultaneously *raises* the team's confidence about the desired outcome. It couples research to design, using design as a research vehicle. Because this happens within the problem space, business stakeholders are actively involved, monitoring how customers react to their desired value propositions.

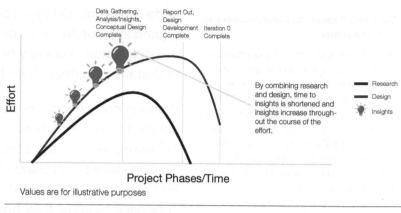

Figure 8.7 Research and design effort and insights (agile/PrD)

Recall a key tenet of agile: Maximize business value. Software developers achieve this by getting working code in front of customers as soon as possible. It's an important point. With a working product the organization has begun earning revenue and enabling its customers. By putting a real thing in front of customers, they can respond to it with feedback for the next cycle. The approach makes a large assumption: External stakeholders have communicated their needs and we have accurately understood them. Recall from Chapter 6 the revised version of the agilists' Pharaoh story.

Moving Fast While Staying Real

PrD and agile agree in principle: We need to get real stuff in front of our stakeholders before they can show us how wrong we are. The challenge is to reduce the investment of producing that stuff. And, of course, we need to agree on what we mean by "real stuff." For designers and researchers, a smoke-and-mirrors artifact is real enough, *as long as it provokes the right conversations*. For some agilists, working

Get Real

117

Presumptive Design
DESIGN PROVOCATIONS FOR INNOVATION

We Can't Expect the Right Answers to Our Questions

A chief source of such misunderstanding comes from thinking we can simply ask external stakeholders what they need, want, prefer, or will use. Analyzing 113 pairwise comparisons, Jonathan Levy and Jakob Nielsen found that the correlation between users' stated preferences and their actual measured performance was only $r = .44$![6] Squaring this to see the variance accounted for we get $r^2 = 0.19$, which means less than 20% of the variance in external stakeholders' performance is captured by asking them what their preferences are. Stated otherwise, if all we do is ask users, what they say may only have a 19% overlap with what they then actually do. If we want to understand and/or predict our external stakeholders' behavior, we shouldn't ask them because they don't know. We can't just ask—we must *watch* them using stuff. This is also a problem for agile's feedback loop. Agile has us build user stories, and then base changes on unfiltered user feedback. But again, how sound is that feedback? Nielsen has found users not only can't tell us what they will or won't use but also, if asked, they'll freely offer copious amounts of feedback on features that don't even exist![8]

code is the only definition of real. But what would an organization prefer: A quick-and-dirty artifact eliminating a possible solution entirely or working code for a narrow slice of that solution (that might be entirely wrong)?

Working code brings an additional advantage: It proves the solution *works*. And herein lies the problem: the word "solution." A truly robust solution comprehends user needs. Agilists leave the crafting of user stories to Product Owners (POs), but POs never work with code. How are the POs supposed to know they have the right stories? Poorly written user stories not generated from a legitimate UCD research method result in lowered quality (from the stakeholder point of view) forcing refactoring down the line. PrD ensures the validity and robustness of the *stories*, before the tasks and work breakdowns begin. (See sidebar for a wonky deep dive into the challenges of reliably capturing user needs.)

Rapid Iterative Testing and Evaluation (RITE) is an established method of iterative *testing* (as its name suggests) of a candidate product.[7] It has many of the hallmarks of PrD in that it is iterative, expects the product to change rapidly between sessions (perhaps in the same day), and involves direct engagement with external stakeholders. Historically, researchers and usability engineers employ RITE after there is a working product, again, using real code. RITE brings its own challenges to the table: Rapidly changing the code itself, in almost real time, depends on a highly mature development process (or a relatively simple set of problems being iterated).

Both RITE and working code are important ways to move quickly and keep things real. Because both operate in *solution space*, both fail to identify the big picture concerns of stakeholders (the "elephant" in the pyramid as we discussed in Chapter 6).

Sketching, as Buxton[9] describes it, is not only a natural tool for designers but also exactly the thing to move forward with external stakeholders *today*. A whiteboard and a marker may be all that is needed to get the conversation going, *today*. Delaying these conversations increases insight overhead and adds risk, especially when critical decisions about infrastructure, platforms, and requirements could use the information. Sketching allows us to race forward with our stakeholders. It helps identify potential risks of infrastructure decisions (including purchasing third-party software or tools). In the happiest of circumstances such sketches influence the decision point before development begins in earnest.

Real Is in the Eye of the Stakeholder

In The Case of the Constricted Collective Conversation (about civic engagement in Englewood, IL) the research team mentioned how academics had spent years studying such communities before advancing possible solutions. These researchers didn't have the time or the luxury to deeply study the culture they were hired to help. Their approach (placing a chalkboard at a busy intersection and offering journals at well-frequented business establishments) moved quickly: Within a period of a few days, the team captured substantial information and, equally important, helped the community discover novel methods of engagement to improve neighborhood dynamics.

Waiting is expensive. Few teams have that luxury; typically we need to hit the ground running.
See Appendix A: The Case of the Constricted Collective Conversation

PrD's velocity depends on the team's ability to quickly switch between analysis and synthesis, a hallmark of design thinking, discussed at length in Chapter 2. One way to guarantee teams use design thinking is to have designers on the team who are good at design thinking. Imagine that!

Reasoning abductively, a key part of design thinking, is required throughout PrD. During initial artifact creation, designers quickly sketch ideas they're hearing from other team members. During the fielding of the artifacts, the

Risk Factors

The Need for Design Thinking

119

Facilitator quickly offers alternative expressions of the artifact. At a minimum, she is able to mirror back alternative interpretations of the artifacts based on stakeholder reactions.

A lack of design thinking on the team impacts PrD's velocity.

Analysis Paralysis

This risk appears at any time: In the beginning when the team is uncertain how to start, in the middle when stakeholder feedback appears confusing, and even at the end when the iterations have stopped and the results need to be comprehended and communicated.

Apparently it's a part of our nature: We want to reduce risk to our reputation. We want to be certain of our assertions and we want to ensure the organization is on the right course. All of these issues reduce velocity and for some of us, some of the time, freeze us in our tracks. We'll discuss techniques for overcoming analysis paralysis in later chapters, but a key method is establishing and maintaining a sense of urgency. Timeboxing the team's effort, for example, is one of the ways to reduce overthinking at any stage of the process.

Equally important is to ensure everyone (sponsors, team members, and internal stakeholders) understands PrD is a qualitative research method relying on small numbers. Of course, if the project is betting millions on the outcome, quantitative measures will be needed. But if the team is simply trying to set its sights in the right direction, the niggling details are likely less important than the big directional indicators. To quote Keynes: It's better to be roughly right than precisely wrong. Moving fast and identifying likely risks early is far more important than getting a narrow implementation exactly wrong.

It's the big ideas that matter up front, not the small details. Moving fast is more important than being pedantic. Part of the value of PrD is getting internal stakeholders aligned. It requires individuals to air their operating assumptions up front and it obligates them to *witness* the testing of those assumptions. Alignment sidesteps the quagmire and cost of design by committee. Nothing releases team members' attachment to a bad idea faster than witnessing, first hand, external stakeholders trashing it. Rapidly assessing an idea, over multiple iterations, improves team members' understanding of its validity far more quickly than offering them a written report or presentation deck.

Summary

- Time to insight is crucial. This means the more we learn about our external stakeholders as quickly as possible, the better. We achieve the greatest velocity by capturing their needs, goals, and work while simultaneously having them vet our assumptions.

- Multidisciplinary teams working together from the start reduces insight overhead by increasing insights and dropping time investments.

- Build the least-cost (time, effort) artifact to capture the most information. Working code can't offer insights into the big picture; PrD identifies the right thing to build.

- The faster and cheaper we iterate through this process, the more we increase the ROI of "being wrong," speeding time to insight. PrD's results are not improved by having more time.

Chapter 9: The Perils of PrD

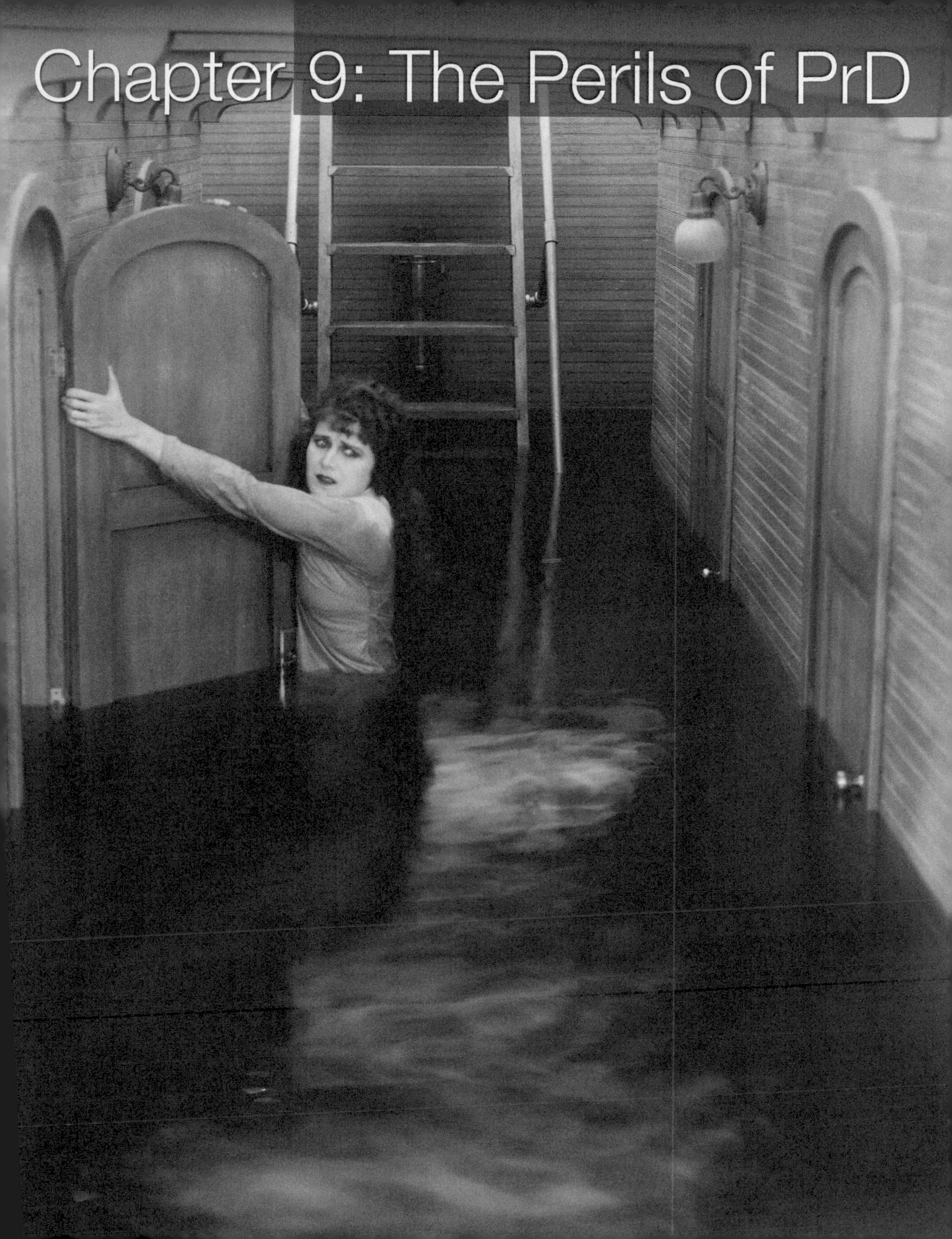

Presumptive Design
DESIGN PROVOCATIONS FOR INNOVATION

A ship in harbor is safe, but that is not what ships are built for.
—John A. Shedd

Overview

In a recent PrD workshop, one of the attendees asked, "What sorts of projects won't work well with this method?" Leo had to pause to consider. PrD isn't limited to a specific *sort* of project, industry, or engagement; rather, it makes the most sense when applied to particular types of *problems*. When businesses face existential threats, in part due to their current processes and strategies, they can't rely on those strategies to move forward. Disruptive innovation (or "possibility thinking"), by definition, conflicts with day-to-day operations. In these cases, PrD offers a cost-effective method of moving forward. Outside such contexts, PrD may not return the results sponsors and stakeholders expect.

In addition to the strategic questions of whether to use PrD, the process can fail for numerous tactical and operational reasons. In each of the preceding chapters (dedicated to PrD Principles) we offer risks associated with the principle in question. The remaining chapters in this part describe additional ways in which the process can fail: team composition, failure to believe we're wrong, poor objectives, poorly executed objectives, and poor facilitation. In this chapter we focus on when PrD shouldn't be considered at all.

Is It the Right Problem?

PrD is not limited in its application. Instead, it is limited by the nature of the problem: PrD is unnecessary for "simple" and "complicated" problems. Recall from Chapter 3 simple problems can be solved by applying standard processes, and complicated problems are solved by experts applying tacit knowledge. In both of these contexts, the problem can be resolved through mechanistic or analytic approaches. In "complex" or "chaotic" problems, however, no amount of analysis or process will identify the right way to proceed. In these situations *action* must come first, and through taking action, produce results on which the team reflects. PrD is best applied when the problem requires taking action first.

Software development is one such situation. The best outcome for a new feature or product cannot be predicted ahead of time. It is unknowable without a series of experiments. Substitute "design" or "strategy" for "software development" and the statement still holds true. The nature of design problems is we can't predict their solutions without a series of guesses.

Design thinking comes in handy for almost any sort of problem, be it simple, complicated, complex, or chaotic. PrD however, though it depends on design thinking, will be too "heavy" for situations in which we already know "enough."

PrD requires two components to succeed: an artifact and a focus on the external stakeholders' problems. With those two ingredients, PrD applies to a whole host of problems. As we discuss throughout, the artifact can be almost anything— as long as it provokes conversation in service of the internal team's objectives. The second ingredient, sincere interest in the external stakeholders' problem space, rarely limits the sorts of things PrD can be used to discover.

Without these two components, either PrD won't work or it isn't PrD.

PrD Needs Two Things

As part of a PrD workshop focused on next-generation drawing systems, a team crafted a "dreamcatcher," a device that could record an individual's dreams and redisplay them on request. The artifact was envisioned to be worn over the ear, similar to a wireless headset. But after the team's Engagement Sessions, it realized it didn't have to build such a

A Provocative Artifact

Presumptive Design
DESIGN PROVOCATIONS FOR INNOVATION

Figure 9.1 An over-the-ear dream catcher could just as easily have been a paper dot

David MacKenzie realized a cardboard box would have sufficed to drive the desired conversations.

See Appendix A: The Case of the Balking Bicyclists

sophisticated artifact at all. The team could just as easily have put a small dot above the stakeholder's ear to achieve its objectives (Figure 9.1). In The Case of the Balking Bicyclists, David MacKenzie quickly realized the key conversations didn't require him to build anything fancy—a cardboard box would have sufficed. The point is the artifact need not "mock up" an envisioned design at all: All it need do is represent the internal team's assumptions enough to provoke a conversation about them with the external stakeholders.

Suzanne Howard, Partner and Managing Director of IDEO's Learning Platform, suggests the artifact should push boundaries of the known—to be "from the future."

Sacrificial concepts—In order to solve the challenges at hand, design thinking involves early prototypes or tangible, conceptual versions of what the future might be in order to help engage participants in imagining new realities.[1]

As Arthur C. Clarke said, "Any sufficiently advanced technology is indistinguishable from magic."[2] If the artifact isn't sufficiently futuristic to be magical, PrD will not produce good results. Consider a drinking glass from the future. Perhaps it has embedded sensors, is networked with other glasses in the area, and both feeds and is fed from big data sources. This isn't such a far-fetched idea. All sorts of magical things could go on with that glass: biometrics, assessment of water quality, social networking, and so on. A magical artifact must express those qualities in service of testing the team's assumptions.

Whether to use PrD or not depends on the magic of the artifact. At first glance it would appear PrD is suitable only for product-type engagements (and by product we mean anything from hardware to software to web designs to services). Requiring a magical artifact would appear to eliminate such things as new org chart, a strategy statement, or a new logo. In reality, PrD can test abstract ideas just as well, if they can be crafted as an artifact *that can be used*. As Steve Sato relates in The Case of the PowerPoint Play, his team did exactly that: They crafted provocative slides to test how far their VP could be expected to advocate for design.

In PrD, the artifact must be magical, and stakeholders must use it to complete a relevant task. PrD relies on the stakeholder's multimodal thinking—not just thinking aloud but also manipulating the artifact *while* thinking aloud. If the team can't devise a task where the stakeholders work with the artifact, then PrD is not going to deliver useful results.

Magical Artifacts

Thought Experiment

So, what about an org chart, strategy statement, or logo? Can you imagine a way to make these suitable for a PrD? How would you construct an artifact that allows stakeholders to test our org chart? Think about what task you would need them to complete and how that might test your assumptions about the new organization. Similarly for a strategy statement. What would the artifact be and what task would you expect stakeholders to complete? For the logo, the artifact appears to be obvious (the logo!), but what task would stakeholders need to perform? Further, what does it mean for a logo or business plan to be "from the future" or "magical?"

As long as stakeholders can use it, an artifact can test abstract ideas, such as how far an advocate will go to defend your position.

See Appendix A: The Case of the PowerPoint Play

An Artifact to Use

Additional Ways PrD Can Fail

Talent

Perhaps the most important consideration in choosing to use PrD is whether the team has the talent to do it. In spite of it being conceptually easy to describe, it is an advanced technique. This book allots considerable space to facilitating in PrD because it is the most difficult part of the process to master (see Chapters 14–16). PrD requires very real and legitimate facilitation expertise. In addition, teams will need creative experts in design, user experience, and user interviewing. When Leo was building a UX team for a large enterprise project, he discovered even folks with years of experience in UX design and research were unfamiliar with the kind of facilitation PrD requires. Only after training and participating in several Creation and Engagement Sessions did the team begin to understand the subtleties of the process. See Chapters 14–16 for more details on facilitation. See Chapter 10 for details on roles, reasoning skills, and personality types that contribute to PrD's success.

The bottom line: PrD won't work, and we advise against using it, without access to an experienced interviewer or facilitator. Not only will the results be disappointing, but the team also may not even know the process has failed until it's too late. Again, see the following chapters for details on who may be experienced enough to make the process a success.

Courage

PrD is not for the faint of heart. It requires team members to keep two opposing and equally passionate beliefs in their minds: The artifact they've created is truly what external stakeholders want and need and that something (if not everything) about this presumption is wrong.

This takes extraordinary courage, but it is the courage that drives team adrenaline and subsequently the focus and clarity of purpose.

Every time we've used the process in the past 15 years, we've doubted whether it would work. Every time. And every time the process has worked. But it's nerve wracking.

So, for teams trying this for the first time, they must have the courage of their convictions: courage to convince internal stakeholders and sponsors this foolishness will work and it is worth getting in front of real customers. And, most important: The team must have the courage to learn from and reflect on its failures.

Another important limitation of PrD is the need to engage in real time and real space. As we describe in detail in Chapter 15, internal stakeholders come together to craft the artifact in the Creation Session. With a few exceptions, achieving the objectives of the Creation Session without collocating the team members is almost impossible. One notable exception is an abstract idea (as we discussed in the Section "A Provocative Artifact"). In The Case of the PowerPoint Play, Steve Sato worked with associates around the globe, both asynchronously and remotely. He could do that because the artifact was virtual, and it was intended to be used in a virtual context by his stakeholders. Few artifacts meet those requirements, including software screens, web pages, and the like. While they certainly are abstract, they are generally used by an individual interacting with a screen. To *test the assumptions* behind them requires an artifact that is used in the "here and now."

Building the Artifact

If in PrD the artifact is real-world, how do people remotely contribute to it? We've heard of a Creation Session in which a remote team member directed local team members to craft an artifact, but it was cumbersome and slow. Equally important is aligning team members on their assumptions. While we can imagine using remote collaboration

Must Be Present to Win

Generally PrD requires teams work together, collocated, to craft the artifact. But there are exceptions to every rule.

See Appendix A: The Case of the PowerPoint Play

technologies to debate assumptions, alignment occurs when team members fully engage with each other and the artifact. In sum, being present is a must for creating the artifact.

In Chapter 16 we introduce the second half of PrD: the Engagement Session. Similar to the Creation Session, it is *possible* to run the Engagement Session remotely, but it may be more trouble than it's worth. We've heard two rationales for doing the Engagement Sessions remotely: convenience and cost.

Convenience

It's true—meeting with an individual at their desk using a phone and screen capture software may be just fine for artifacts easily represented in a digital format (presentation software, prototyping applications, HTML mockups, and the like), especially if that's where the stakeholder is likely to do his work. The additional burden to set up a screen sharing application, video camera, and other minimal infrastructure may take less effort than meeting the stakeholder face to face. The convenience may warrant the additional risk introduced by the intermediating technologies. If Engagement Sessions are less than 30 minutes, a quick remote collaboration call may be perfectly sufficient to achieve team goals and reduce the bother of a face-to-face meeting.

But these sorts of artifacts are frequently too refined to provoke the conversations for which we use PrD. Also, most web prototyping tools require *more* work to make the results appear as rough as a quick sketch on a sheet of paper.

Cost

In general, though, the rationale most organizations use to avoid face-to-face meetings is cost. We take a sensible approach to most of our design budgeting, whether during the research or execution phases: Spend between five and

10% on the total estimated cost of the project. If a project is expected to cost $10K to complete, clearly flying a team all over the country isn't going to make sense. But if the cost is estimated to be $5M, cutting corners using digital approaches to save a few dollars merely increases the overall risk of the project.

PrD is an extraordinarily powerful risk reduction technique. Saving costs up front doesn't necessarily translate into overall project savings—if the PrD team discovers a completely different way of proceeding as a result of something they witnessed at multiple customer sites, the project may be cancelled early or may have an improved ROI. Either way, the cost of the Engagement Session is a pittance compared with that of fielding a failed product months later.

In Chapter 16, we provide additional details about the challenges of remote facilitation. In brief, remote facilitation requires even greater expertise in facilitation and increased investment in collaborative technology.

Consider the options if the artifact is real-world and the team is remote. Teams need to figure out how to have the participant work with the artifact in their location. Do they mail it to them? Is there a remote facilitator? If the artifact is digital, it's a little easier. Videoconferencing tools such as Lync, WebEx, and even Skype and Hangouts can share screens, allowing the team to observe and facilitate the session much like a remote usability test. But as with remote usability tests, much information is lost: body language, nonverbal facial cues, distractions, hesitations, and even potential for attention slicing (e.g., remote participants may choose to answer a high-priority e-mail, unobserved). And, as discussed throughout, crafting a digital artifact often requires far more investment than the typical junk artifacts we rely on for PrD.

Presumptive Design
DESIGN PROVOCATIONS FOR INNOVATION

In sum, a major consideration in using PrD is the very real need for very real-world engagement on the teams' part—both in creating the artifact and in engaging stakeholders with it.

Summary

- PrD is more successful in problem spaces requiring taking action first. In these types of problems, the right solution cannot be intuited or reached through analysis alone: They require experimentation and reflection to determine the next best way to proceed.

- PrD is not limited by the type of product, service, industry, or application. As long as the team crafts an artifact stakeholders can *use*, PrD will work.

- PrD will not succeed without masterful facilitation and courage!

- PrD works most effectively when teams are collocated, whether during the Creation Session or Engagement Sessions.

Presumptive Design
Design Provocations for Innovation

If two men agree on everything, you may be sure that one of them is doing the thinking.
—Lyndon B. Johnson

Overview

A successful PrD Engagement Session requires a multidisciplinary team to craft and interpret the results.

See Appendix A: The Case of the Pushy Pillboxes

It was a typical PrD session: The teams had worked feverishly to create artifacts and prepare for their first Engagement Session. Excited and anxious, they sat at the tables in the assisted living center and began working with the women, trying to capture their reactions to the pillboxes they'd created (Figure 10.1).

As The Case of the Pushy Pillboxes describes, the sessions didn't go as planned, or as the teams had expected. But it's what happened the next day back at the workshop that was eye-opening for the facilitators. The *designers* were crushed by the women's responses to their designs, believing they had to start over. The *researchers* took away completely different impressions: They felt the teams were on track and just needed to make modest adjustments to the designs. What everyone learned from the experience was a successful PrD engagement requires a multidisciplinary team: a team including more than just designers and researchers.

This chapter begins by discussing the ways in which PrD fails due to homogeneous teams,

Figure 10.1 "Junk prototype" mock-up of an intelligent pill dispenser

134

regardless of their membership: designers, researchers, product managers, engineers, or business leaders. Further along, we discuss how the characteristics of multidisciplinary teams contribute to PrD's success. The bulk of the chapter describes each of the roles on a PrD team (as well as possible professions in the organization adept in those roles), team member responsibilities, and the methods for balancing team composition.

Although we spend considerable time describing large-scale PrD projects, PrD truly is a lightweight process, usually requiring only a few people on the team. This chapter focuses on large-scale efforts, simply because they have greater opportunity for things to go wrong and are more difficult to manage. The issues we discuss, such as groupthink, social conformity, and the need for diversity in reasoning, are just as applicable to small teams as to large teams.

Figure 10.2 A flock of sheep as social conformity

The Hazards of Homogeneity

Social Conformity + Homophily = Groupthink

In 1951, psychologist Solomon Asch conducted the first of many experiments focused on the notion of social conformity (Figures 10.2 and 10.3).[1] The experiment was simple: Two flashcards were shown to a group of eight people. On the first card was a single vertical line; on the second was a set of vertical lines of varying heights. The people in the room were then asked to indicate which of the lines on the second card most closely matched the line from the first.

Presumptive Design
DESIGN PROVOCATIONS FOR INNOVATION

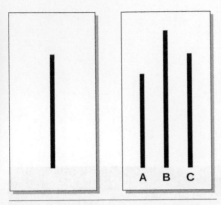

Figure 10.3 Asch (1951) social conformity study

Unknown to the participant, the seven other people in the room were confederates, who were, on certain trials, instructed to unanimously answer incorrectly. On these trials, 75% of participants answered incorrectly at least once. In the control group, where there was no pressure to conform to confederates, participants answered incorrectly only 1% of the time. Asch later varied the number of confederates present in the room. When there was a single confederate (the only other person in the room), the participant erred only 4% of the time. With two this more than doubled to 14%. With three it shot up to 32% and, interestingly, leveled off at four (at 35%).[2]

We avoid people different from us. The sociological term "homophily" suggests we prefer to be with people who we perceive as being like us. Homophily along with social conformity results in the well-known phenomenon of *groupthink*.

Disagreement Deficit

Kathryn Schulz suggests close-knit communities suffer from an effect she calls "disagreement deficit."

> … [O]ur disagreement deficit … comes in four parts. First, our communities expose us to disproportionate support for our own ideas. Second, they shield us from the disagreement of outsiders. Third, they cause us to disregard whatever outside disagreement we do encounter. Finally, they quash the development of disagreement from within … Whatever the virtues of our communities, they are dangerously effective at bolstering our conviction that we are right and shielding us from the possibility that we are wrong.[3]

How Groupthink Impacts PrD

Given PrD expects everyone to be wrong, what difference would a team's composition make? If everyone agreed on an artifact, the process to create it should take *less* time. But since PrD depends on external stakeholders to set the team straight, the process should correct for groupthink.

And it will.

But phenomena such as groupthink, idea anchoring, and social loafing reduce the number of possible outcomes the team will explore, slowing down the process. Social loafing says if 20 people generate ideas in isolation, there will be 20 ideas. If they generate ideas as a group, there may be only five real contributors. Some team members will not reveal their assumptions, choosing instead to agree with what's been offered by others. Regardless, without a group dynamic supporting opposing points of view, assumptions and ideas will be left unstated.

Figure 10.4 Results of brainwriting

In Appendix B we offer an antidote to social loafing, a form of brainstorming called "brainwriting." In brief, team members brainstorm silently by themselves before sharing their ideas with the group (Figure 10.4).

Homophily and Schulz's disagreement gap cause a homogenous (or nearly homogenous) group to quash disagreement from within. The minority voice won't stand up to the herd. These dynamics reduce possibility thinking and wild idea brainstorming. As we mention in the prior chapter, PrD requires teams offer artifacts from the future with "magical" qualities. Magical artifacts need crazy ideas. For PrD to be successful, both the Creation Session and the Engagement Sessions demand multidisciplinary teams with an appropriate amount of diversity.

Diversity in a small organization can be a challenge. But small organizations are not off the hook. Even if the team

Homophily Delays Action

Some types of homogeneity may also delay the team's agreement on the artifact. During a Creation Session we had several teams all working on aspects of a large-scale, corporate-wide problem. We realized one of the teams was consistently underperforming from the rest. In fact, throughout the session, that team was consistently slower, produced fewer divergent ideas, and all in all had trouble coalescing around a concept. After looking at the roster and then at the team members, we laughed: It was a table composed of male engineers. Irrespective of whether it was their job role or sex, team members displayed highly competitive behavior that prohibited them from moving forward.

PrD is most successful with diverse teams. Small teams must find ways to increase diversity.

See Appendix A: The Case of the New Case and The Case of the Business Case

is too small to be diverse, it must find ways to broaden its membership. In The Case of the New Case, Leo had only two team members other than himself: an Analyst and a Builder (see below for definitions of these terms).

In this case, he played the role of Facilitator/Researcher and brought in a Designer to help. Similarly, in The Case of the Business Case, an Analyst, a Builder, and a Researcher comprised the entire team. In that case, they brought in a couple of Designers, a Researcher, and a Facilitator to help them with both the Creation and Engagement Sessions.

In the Engagement Sessions, Schulz's third disagreement gap comes into play: When stakeholders disagree with our presumptions, and we are all of one mind, we downplay the input. Further, it isn't enough for one of us to advocate for the minority position. We all must let go of the erroneous presumptions (or at least a majority of us) lest we fall prey to Asch's conformity behavior. Alternatively, we may not hear the subtlety of the critique offered by our stakeholders; we may bucket it all together as the Designers did in The Case of the Pushy Pillboxes described at the start of this chapter.

Without diversity, teams risk missing subtleties of stakeholder critiques.

See Appendix A: The Case of the Pushy Pillboxes

But what sort of diversity are we seeking on these teams? And is it the same set of differences during the Creation Session as it is during the Engagement Sessions? And how many people are enough, and how many are too much?

Diversity of Reasoning

What we're recommending is diversity in *thinking and reasoning*. "Right-brain" and "left-brain" thinkers, analysts and synthesists, deducers and abducers—the team must have a balance of different kinds of reasoners. We are not suggesting all analysts think alike or all business leaders think with one mind. We are suggesting, to reduce the risk of groupthink, teams should comprise people who naturally reason differently. Often people choose a job function or role that best fits their problem-solving approach or style of reasoning. It's natural: We go with our strengths; we gravitate to job roles supporting those strengths.

But as Charles Owen suggests (when he introduced the four-square design thinking model), just because a profession or domain has a center of gravity in one of the quadrants doesn't mean individuals from that domain reason only within that quadrant.[4]

In short, building teams with individuals from different job roles may be all that's needed for enough diversity in reasoning to make PrD a success. Maybe, but not necessarily. We look to other characteristics, in addition to job role, to help us build balanced teams. One approach we've taken is to balance the team based on where an individual sits within the design thinking model.

Figure 10.5 Reasoning roles, all

Reasoning Roles

We suggest five different roles for balancing a team (Figure 10.5). Although we use names like "Researcher" or "Analyst," we're not suggesting job roles; we've simply assigned a title to the types of skills and reasoning appropriate to the quadrant. The designations are shorthand for the types of activities going on in those quadrants.

The sorts of activities in which each role engages will differ between the Creation and Engagement Sessions. In the following, we offer an overview of each role's activities within each type of session.

Researcher

The Researcher is focused on the real (here and now) as opposed to symbolic (Figure 10.6). Researchers are adept at active listening, are concrete, and are concerned about maintaining consistency and coherency between the artifact and the purpose of the research. The Observer role occurs only during the Engagement Session. Typically, a market researcher, UX researcher, business analyst, or human

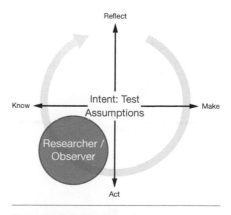

Figure 10.6 Reasoning roles, Researcher

factors engineer can easily perform this role, in both the Creation and Engagement Sessions. The Researcher is responsible for curating *how* things are done *currently*.

Activities in the Creation Session

In the Creation Session, this individual assists the team by confirming the artifact best addresses the team's objectives and assumptions. In contrast, during Engagement Sessions, the Researcher is one of several roles potentially becoming the Facilitator. Because of this duality, the Researcher is constantly imagining how the artifact will be used as the team is building it. As the assumptions are being expressed, both verbally and in artifact form, the Researcher captures them and begins to construct the Engagement Session "script."

Activities in the Engagement Session

In addition to transitioning to the Facilitator, the Researcher may be responsible for planning and logistics—recruiting and calendaring participants, finding the right rooms, incentives, and the like. Alternatively, these activities could be handled by a project manager who may not participate in the actual sessions. If there is more than one Researcher during the Engagement Session, the second Researcher becomes an Observer, capturing notes, interactions, expressions, body language, and other "tells."

Analyst

Analysts are comfortable working with symbols, drawing "box-and-arrow" diagrams to describe processes, software stacks, and the like (Figure 10.7). They are concerned about economies, architectures, and other elements driving system performance. They are, well, analytical: able to categorize, decompose, rearrange, and organize information often in service of *normalizing* it. Several different types of analysts are found in large organizations: business analysts, system

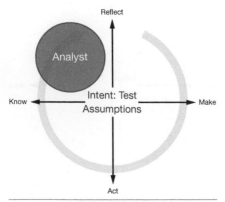

Figure 10.7 Reasoning roles, Analyst

analysts, enterprise architects, system architects, data analysts, and the like. The Analyst is responsible for curating *why* things are done *currently*.

Activities in the Creation Session

During the Creation Session, the team is trying to identify an *ideal* experience from the perspective of the external stakeholder, based on the team's assumptions. The Analyst can provide an ideal state for the *system* or *business processes* and argue for those to be part of the team's assumptions.

Analysts may be uncomfortable during the Creation Session because of their strong desire to normalize. We've seen cases (when the team comes up with outrageous notions violating all sorts of existing conditions) where Analysts become agitated and question the entire process. If it is too uncomfortable for them to set aside their day job, and they are compelled to offer reality checks, then the Facilitator must step in to prevent delays and confusion.

Analysts *can* document and track the differences between the proposed experience and current realities as the team comes up with wilder and crazier ideas. If the Analyst is channeling his energy away from being hypercritical, he can highlight potential risks, costs, and performance impacts. Although this information could be critical, much of it may be irrelevant after the Engagement Session, as in the case when external stakeholders disagree with the team's assumptions and the idea is thrown out. Remember, in PrD it's perfectly okay if the artifact suggests something that can't actually be built or that could even exist! If creating a putative time travel device vets the team's underlying assumptions, the Analyst must be able to suspend his disbelief.

The Analyst can also direct his energy to capturing ideas as they flow, before the Designer can express them in the artifact. Wielding the marker, the Analyst becomes the scribe, helping organize ideas, letting the Facilitator focus on her tasks.

Activities in the Engagement Session

In complex offerings, the Analyst is required during the Engagement Session. Generally, the Analyst becomes an Observer, but he is specifically listening for key elements impacting the systems and/or business processes. Without saying a word, the Analyst captures the ideas presented by the stakeholder, and in those instances where there are surprises, marks them for later discussion during the debrief session.

If the conversation turns technical, as some sessions require, the Facilitator may turn to the Analyst to get a brief set of ideas about how the stakeholder's proposal might be accommodated. In exploring some of these structural considerations with the stakeholder in these early sessions, the stakeholder may adjust her thinking, helping the team understand what is a "must have" versus a "nice to have."

Seeking such ideas from the Analyst should be done sparingly, especially during early iterations, as the true purpose of these sessions is to capture the mental model of the stakeholder rather than the realistic potential for execution of ideas.

Designer

Because PrD depends on design thinking, the team must have at least one Designer as a member! Designers are possibility thinkers and lateral thinkers, and often provide other-worldly perspectives on the discussion (Figure 10.8). They think symbolically while simultaneously making things concrete. The Designer riffs off others' suggestions, building on them, supporting ideas, capturing them, and cheerleading others to come up with more. Most importantly, the Designer *makes* things. She glues paper to paper, and googly eyes to pipe cleaners. Naturally we expect to see anybody with

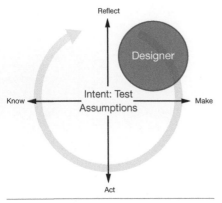

Figure 10.8 Reasoning roles, Designer

"design" in their title, but for some organizations the job role may be difficult to find. Interaction, UX, visual, graphic, web, industrial, game, and curriculum designer are just a few titles that make sense. Design engineer is another possibility, and we've had great success with software architects and software designers even though those titles often refer to activities far removed from design as we've been discussing it. The Designer is responsible for curating *why* things should be done *in the future*.

Activities in the Creation Session

The Designer captures and expresses the assumptions posed by the team in the form of an artifact. The Designer is free to offer her own suggestions as well, but must do so explicitly, not silently. While everyone is permitted to craft the artifact, the team generally looks to the Designer for expertise and creative approaches to express their thoughts. We've found in some cases having two Designers is necessary, especially if the remainder of the team does not have much comfort with the "make" side of the model.

The Designer may play her role quietly, allowing the team to explore and brainstorm before swooping in with a representation of what's been discussed, capturing the essence of the conversation.

As a synthesizer, the Designer constantly puts two and two together, coming up with five. With teams that aren't flowing, this can add tension and confusion into the process; in most cases it provides humor and the right touch of lightheartedness and fun.

Activities in the Engagement Session

With one exception, the Designer is an Observer during the Engagement Session. In some cases, the Designer captures and expresses any changes proposed by the stakeholder *as necessary to move the conversation forward*. Normally, the Facilitator can handle most conversations around the artifact with a little imagination and framing. Sometimes, however, the stakeholder has suggested something so radically different from what the team had presumed that the conversation would stop if not for an addition or change to the artifact.

Either the Designer makes the change directly or the Facilitator suggests the stakeholder make the change and the Designer assists as needed.

The Builder

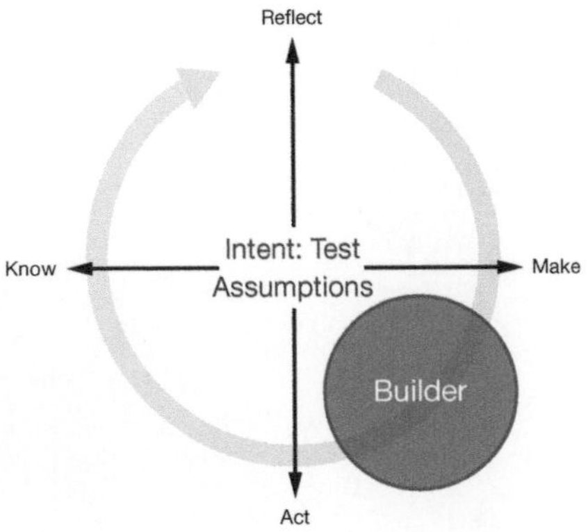

Builders are the ultimate realists (Figure 10.9). They work with material things, even if they are writing symbolic code. As their name suggests, they build things. They are concrete. They don't do well with ephemeral concepts and diagrams. At the same time, they are deeply immersed in the technical details of the solution space, and for that reason alone, it is crucial to have them on the team. Anyone with "engineer" in their title is likely to be a Builder, but, again, it has more to do with their reasoning and thinking styles. The Builder is responsible for curating *how* things should be done *in the future*.

Figure 10.9 Reasoning roles, Builder

Activities in the Creation Session

During the Creation Session, Builders face the same tensions as the Analysts, only more so. As we have said throughout the book, during the Creation Session, "Reality bats last," but Builders are the ultimate realists. The team needs to enlist their service not to shoot down ideas, but to begin to consider how to build those ideas.

This requires a special sort of developer/engineer, one who is dedicated to making a difference, who really wants to build something stakeholders will clamor for. Builders who get early insight into the team's assumptions can also begin to think about where the existing system's structures and capabilities aren't going to cut it.

Activities in the Engagement Session

As with the Analyst, the Builder becomes an Observer. Having a Builder at the Engagement Sessions is important for two reasons:

1. The Builder hears, with her own ears, and sees, with her own eyes, exactly what the stakeholder is saying and doing. This uninterpreted raw engagement is transformative, especially when a stakeholder is passionate about his point of view. Few Builders come back from Engagement Sessions unswayed by customer feedback. In fact, Builders often swing far to the other side, becoming overly avid customer advocates. Builders must attend the debrief to ensure their points of view are calibrated with the rest of the group.

2. True science-fiction scenarios may need to be explored further. If the stakeholder requests something of the system that would violate laws of physics, for example, the Builder should signal to the Facilitator to dig for additional information. Without the Builder's real-time intervention, the process may get delayed as the team returns to discuss what they learned, only to discover the proposed ideas are truly not buildable, at all. Again, this intervention must be handled extremely carefully, and generally rarely. Similar to the Analysts above, the real issue is not whether something can be built but rather why it's important to the stakeholder in the first place.

The Facilitator

We've dedicated Chapter 14 to facilitation in the Engagement Session. In Chapter 15 we discuss the role in the context of the Creation Session. Here we briefly sketch the key attributes of the Facilitator role. The Facilitator is ego-less: empathically in tune with everyone on the team (Figure 10.10). Any of the roles can be a Facilitator, if the individual is good at it.

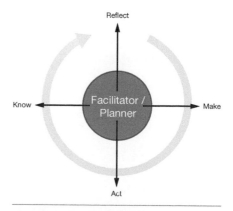

Figure 10.10 Reasoning roles, Facilitator

Activities in the Creation Session

The Facilitator maintains an open mind, listening to the flow of ideas, making sure every voice is heard. He gently shuts down overenthusiastic contributors to let others chime in.

The Facilitator is not overly critical about any offering but offers probing critique if the artifact (or the assumptions on which it is based) isn't clear. He constantly checks the mood and energy level of the team, adjusting as needed and calling time when the team is too tired to be productive. The Facilitator keeps time, making sure the team understands the urgency of the exercise and the finality of the clock. He uses the clock as a gentle prod to get people thinking.

Activities in the Engagement Session

As in the Creation Session, the Facilitator makes or breaks the Engagement Sessions. Any one of the team could be a Facilitator, as long as they are good at it and they understand the process. As mentioned above, often the Researcher becomes the Facilitator.

The Facilitator keeps a tight control over the process, allowing only the stakeholder to talk, accepting questions or prompts from the Observers through some silent mechanism (passing of notes, IM window, etc.). The Facilitator keeps time, moving the stakeholder along if she gets sidetracked, allowing her to linger if the specific point she's making is worth a deeper dive. He is present, moving real time where the stakeholder wants to go. The Facilitator watches the clock, not because he wants to hurry the stakeholder along but to respect the stakeholder's time. In our experience, once an Engagement Session gets going, stakeholders are typically happy to stay far longer than they initially had committed to.

How Many Again?

Figure 10.11 shows the desired number of team members for both Creation and Engagement Sessions.

At a minimum, the team should have four members during the Creation Session and two members during the Engagement Session. This is in line with the purpose of having diversity in your teams: Teams need maximum diversity during the Creation Session; during the Engagement Session less diversity is required.

Role	Desired # for Creation Session	Desired # for Engagement Session
Researcher	1	0-1
Analyst	0-2	0-2
Designer	1-2	1-2
Builder	1-2	0-2
Facilitator	1	1

Figure 10.11 Number desired, role by session type

The Creation and Engagement Sessions may have as many as eight individuals. As we discuss in Chapter 16, having five team members working with a single stakeholder can be overwhelming to the stakeholder; the advantage being it accelerates alignment across the team. Builders and Analysts often don't have the opportunity to engage with external stakeholders; participating in the Engagement Session is a transformative experience. One way we avoid overwhelming stakeholders is to mix and match individuals on the team, keeping any one session limited to three people. For example, we have a Facilitator/Researcher and a Designer, and we rotate in one other role. Over the course of all sessions, team members will have had a chance to participate in at least a couple.

At the end of the chapter we discuss the risks of teams with too few individuals in both the Creation and Engagement Sessions.

Presumptive Design
DESIGN PROVOCATIONS FOR INNOVATION

Personality Attributes

When we are involved with large Creation Sessions, we need to consider more than just team members' approach to reasoning. Large Creation Sessions may have several teams working independently—the largest we've run had six teams of eight. In these contexts, we are careful to identify other aspects, such as extroverts, introverts, dreamers, realists, and, if it's possible, any known relationships among participants that might be problematic (Figure 10.12).

With large sessions, we ask participants to answer a short questionnaire. We also gather information about them (if they

Figure 10.12 Multiple teams at a Creation Session

148

are not known to us personally) from trusted associates who can attest to their style of engagement, relationship, and personality. We do this research at least a week before the Creation Session and, based on the information, we adjust team membership accordingly.

Sometimes we don't have the luxury of capturing intelligence about the team members beforehand and must create teams during the Creation Session itself. When we run workshops on PrD, for example, we don't know in advance much about the attendees. Instead, we run a small creative exercise helping people separate themselves by self-evaluating their reasoning styles.

Thinking Style Questionnaire

We send out the questionnaire given in Figure 10.13 in advance if we have the time and if:

- The situation calls for it.

- The attendees aren't people we know.

- We have more than two teams participating in the Creation Session.

- We offer these instructions to the participants when we send out the questionnaire:

  1. For each *row*, circle the *one* word that best describes you. The total of items circled should equal 20 (one item/word for each row).

Column A	Column B	Column C	Column D
Analytical	Organized	Imaginative	Expressive
Problem-Solver	Administrator	Inventor	Communicator
Logical	Disciplined	Intuitive	Perceptive
Sensible	Careful	Relaxed	Co-operative
Profit Driven	Task Driven	Idea Driven	Values Driven
Researcher	Doer	Thinker	Co-coordinator
Rational	Controlled	Spontaneous	Flexible
Quantifying	Evaluating	Estimating	Sensing
Diagnosing	Planning	Speculating	Supporting
Examine	Construct	Experiment	Illustrate
Debate	Discuss	Ask	Listen
Financial	Tactical	Strategic	Personnel
Critical	Detailed	Holistic	Intuitive
Technical	Operational	Innovator	Trainer
Calculated Risk	Risk Avoider	Risk Taker	Consensus Risk
Reader	Assembler	Artistic	Spiritual
Critical	Conservative	Creative	Emotional
Knowledge	Action	Thinking	Communication
Evaluate Ideas	Implement Ideas	Generate Ideas	Express Ideas
Fact	Form	Fantasy	Feeling

Figure 10.13 Thinking style questionnaire

  2. Next, add the number of items you have circled in each *column*.

3. Send your totals for Columns A, B, C, and D to
   <Facilitator>. For example, your totals might look
   something like the following: Column A, 8; Column
   B, 2; Column C, 6; Column D, 4.

Hidden from the participants are the qualities associated with each column: Column A, Logical; Column B, Organizational; Column C, Imaginative; Column D, People.

By making sure each team comprises individuals scoring high in one of the columns, we increase the likelihood of balancing team membership.

Team Balancing Exercise

Sometimes we don't have the ability to know, in advance, who is coming to the Creation Session, especially when we are running workshops at conferences or in large organizations. In these cases, we use an ice-breaking exercise at the beginning of the Creation Session to help balance the teams.

We have everyone get on their feet and offer them the following instructions:

> We're going to divide ourselves up using a self-assessment based on four labels I'll announce in a moment. This is a bit forced, as it is impossible to categorize yourself based on one label, but for now, go with your first impulse. Don't overthink the words, or their association. Just go with your gut instinct.
>
> I'll read off four labels. When you hear a label that best fits your own self-assessment, please move to the corner of the room I'll associate with the label.
>
> Everybody understand?
>
> Okay. The four labels are: Scientist, Artist, Engineer, Designer.
>
> If you consider yourself a Scientist, go to that corner of the room.
>
> If you consider yourself an Artist, go to that corner of the room.
>
> If you consider yourself an Engineer, go to that corner of the room.
>
> And if you consider yourself a Designer, you're excused, you can leave.

(Obviously a joke.)

As you can see, the exercise expresses design thinking and introduces the four-square design thinking model at the very start of the Creation Session.

Neither approach is perfect. In the case of the questionnaire, it's unclear whether those words really are indicative of the categories in which they have been associated. In the room exercise, if working with a homogenous group, it may be difficult to get enough variance to balance the teams. Still, doing something is better than relying on pure happenstance.

Establishing the team composition beforehand, as described above, is key to establishing diversity, especially for the Creation Session. For the Engagement Sessions, as we've mentioned and as Figure 10.11 suggests, at a minimum we should have a Designer and a Facilitator. What should we do if in spite of best efforts we're not able to achieve a diversity of roles on the teams?

For the Creation Session, it is *possible* a single individual, let's say the Designer, can generate assumptions and artifacts. That is, a Designer, working solo, could create the artifacts (and, by definition, her assumptions) to support an Engagement Session. But it is the rare Designer who can also draft the script and who can step outside her worldview enough to see the assumptions she's making. Other than the Designer, it is *possible* the Facilitator/Planner could craft artifacts expressing assumptions, but (by definition) these roles are not artifact makers, so what the Facilitator creates may fail to have the future-leaning, magical qualities on which PrD depends.

Regardless of whether it is *possible* to have a single individual craft a magical artifact misses the point. The point of the Creation Session is to generate divergent ideas, get assumptions out in the open, and continue aligning the team on the goals for the project. That just won't happen if a single

Where Things Go Wrong

How Many Is Too Few?

Lack of Diversity

individual is doing the work in isolation. Yes, the *individual's* assumptions will be surfaced, but those may be completely insufficient in the context of the team's or business's needs.

For the Engagement Sessions, going solo is a recipe for disaster. While going solo may be possible with standard user interviews (and even there, having at least one partner is often essential), PrD requires more effort of the interviewing team than a single person can muster. PrD requires a Facilitator and a Designer, at a minimum. If we can't field these two roles, we don't bother proceeding (Figure 10.14).

Figure 10.14 A stakeholder with a Facilitator and five Observers at an Engagement Session

Here again, fielding the minimum number of team members makes the process *possible*, but it still misses a key benefit of PrD: gaining alignment across the organization on potentially disruptive innovations. It is nice to have additional team members in the Engagement Sessions to observe and collect data. Of greater benefit is having them gain firsthand knowledge of customer insights. The more team members who have heard and seen stakeholders' points of view, the more advocates there are for the ideas that ultimately make it through the process.

So there is a minimum below which the Creation and Engagement Sessions will likely not be successful. Of course, crossing a minimum threshold doesn't guarantee success. In spite of best efforts at creating diversity, the Creation Session may not bear fruit. In the example of the all-male engineer team mentioned in the sidebar in the Section "How Groupthink Impacts PrD," the team just didn't get itself together and was consistently falling behind in the exercises.

We've had similar dysfunctional teams at workshops in which the attendees were all from a similar domain. In one such workshop, individuals on one of the teams consistently responded they didn't feel their ideas were being heard, and the outcomes they drove were not the best they could have imagined. We helped the team better understand the goal of the exercises they were doing, reducing some team members' performance anxieties so that, as a team, they could move forward. The symptoms of this malaise are relatively easy for the Facilitator to spot: delays in making decisions, sour faces, disengagement, and less than hearty fun. In some extreme cases, the Facilitator may need to "reset" the entire session, perhaps even scheduling a separate session. In most cases, however, the problems are resolved through assertive Facilitation and intervention. In Chapters 14 and 16 we offer

Failure to Cohere

more details about facilitation to improve the likelihood of success.

Detractors   To begin the process of aligning a very large project team, we ran a three-day Creation Session. We balanced the teams, established clear objectives, provided background to the process, and offered ongoing positive reinforcement for the team's effort. In spite of all that, we had more than one upset participant. In this case it was an Analyst and a Builder who couldn't accept several tenets of PrD: Letting go of reality and junk prototyping were just too much for them to accept. Thankfully, they reserved their concerns until the "hot wash" critique at the end of the Session.

Detractors, especially outspoken and passionate detractors, can spoil the suspension of disbelief required to make magical artifacts. If their concerns and anxiety are not addressed, their attitude infects their team and perhaps the rest of the participants. Every large event has at least one individual who doesn't quite resonate with the purpose of the event, no matter how much prework and preparation one does. Builders' and Analysts' key concern is often *cost*, even if they don't express it in those terms. Sometimes it's expressed in terms of complexity, sometimes in terms of technical gaps, but in the end, their concerns are about how costly an idea might be. The Facilitator listens to those concerns but continues to remind the team that costs are only one half of the equation. If the ideas the team generates are truly disruptive, the business may have discovered a completely new opportunity—an incremental revenue stream with an extraordinary ROI.

In short, the Creation Session is way too soon to know what *too expensive* looks like.

The irony is that many of these same individuals become the biggest proponents of PrD once they get past their concerns. So we don't want to exclude them from the Creation Session and even if that was desirable we can't predict who they will be. The best we can do is assist them in overcoming their concerns through strong facilitation. Fortunately, we've never had to resort to escorting a participant out of a session, but in extreme cases it could come to that.

Summary

- PrD depends on teams and diversity within those teams. Groupthink, resulting from homogeneity on teams, isn't fatal, but it will slow the process down (and risk dismissing stakeholder criticisms).

- By "diversity" we mean diversity in thinking and reasoning. Getting members from each quadrant of the design thinking framework is a good way to balance teams.

- Each role plays a part in both the Creation and Engagement Sessions. Sometimes individuals shift roles when transitioning from Creation to Engagement.

- For large Creation Sessions, we pre-staff teams, based on information we glean from associates about characteristics, or use a questionnaire or self-assessment activity to improve team diversity.

- PrD works best with at least a few people on a team for a Creation Session, and at a minimum two people at the Engagement Session. But minimums miss the point: PrD is about alignment. Having more team members present improves alignment on assumptions and stakeholder reactions.

- In spite of our best efforts, some teams (or some individuals) may not work out. Masterful facilitation usually resolves these difficulties.

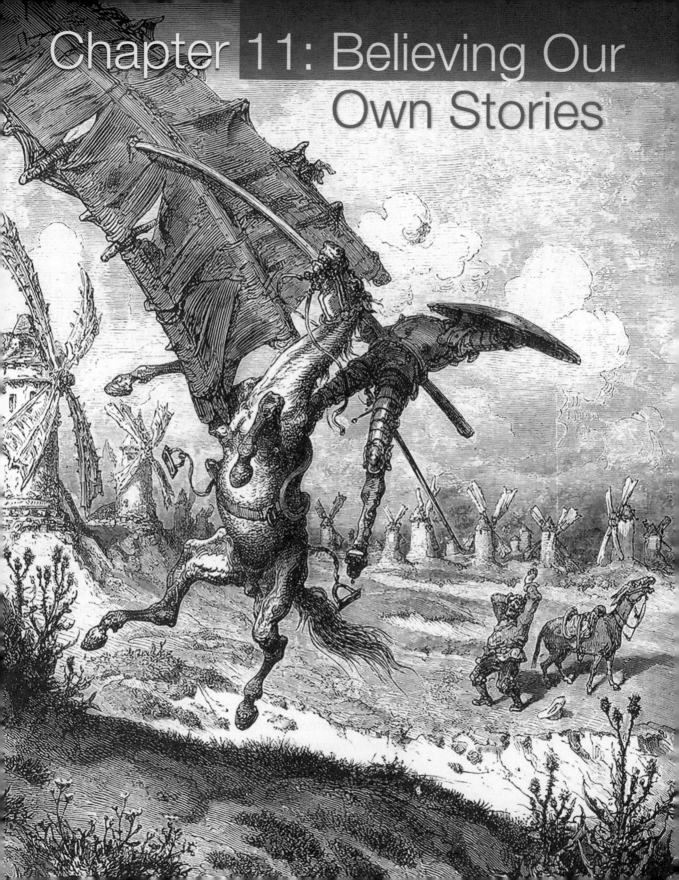

Presumptive Design
Design Provocations for Innovation

The human understanding when it has adopted an opinion ... draws all things to support and agree with it.
—Francis Bacon

Overview

Though called Presumptive *Design*, PrD is fundamentally about research, not design. Design is the medium; research is the activity. Irrespective of its name, the process challenges both designers and researchers, because it requires each to rethink the way they've approached their disciplines. Another challenge (to everyone, not just designers and researchers) is PrD's insistence we enter engagements with stakeholders *believing we're wrong*. The principle of Design to Fail was discussed in Chapter 4. Here we'll discuss the flipside of this principle—the hazard of believing our own stories.

It's difficult to imagine spending (or perhaps wasting) our and our stakeholders' time exploring things we know to be wrong. We hold onto our belief in the value and fitness of our ideas; that's as it should be. Once we've spent time crafting an artifact expressing those ideas, we become intimate with it. We go over it in our minds, thinking deeply about it, ready to explain each of the decisions we made when creating it. In this way, we convince ourselves we have a really good idea. It might very well be. But PrD necessitates our disproving that position. Even if we're confident in our assumptions, we must at the same time honestly seek to hear how, and in what way, they are wrong.

We must get good at harboring these *seemingly* disparate notions simultaneously: It's a great idea (given what we currently know) *and* it's wrong. We're looking for that "Aha!" moment of surprise that shifts our perspective. Consider the delight we feel when we look at visual illusions, perceiving the image first one way and then another. In Figure 11.1a, for instance, is Edgar Rubin's famous figure-ground vase. In Figure 11.1b is William Ely Hill's (1915) drawing of the "my wife and mother-in-law" illusion, from an older (1888) German postcard. Also see Figure 11.2.

Keeping two completely opposite notions in our heads at the same time is challenging. In the case of visual illusions, it's impossible. Instead, we rapidly shift from one to the other. But in the case of a point of view or assumption, once we have seen it is "wrong," we can never go back and believe it to be true. That moment of transformation can be delightful, surprising, and sometimes embarrassing. In PrD, we prepare ourselves for it in the belief it is inevitable. Still, it is always a surprise.

(a) (b)

Figure 11.1 (a) Vases and faces (b) my wife and my mother-in-law

Consider a scenario we encountered with a design team member (we'll call him Jason). Jason was taking the first step to envision a completely different intranet experience for his group. Jason had over 20 years of design experience, was great with stakeholders, and knew his way through the design process. He wasn't that strong with user research, however, having had only a smattering of engagements over the years. Until he got involved with PrD, he'd never really taken an interest in research. But Jason became enamored with PrD when he was introduced to it. PrD gave him a chance to use his design skills in service of better understanding his stakeholders. Jason went through formal training and had several opportunities to experience PrD Creation and Engagement Sessions.

Increasing Investment Increases Belief

Jason had a presumption about the intranet and how a visitor's homepage should work. He was adamant

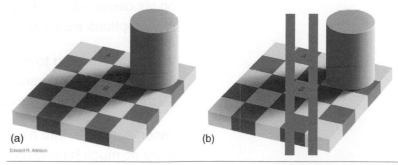

(a) (b)

Edward H. Adelson

Figure 11.2 (a) Edelson's checkerboard (b) Edelson's checkerboard proof

about it being a novel mash-up of widely varying content, tools, feeds, and the like. In addition, based on substantial research already completed, Jason had a metaphor for the homepage: We'll call it "Main Street." Jason was most concerned about getting his vision *right* and getting his story out there. Relying on his 20 years of experience, he knew he had to present something to sponsors that would make them salivate and want more. Alarm bells went off, however, as he explained he expected to run his PrD sessions *after* he presented his vision. He suggested he might use PrD to test a rollover interaction or perhaps an approach to navigation.

After making it this far into the book, we hope you appreciate Jason's misunderstanding about PrD. Over a couple of beverages, he and Leo discussed how PrD enabled him to get external stakeholder feedback on his initial story. He could use the process to test his metaphor and his initial *assumptions*. Especially because he felt so strongly about his story, he needed to quickly understand whether external stakeholders would want or understand it. Most importantly, the stories he told his sponsors shouldn't be *his*, but rather his external stakeholders'. Thankfully, light bulbs went off and he got it. His presentation to his sponsors would be more powerful if he showed how visitors to the homepage understood and had shaped the concept. He understood PrD wasn't limiting his design proposals. PrD wasn't about asking stakeholders for design reviews or feedback on his design ideas. He understood and appreciated his presumptions were extraordinary and in need of vetting.

What was amazing to the rest of us was why Jason hadn't internalized his understanding of PrD even though he'd had so much experience with it in the past.

Jason had fallen into a common trap: He believed his own story so much he couldn't see past it to test it. After the happy-hour chat with Leo he was able to envision the PrD session, imagine the artifact he needed to create, and had a sense of how the script could go. Now Jason was prepared *to be wrong*; he was setting up the session to help him find out *how* wrong he was as quickly as possible. "Better to figure that out now, before we spend a lot of money building something," he confirmed.

Jason had seen the light: Believing his own stories could have been costly. Jason's experience is not unusual; it illustrates a pitfall many experienced designers encounter. Designers spend a lot of time thinking about their approaches, crafting solutions and concepts, and reflecting on them again and again. By the time they are ready to talk to stakeholders, they have thought it all through. PrD asks them let go of all this.

Designers are not alone in tripping over their beliefs. Researchers also fall prey to believing their own stories, but in different ways. We'll illustrate a few of the common traps related to believing our story: pitching, presenting, and arguing. We spend the bulk of the chapter exploring the underlying psychological basis for believing our own stories, or, as cognitive psychologists call it, confirmation bias.

The Three Traps

Pitching the Design

Designers are most likely to fall into the trap of pitching the design. Anyone who's been part of a design group knows the "pitch" is a key part of gaining support from clients, sponsors, or other stakeholders. It can take a designer years to develop the ability to effectively pitch an idea. We shouldn't be surprised experienced designers expect this to be part of the process. But as we discuss in Chapters 14 and 16, it's exactly the wrong thing to do during the Engagement Sessions. After Jason had internalized the process, he realized *his* idea, *his* story, and *his* concept didn't matter one iota. What mattered was his ability to get external stakeholders to tell *their* stories in reaction to the artifact.

Presumptive Design
DESIGN PROVOCATIONS FOR INNOVATION

Presenting the Design

The seemingly innocent cousin to treating an Engagement Session as a pitch is the impulse to present or explain the design to external stakeholders.

This trap occurs when the team *explains* the design *as envisioned*. Establishing rapport at the beginning of the Engagement Session is vital (as we discuss in detail in Chapter 14). Team members new to PrD may be tempted to build rapport by explaining the design. These initial remarks are intended to put the stakeholder at ease, but they cause considerable damage. Presenting the idea, by way of introducing the artifact to the external stakeholder, ruins the session; it's as good as over. By the time the introduction is finished, the team has filled the stakeholder's head with its own notions, irrevocably losing access to the stakeholder's own thoughts. Explaining or presenting the design is often accompanied by a team member holding the artifact, preventing the stakeholder from engaging with it. The opportunity for PrD is lost—the team has told the stakeholder *its own* story, wiping out the stakeholder's story in the process, and the team never crossed the threshold of offering the artifact as a "social object." (We discuss artifacts as social objects at length in Chapter 14.)

Team members may also feel an urge to explain the design when the stakeholder is confused about something or asks a question. The impulse to help, to *answer* the stakeholder's questions is a natural response; we want to be helpful and not alienate our participants. Such questions and confusion indicate a mismatch between the external stakeholder's mental model and what she *thinks* the artifact is trying to communicate. These tender green shoots are easily trampled by the team's explanations.

The only time we explain the design is *at the conclusion of the Engagement Session*. The stakeholder may need closure about what the team had in mind and it is a common courtesy to answer her questions. During these postsession discussions the team gleans additional information, but keep in mind we're no longer doing PrD; this is now a traditional user interview—with the same benefits and risks.

The final trap teams encounter is approaching the Engagement Session as a contest of wills. When the stakeholder appears to misunderstand the purpose of the artifact, she reveals an important perspective. We're looking for those revelations. Such misunderstandings are the most important provocation the artifact offers. It is expressly forbidden for anyone on the team to contest anything the stakeholder says about the design, artifact, or concept. *Correcting* the stakeholder not only quashes insights but also exposes the team's misconception about the process. The only people who are wrong are the team members.

Arguing with Stakeholders

Resisting the impulse to answer questions, to help, to explain the concept can be hard to do. We think we have a good idea. We think our assumptions are mostly correct. We think we're really onto something. How can we possibly want to prove ourselves *wrong*? It feels unnatural, and that's because it is. Wanting to disprove our own world view is not how we naturally think. When assessing our hypotheses, we selectively seek evidence we think supports them.

Confirmation Bias

Seeking Supporting Data

Tell someone a series of three numbers, such as "2-4-6," and tell him the numbers adhere to a rule. The rule is a secret, but he can try to figure it out by offering other three-digit sequences and being told whether or not they also adhere to the rule. What will he probably do? He'll probably make a guess as to what the rule is, such as "even numbers that increase by two." Then he'll throw out sequences that adhere to his guess, such as "6-8-10," "12-14-16," etc. After hearing "Yes" a number of times, he'll announce his guess—and he might very well be *wrong*. What if the rule was merely any series of ascending numbers? He'd never figure this out *unless he tried to prove his guess wrong*. In Wason's classic study on the confirmation bias,[1] in which exactly this exercise was done, only 21% of participants ever figured out the correct rule.

Resisting Effort

We don't just fail to violate our hypotheses in general, we also remain fixated *on a specific hypothesis we've generated*. In short, once we form a hypothesis, conceive of a solution or a design idea, we slip on blinders. We home in on that single idea. Rather than generating as many alternate ideas as possible, we become defensive. Rethinking things takes effort and we naturally resist it. When people are presented evidence for both sides of an important social issue, they are prone to rate evidence conforming to their stance as being of better quality than the evidence against.[2] In another classic study, this still occurred when people were explicitly instructed to be "objective" and "unbiased" (an impossible ask!).[3]

Experience Is Not Our Guide

From experience we've witnessed being right about our design intuitions. So while all of the introductory material about confirmation bias might be true for *other* people, *our* hunches are, well, gold, and we have the evidence to prove it. But even our own experiences can be misleading![4] Say we have a good track record. We've done lots of projects and most of them have been successes. We've approached them in much the same way and consistently know how to produce such successes. These repeat performances increase our confidence in our abilities and hunches. Here's the problem: What we learn from experience is what we're operationally reinforced to think, but such knowledge is situational. Depending on the environment, what we're reinforced to think may not constitute valid knowledge.

Consider the following: We have a problem. We do some research, derive a solution, and execute on it. Sounds pretty straightforward: We've identified a good solution to the problem as we understand it, based on our upfront research. The solution is built and we consider it a success. Should we notch that up as another good design call? Maybe not. It's not just a matter of making a decision and observing its outcome. If only the world worked that way!

As Einhorn and Hogarth stress in their seminal work on the relationship between our confidence and accuracy,[5] what is left unspoken are all of the "meta" variables at play in this simple dynamic. Relevant variables include:

Success Is Not So Easily Defined

- Our decision to go with a certain solution

- Our criterion for making the decision

- Our assessment of the outcome of the decision

- The criteria we use to make the assessment

- The selection ratio of how many possible solutions are tried out and assessed

- The base rate of how many solutions would be deemed successes given our criteria

- How well our judgments *actually differentiate between good and bad solutions*

This gets complex.[6] Imagine our criteria for assessing the outcomes of our decisions aren't particularly strict. Let's say we're interested in profitable outcomes or high rates of task completions. Perhaps we define success as an absence of "showstoppers."

No problem, right? Wrong. With such lax criteria, we'll incur high opportunity costs. So what if users are able to successfully complete key tasks? What about other solutions that might have enabled them to complete the same tasks quicker? So what if we were profitable? How much money did we leave on the table? Was there a better way to achieve the same results, or a way of producing even better results? Forget a lack of showstoppers. What about user delight or customer satisfaction? What about solutions disrupting the *status quo*, whether that's user productivity or market penetration?

In a Small Pool, Any Fish Looks Big

There may be a lot of possible solutions to our problem we didn't choose to explore. And whenever the proportion of possible solutions tried is less than the base rate of how many would be deemed successes (given our criteria), we'll be reinforced to think our hunches are good even if they don't really differentiate between good and bad solutions at all! The more lax our criteria, the bigger the problem, and this is a costly trap to fall into.

The way out is discussed in the next chapter. In brief, we must remain skeptical of our own stories. We're wrong. We just don't know in what ways. The antidote to Believing Our Own Stories is to actively imagine the opposite is true. We think our design idea is the right solution? We think we know what users need? We think we know how they'll respond to our artifact? We need to consider the opposite. How might our assumptions be unfounded? How might the narrative we've weaved about the users and their needs be wrong? We're there to uncover the external stakeholder's story, not to confirm our own. Our posture, approach, and demeanor are that of a student learning from the master. The external stakeholder is the master. We are the student. Only she knows her story. We don't. To counteract our beliefs, we must view our work through this lens.

The last pitfall around Believing Our Own Stories is fatigue: After several Engagement Sessions, we hear external stakeholders tell the same stories. This influences our beliefs in two ways: (a) Our story changes the more we work with external stakeholders and (b) external stakeholders may continually reinforce our initial assumptions.

Been There, Done That

It doesn't take very long for a team to begin to believe the external stakeholders' stories, especially if it hears the same ones over and over again. Something funny happens; the team subtly shifts its thinking and begins to own the new story. That's actually a great thing! But it also means it's time to move on and find something else to talk about. If the team encounters the same "new" story again and again, it's not learning anything new.

Owning the Stakeholder's Story

When the team encounters stakeholders who validate its assumptions, this should be cause for celebration! We always appreciate the jolt of pleasure that comes when a stakeholder expresses our assumptions back to us without any prompting on our part. We've succeeded! So why do we put this into a pitfall? Two reasons:

The Stakeholders' Stories Reinforce the Team's Assumptions

1. Once we've learned stakeholders believe the same thing we do (a majority use the same language, bring up the same idea, or consistently display the same re-actions to the assumptions), we must remove the line of inquiry from the script and focus on something else. If we don't, we just waste time.

2. Equally important, we must still question the valid-ity of our understanding. Although we may have heard the same story multiple times, we still must accept the possibility we're wrong. After all, we've heard it only a handful of times. It isn't predictive of the entire population we're trying to serve. It serves as

Believing Our Own Stories

a *signal*, and if big bets depend on being absolutely certain, the team needs to use a different method (perhaps a quantitative instrument) to be certain that signal is real.

Summary

- PrD is fundamentally about finding out how wrong we are in our assumptions, but it is human nature to believe in those assumptions.

- We must avoid *selling* our ideas to stakeholders by pitching, presenting, or arguing with them. Hand the artifact over and let them pitch, present, and argue with *us*.

- Psychologically, the cards are stacked against us: We seek data supporting our position, we resist the effort required to change our minds, we rely on experience even when it isn't a reliable guide, and we never generate enough disparate solutions to truly know how wrong we might be. Still, by simply keeping an opposite frame of reference in mind, we can counteract our bias toward confirmation.

- If we're lucky, we'll have guessed more right than wrong, or if we're sensitive, we'll begin owning the stories our stakeholders tell us. In either case, it's time to move on to something else.

Chapter 12: Unclear Objectives

Would you tell me, please, which way I ought to walk from here?"

"That depends a good deal on where you want to get to," said the Cat.

"I don't much care where— " said Alice.

"Then it doesn't matter which way you walk," said the Cat.

Presumptive Design
Design Provocations for Innovation

A goal properly set is halfway reached.
—Zig Ziglar

Overview

There are many reasons why any endeavor fails. A quick review of the topic reveals such things as poor management, undefined objectives and goals, lack of planning, lack of user input, poorly defined roles and responsibilities, inadequate or vague requirements, scope creep, and on and on.[1] But stepping back we can put these into two large buckets: a structural failure (strategy, requirements, objectives) or a failure of execution (management, tools, operations).

This chapter discusses the first category in the context of PrD, but its lessons are applicable to any project in which the team must first define *what they're going to do* before actually doing it.

Throughout the rest of the book we've covered many ways to fail (and avoid failing) in execution of PrD. In brief, PrD, like any other form of research (e.g. Lean UX discusses the notion of crafting "hypotheses" suitable for testing), requires a clear set of objectives or experimental questions. For the purposes of PrD, *we define an objective as a statement that helps design, conduct, and ultimately evaluate the results of PrD Engagement Sessions*.

If you already familiar with creating SMART objectives feel free to scan this chapter to see how we define and apply objectives in PrD. In brief, not only do good objectives help the team shrink the Engagement Session "to fit," but they also provide a "definition of done." Using objectives real-time during the session, the team knows when to stop. (When we've achieved our objectives with the external stakeholder, we're done.) For reporting out, objectives provide the skeleton to discuss the results for sponsors and others who couldn't attend the sessions.

The corporate world is replete with objectives: Objectives measure employees annually on their performance, projects are measured based on how well they achieved their goals, and the company itself is measured by stockholders on its performance to goals. So much depends on carefully crafted objectives that few corporate denizens need to be formally introduced to them. Similarly, in the armed services, all engagements are based on well-formed, measurable objectives. Even in these contexts where objectives play such a major part of day-to-day operations, the crafting of clear and precise objectives remains a challenge for many. For those who are befuddled by them, or have little experience building them, this chapter provides a strong foundation for crafting solid objectives.

Objectives come in two flavors: explicit and implicit. In general, the team is free to engage external stakeholders in discussing *explicit* objectives, because revealing them will not change the stakeholders' behaviors or feedback. In contrast, implicit objectives usually remain hidden; talking about them will likely cause stakeholders to change their answers or reactions, simply because they now know what the team is looking for. In the next section we offer suggestions for creating explicit objectives; here we offer examples of implicit objectives.

All PrD investigations have at least one underlying implicit objective: Collect reactions by stakeholders to the team's assumptions about the stakeholders' world. Even though the Facilitator may reveal this objective in a variety of ways, she likely won't explicitly say: "Today we'd like to hear your reaction to our assumptions about you, our assumptions about your work and our assumptions about your expectations for improvements to the boaconic confabulator." She *may* say: "Today we're also interested in learning where we've got things wrong about your work and about our proposed solution to the challenges

Explicit and Implicit Objectives

we believe you face." There is a subtle but important difference.

Here are a few more implicit objectives:

- *How well does our concept work (because our sponsor really likes it)?* While we would prefer to think our sponsors are as eager to be wrong as we are, that's not necessarily so. If a sponsor really likes an idea, the team may harbor a strong implicit objective to find data supporting the sponsor's desire.

- *This is our job and we enjoy doing it.* This isn't a bad objective; we hope it's implicit in the work we do! We may share it with a stakeholder (and thus make it explicit), but not until after the session is over. Our passion for our work is likely inherent in the way we comport ourselves during the session.

- *We are on a quest for the truth.* As researchers, we seek knowledge; it's implicit in our reason for being with the stakeholder. Whether we achieve that goal is immaterial and certainly not something we'd likely share with the stakeholder.

There are dozens of other similar implicit objectives in any team and organization.

It Takes a Village …

Objectives are best constructed by a multidisciplinary team rather than by a single person. The more eyes on an objective, generally, the more likely it will have the right impact. At a minimum, the team should craft the objectives for a PrD session. In addition, the sponsor should participate. The last thing the team wants to do is return from an otherwise successful set of Engagement Sessions to learn the sponsor wasn't happy with the purpose of the endeavor!

But crafting excellent objectives is only half of the challenge: Once the team has decided on the objectives, it needs to construct the artifacts and scripts to achieve them. The remainder of the chapter describes all of the ways PrD can fail due to poor attention to objectives. In the first part, we discuss the strategic or structural failures of the Engagement Session due to poor objectives. In the second part, we discuss how the artifact itself may be negatively impacted. In the last section we discuss how the report out relies on good objectives to communicate the results to internal stakeholders and sponsors who couldn't attend.

Structural Failures

In the absence of objectives, PrD's chances of success are practically zero. PrD requires carefully crafted objectives because they form the structural backbone of the entire process, from the building of artifacts to deciding who should attend Engagement Sessions, to interpreting the results.

Lack of Well-Defined Objectives

The mnemonic SMART should be familiar to many readers: Objectives are SMART if they are Specific, Measurable, Achievable/Appropriate, Realistic/Relevant, and Time-bound.[2] We'll cover each in detail. In addition, we often start with a formula to help create our objectives: ⟨action word⟩, ⟨target/metric⟩ ⟨time constraint⟩, where ⟨action word⟩ may come from the list given in Figure 12.1.

A "well-formed" objective, syntactically, would appear as follows:

> Assess six characteristics of the bottomography process within 15 minutes of engaging the participant.

Of course, just because it is well formed doesn't mean it is useful or applicable, or meets all of the SMART attributes.

Specific

An objective describes *one* thing. If we are interested in multiple things, we have multiple objectives. It's really that simple. With the exception of the measurement criteria, specific objectives do not include a list, the words *And* or *Or*, or lots of comma-separated clauses.

Action Words for Objectives	
Assess	Judge
Clarify	Justify
Define	List
Demonstrate	Prove
Describe	Record
Determine	Relate
Evaluate	Show
Examine	Specify
Explain	Test
Identify	Validate
Illustrate	Verify
Inspect	

Figure 12.1 List of Action Words for Objectives

Presumptive Design
DESIGN PROVOCATIONS FOR INNOVATION

Take a look at the following good and bad examples of objectives with respect to their specificity. Before looking at our choices, take a moment to indicate which objectives are specific and which are not:

1. Determine the key elements involved in stakeholder decision making as defined by the top 10 elements mentioned during the PrD session.

2. Solicit updates and new material for the website from stakeholders.

3. Identify 12 changes to the application most needed by stakeholders.

4. Assess the quality of the application and the performance of the search capabilities within the first five minutes of the PrD session.

5. Judge stakeholder reaction to 16 distinct examples of cromulence in the fluddle portion of the application and rank and rate their dissatisfaction with them.

While some examples are obvious (2, 4, and 5 are all multiples with the word "and" in them), some are a little trickier. We believe 1 and 3 are specific, even if 3 fails on other characteristics. 1 is specific because it focuses on a single thing: "key" elements, as defined by the metric ("top 10 elements"). 2 fails the specificity test on two possible counts: Updates *and* new material may be two very different things. But there is no upper limit to the number of updates the team might acquire, failing the "definition of done" test.

If we have more than one thing in an objective, we won't know when we're done. One thing might be achieved, and the other not. Should we declare success or keep going? When we encounter multiple things in a single objective, we split 'em up and decide if both are truly required.

Measurable

This one is (or should be) the easiest of the bunch—
we define a *quantity* that can be measured *during* the
Engagement Session so we know when we can move
on. Quantities can be anything: a unit of time, number
of attempts, number of paths pursued, number of ideas
generated, and on and on.

Really, the only gotcha with measurable is whether it's
achievable and/or relevant. Still, many objectives we've
encountered simply fail to include any measures at all.
When we evaluate our objective, we must ask ourselves:
"Will we know when we've accomplished it?" Measurable
cannot be separated from achievable and time-oriented.
The three work in concert—but without measurable we
won't know where we are in the process. Here are a
few bad and good examples to consider with respect to
measurable:

1. Determine the key elements involved in stakeholder
   decision making as defined by the top 10 elements
   mentioned during the session.

2. Solicit more than 12 updates for the website from
   stakeholders.

3. Identify 15 changes to the application most needed by
   stakeholders.

4. Evaluate stakeholders' impressions of the home page
   within the first five minutes of seeing each variation.

5. Judge stakeholder reaction to 16 distinct examples
   of cromulence in the fluddle portion of the application
   and rank and rate their dissatisfaction with them.

6. Collect as many reflections as possible from
   stakeholders on the diator function within the first
   15 minutes of the session.

With the exception of 4 (and the hanging clause in 5),
we would rate each of these as measurable. *Note*: To be

measurable, an objective requires either a lower or an upper limit (or both). In 2, for example, as soon as the stakeholder provides 13 updates the team can decide to stop; the objective has been achieved. You might argue about 6, but here's where the time-bound constraint provides a means of measuring, and therefore defining, when the objective has been achieved.

Achievable

The A in SMART has the greatest variability among the many definitions we've looked at. Achievable is a fine attribute, but it often is confused with Realistic, so various authors have substituted Attainable, Applicable, or Appropriate for the A, or Relevant, Resourced, or Realizable for the R.

We'll stick with Achievable: The team has to look at the objective and say, "Yep, we can get that done in the time we've got with the stakeholder," or "Hmmm, do we really think we'll collect that many reactions in the time we've got?"

Achievable requires both an analysis of internal consistency with the objective and the overall plan for working with the stakeholder. In general, stakeholders don't have a lot of time to offer us; let's say in the most generous cases they'll give us 90 minutes, total. Some amount of that time will require introductions and helping them get situated with the process. Some amount of that time will require debriefing and closure with them. At best we've got 60 minutes and maybe only 45. Can we achieve the objective in that time? Do we have several objectives? How likely is it we'll be able to achieve all of our objectives in the time we've got?

Realistic

Because Realistic feels a lot like Achievable, we also think of the R as Relevant. The entire point of an objective is to achieve something useful to our cause, to move our agenda forward. If the objective doesn't make sense in the context of the team's effort, the objective won't lead to a useful outcome.

An objective can be well formed and not realistic: It can have a specific target, with great measures, be achievable in the time allotted, and be completely irrelevant to the purpose of the Engagement Session.

Realism and relevancy are not very difficult to comprehend or to reconcile, as long as the team is all on the same page. Remember, objectives have three primary purposes: to help align everyone on what we're going to do (team and sponsors), keep things straight *during* the sessions, and provide a structure for reporting out the results. When the team evaluates the objective on its relevancy, it is using the objective to align all of the team members and get things straight before expending any additional effort.

Time-Bound

Building a deadline into an objective should be obvious, but it is often overlooked. For many objectives the time frame can be days, months, or even years, but in the case of PrD, we're expecting to complete the objective within the span of the Engagement Session. That provides an *upper* bound by which the objective must be achieved. But there's no guarantee we'll actually accomplish the objective by the end of the session. It really doesn't matter *how* we fail to achieve an objective (either we didn't facilitate the Engagement Session toward an objective's metric or we ran out of time); the end result is the same: a failed session.

So, an objective can't take longer than the proposed length of the session; that's the upper bound. The lower bound may be much earlier than the time we've allotted to the Engagement Session. What happens if an objective can be completed in the first few minutes of the session and there are no other objectives? There's no reason to continue taking up the stakeholders' time.

So building a time frame into the objective is key to pacing the sessions. If we think we can accomplish the objective in the first five minutes, we make sure we have another one to move on to. In this way we create a rhythm for the sessions. Depending on the objectives, we may do them in sequence or we may be able to accomplish them simultaneously. If one objective depends on another, clearly we design the session to complete the independent objective first. In some cases a single objective may take the entire session to complete, but we know we can achieve it even as we pursue others.

Regardless, once we've completed the objectives, the session is over.

Too Many Objectives

Just because we've crafted a set of SMART objectives, we still don't know if we can accomplish all of them together.

While each objective may be perfect, and even together we're convinced we won't exceed the time frame of the session, we still could fail to achieve all of them. Every objective we create adds complexity into the session: measures, questions, observations—the team will need to keep their eyes and ears open to make sure all of the objectives are being addressed. As the number of objectives increases beyond a handful, the team won't be able to keep track (Figure 12.2).

A good rule of thumb is to develop between three and five objectives. In general, three objectives can easily be achieved within an hour, and depending on the type of engagement, three objectives can be completed within 30 minutes. More than five objectives require a bit more thought. Are all of them truly necessary, or are a few just variations of each other? Are there several that focus

Figure 12.2 Too many objectives becomes a juggling act

on specific, related measures? Remember, PrD isn't about highly resolved quantitative measures. Consider consolidating the detailed objectives into a single objective with a more general term for the individual elements. The example we provided earlier ("Determine the key elements involved in stakeholder decision making as defined by the top 10 elements mentioned during the PrD session.") uses a generic term in one objective instead of crafting as many as 10 separate objectives.

What if, after consolidating and reviewing, the team has a dozen separate objectives it needs to address? A project with that many objectives is complex. In this case, the team needs to sanity check its charter and confirm its understanding of the business's needs. At a minimum, the team will need to have a heart and soul conversation with the sponsor to calibrate everyone's expectations. This level of complexity raises the cost and effort of the entire process, something the sponsor will need to buy off on.

In the rare cases where the team does have more than a handful of objectives, it will need to strategize about getting the work done productively. One strategy is to break the sessions into multiple parts. Either set up two sessions with the same stakeholders (each session focusing on a subset of the objectives) or find twice as many stakeholders (covering half the objectives with some and the other half with the others). Remember, because there's nothing statistically interesting about the sessions, there's little reason to worry about randomization or counterbalancing. Instead, on a project this complicated, the team is likely working with different types of stakeholders; some of the objectives may not apply to all of the possible stakeholders.

In any event, stakeholders aren't the issue when the project has so many objectives. The issue is with the artifact. As we discuss in the next section, no single artifact will cover all of them, in which case the team will need to build separate artifacts. Now, with separate artifacts, the team can just as easily run separate sessions—whether with the same stakeholders or different ones—as if they had separate projects, or separate objectives.

All of this discussion about objectives may sound distinct from the underlying principle behind PrD: to test the team's assumptions about the stakeholders' world, but it isn't. Our stakeholders' mental model is an unknown landscape, filled with all sorts of interesting cul-de-sacs, byways, and detours. Defining clear and achievable objectives keeps the conversations and stories focused on the stuff about which we are interested in learning.

The Artifact Serves the Objectives

Doing Too Much

Assuming we've got the right number of well formed objectives and we're confident we can get them accomplished in the time available, we'll want to be sure the artifact(s) support our objectives.

This requires immense discipline, mostly because the design team will enjoy the possibility of exploring all sorts of different ways to craft the artifact. At some point, and hopefully all along the way, the team needs to step back and evaluate the fitness of the artifact. We use two primary criteria: Will the artifact inspire the right conversations (focused on the team's assumptions), and will it achieve the objectives? Anything not meeting those two criteria can be safely removed, no matter how creative it is. When the artifact has too much going on, the Engagement Session is put at risk. First, the stakeholders may become confused by what they're being asked to consider. Second, the team may become confused and have trouble tracking what's going on (Figure 12.3).

As we cover in detail in Appendix B, less is more in crafting the artifact: Let the stakeholders reveal what they're thinking by projecting onto the artifact. Better to have some squiggly lines representing...something... than to have complete text. Who knows? The stakeholders may not think it's supposed to represent text at all, raising all sorts of possibilities and revealing interesting insights into their mental models.

Figure 12.3 An artifact addressing too many objectives

There are plenty of resources to help the team devise clever artifacts.[3] First and foremost, the point is to craft the smallest necessary artifact to achieve the objectives and test the team's assumptions.

In The Case of the Hard-Boiled Eggs, testing the team's assumptions boiled down to a set of plastic eggs and an egg carton. The objective was to understand what stakeholders would do when faced with a componentized experience. It was a single objective taking less than 20 minutes to achieve.

To help the team (and especially the designers on the team) stay disciplined about the artifact, treat the artifact as a miniature design problem. What is its benefit? What is its value to the users? What interactions would it enable? The design brief is to craft the least complicated artifact to drive conversations that will achieve the objectives and test the team's assumptions. In the Creation Session, the

The team's challenge is to craft the minimum necessary artifact to achieve the objectives, even if the artifact is nothing like the intended experience.

See Appendix A: The Case of the Hard-Boiled Eggs

Presumptive Design
Design Provocations for Innovation

design team focuses on crafting the artifact itself, not trying to solve the larger design problem.

As Jason's story in Chapter 11 described, he had made an assumption and was off down the road wanting to test the details of the *design*. His working assumption was the basis for all sorts of interesting design decisions, but none of those decisions mattered if his stakeholders couldn't comprehend his basic premise. His gut told him to illustrate his premise with a bunch of details. In our experience, *not* illustrating the team's assumptions with a bunch of details provides a far richer opportunity for discussion.

As we've mentioned in prior chapters and discuss in Chapter 15 and Appendix B, the design of the artifact should bias toward *ambiguity*. When external stakeholders encounter an ambiguous artifact, they offer up stories to fill in the blanks. Such was the case in The Case of the *Star Trek* Holodeck: Users were asked to evaluate a product with no fundamental "narrative" explaining why it existed or how it might be used. Because of that, users offered their own explanations and stories, enlightening the team about aspects of the experience no one had given thought to.

When external stakeholders encounter an ambiguous artifact, they offer up stories to fill in the blanks.
See Appendix A: The Case of the *Star Trek* Holodeck

Doing Too Little

There is, however, a diminishing return on minimalism. In the practice of Participatory Design, the clean sheet of paper is the general rule. Activists inspire the community to put their thoughts on the clean sheet, out of which they tease a common set of themes. So, the least one can do in Participatory Design is provide a piece of paper and a pen.

But this isn't Participatory Design; this is PrD, in which we are intentionally trying to provoke a conversation about our assumptions. We need to provide enough to inspire the stakeholder to tell us how, and in what way, we are wrong in our thinking. The Case of the Hard-Boiled Eggs illustrates the least amount of rendering we've attempted to test our

Artifacts need not be complicated; they can be as simple as a set of plastic eggs.
See Appendix A: The Case of the Hard-Boiled Eggs

assumptions and objective. We recently saw a series of Engagement Sessions where the artifact was a plastic cup with sticky notes in it. In spite of it being simple, the team was amazed by the insights they gained (Figure 12.4).

Striking the right balance of details and craftwork takes some practice, but most important is for everyone on the team to agree on the assumptions and the objectives: Even a poorly rendered artifact can be mitigated in most cases with good facilitation.

Figure 12.4 Even a simple artifact can drive the objective

There are cases in which no artifact needs to be *designed*. In these cases, the team uses found artifacts to provoke conversations, test their assumptions, and achieve the objectives. The mini-exercise in Chapter 1 illustrates this approach: Using a smartphone's home page took less effort than the carton of eggs to engage with stakeholders in discussions about a componentized experience. But just because the team finds an artifact meeting its needs doesn't mean it's solved the problem. As we discuss in the next chapter, any artifact is likely to create friction or dissonance in the minds of the stakeholders. A found artifact, such as the smartphone screen, brings with it all sorts of associations and "loose threads" that will require expert facilitation to address.

In the workshop we discussed earlier in the book, in which participants crafted a "dreamcatcher," they concluded they could have used a simple paper dot to represent the device since their objectives were not around the device itself, but rather the images it created during the stakeholder's (simulated) dream. Perhaps. Or perhaps, after trying that in a couple of sessions they would have gone back to the over-the-ear artifact (Figure 12.5).

Figure 12.5 Even a simple artifact may be too complicated for the objective

The last way in which PrD may fail structurally is in analyzing and reporting out the results. In general, the people who need to know the results have already been in on the Creation and Engagement Sessions, so putting a report together may seem wasteful.

It's true that for small projects with a few objectives, all team members will likely have been able to participate in every Engagement Session. But for anything requiring more than a handful of stakeholders, many team members will not have attended every session. In addition, there are always internal stakeholders, such as the sponsor, who may not have attended *any* session, Creation or Engagement. For these people, the team owes a concise and rich report of their findings. With PrD the challenge is to distill out the key insights.

In a single Engagement Session, with a few team members present, we generate several dozen pages of notes. Sure there is duplication, but even when two people hear the same words from a stakeholder, they may draw two completely different conclusions. Boiling down and distilling the raw notes into a comprehensive (and comprehendible) story to retell is already a challenge. But an equal challenge is telling the story supporting the objectives. Without those objectives, the story can meander all over the landscape.

We structure our reports using the objectives as the main outline entries. Because the team ostensibly got agreement from the sponsor on the objectives at the beginning of the process, these are the key touchpoints to refer back to at the end of the process. We use the objectives as a lens through which to view the results.

Without the objectives, the report loses its structure. Even though the team may have gleaned important insights, insights alone do not bear much weight. Any insights from

The Objectives Frame the Report

Even when a stakeholder reaction is interesting, if it doesn't serve the objectives the team must set it aside.

See Appendix A: The Case of the Business Case

the sessions not associated with an objective are suspect and require further investigation. We don't suppress them, but we clearly flag them in the report as unsubstantiated curiosities.

It happens all of the time: A stakeholder goes "off script" and illustrates a fascinating aspect of the experience nobody had anticipated. In The Case of the Business Case, one of the stakeholders, after understanding the initial assumption, leapt several years beyond the team's proposal, offering a completely revolutionary alternative. This was an important finding and it may have had massive implications for the business. But it was on a trajectory so far off from the purpose of the PrD it wasn't clear how to fit it into the objectives. In this case, the team chose to include it in the report as a key insight, but one that required further study to more fully understand.

Without objectives, that's how all of the insights would appear. If we don't have a way of framing the insights, they become completely arbitrary.

Summary

Objectives serve three purposes:

1. Provide a definition of done for the Engagement Session

2. Provide guidance in the creation of the artifacts

3. Provide a structure for the report out to stakeholders who weren't present

Establishing SMART objectives reduces the risk of the Engagement Session going poorly. Specifically, objectives are as follows:

- *Specific*: If an objective isn't limited to a single target, we don't know when we've accomplished it. This could mean too much or too little coverage in the session.

- *Measurable*: When an objective has nothing to measure, we don't know what we're supposed to cover; anything might as well serve as nothing at all.

- *Achievable/Realistic*: Without knowing whether we can actually accomplish the objective during the session we can't predict the pacing. We risk ending the session without capturing everything we had hoped to.

- *Relevant/Appropriate*: We not only have to build the objectives "right," but we also have to build the right objectives. If we fail to serve our internal stakeholders and sponsors, we risk wasting time, money, and goodwill.

- *Time-bound*: All objectives in PrD are automatically time-bound: the scheduled time with the external stakeholder. Objectives must be sized to fit within that deadline. When the objectives have been met, the Engagement Session is over.

- Keep the number of objectives to a handful: about three to five. Too many and the artifact becomes difficult to manage; too few and the session may be over too soon.

- Adjust the complexity of the artifact to serve the objectives; build multiple artifacts if necessary.

- Use the objectives to manage the information provided in the report. Any findings not associated with the objectives may be noted but should be marked as needing further study.

I'm just like a black hole for stuff. No one should ever hand me anything, because I get so easily distracted.
—Florence Welch

Overview

Throughout the book, we've emphasized the purpose of PrD: to elicit and provoke conversations with stakeholders about their mental models through the use of a throwaway artifact. The artifact is the stone we throw in the pond. We're interested in the ripples created, not in the stone itself. This simple proposition creates a tension: Balance the team's investment in creating the artifact with investing enough to drive the right types of conversations.

Just as our assumptions about stakeholder needs are wrong (and we go into our Engagement Sessions with this knowledge), so too the artifact we create must be wrong. The ways in which the artifact is wrong bring additional challenges to the Engagement Session. By definition, and by intention, the artifact may be vague, ambiguous, and unclear. Less intentionally, the artifact is crude, unfinished, and slapped together. All of these characteristics *can* contribute to a rich conversation—but they can also easily drive stakeholders to distraction (Figure 13.1).

Users Catch on Rough Edges

Even the most refined prototypes have edges, places where they are incomplete. By definition a prototype is not a complete product. Usability reviews of prototypes must account for informants pursuing paths poorly defined in the prototype. In usability reviews such meandering must be carefully managed: They focus on specific tasks, task completion, and how the proposed solution addresses user satisfaction in the context of those tasks.

In contrast, PrD artifacts are designed to inspire such meandering journeys. By offering an intentionally vague

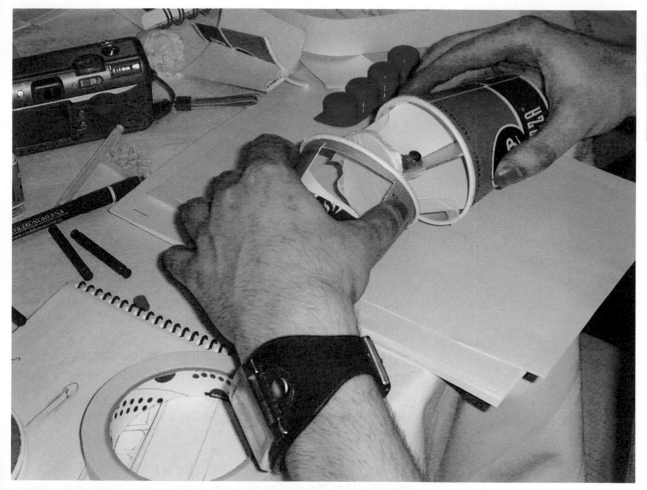

Figure 13.1 PrD artifacts are intentionally ambiguous...and rough (as in this mockup of an intelligent pill dispenser)

artifact, the team aspires to enable these meanderings. It really doesn't know, up front, what does or doesn't make sense to stakeholders. So, the rough edges of an artifact are themselves the source of inspiration and conversation. The challenge is around the types of conversation these rough edges inspire. Consider the following silly but not unusual example.

The team offers a stakeholder an artifact: a set of rectangles in an open frame, perhaps a browser-based wireframe, perhaps a front panel on a machine. Irrespective of its representation, some of the rectangles are outlined in blue, others in black. The team consciously chose to differentiate some rectangles from others. It felt there were categorical differences, and it wanted the stakeholders to opine about that assumption.

A stakeholder looks at the artifact and asks, "Why are some of these rectangles blue and others black?"

The Facilitator anticipates the question and mirrors back, "Why do you think there might be a difference?"

And here's where things go off the rails.

"Well," the stakeholder continues, "that blue isn't a brand standard. If you decide to use a color it shouldn't be a blue that violates our brand standards. Maybe it should be yellow..."

Not only is this observation gratuitous at this stage of the process, but the team also should not be spending any time tracking it or others like it.* Most important, the Facilitator needs to quickly dive in and get the conversation back on track.

"Ahhh, good point. Let's assume for the sake of today's session that the rectangles are using brand standards. You mentioned some appear to be different from others … what do you suppose would differentiate these, other than their color?"

Because the artifact is almost nothing but rough edges, there are more opportunities for these sorts of distractions than not. In fact, this is actually the advantage of PrD

---

*The only possible benefit to pursuing this line of reasoning is to dive deeper into the stakeholder's focus on brand standards. Is that an important aspect of his job or focus on his life? Depending on the objectives, a deeper dive may be called for.

artifacts: Almost every engagement with the artifact will catch the stakeholder and raise questions. It is imperative the Facilitator emphasizes questions around the team's assumptions and deemphasizes questions about the artifact itself.

When Confusion is a Distraction Versus Branch Point

Sometimes a stakeholder will simply be confused by something in the artifact. The challenge for the Facilitator is to understand the basis for the confusion. Is it something about the artifact or is it the assumption itself? In some cases it's not obvious. Consider the following seemingly innocent interchange:

Stakeholder: "What is that doohickey there?"

Facilitator: "What do you suppose it could be?"

S ⟨laughing⟩: "Shit. It could be practically anything..." "I really don't know...a button?"

F: "Okay, let's say it's a button. Tell me about that button."

And here's where we're at the branch point. If the stakeholder is truly confused by the assumption, it will emerge right at this moment. Her description of the things around that button (perhaps what she expects will happen if she presses it) hopefully reveals her mental model about the process in which she's engaged.

S ⟨laughing again⟩: "Okay, well, I assume if I pressed that button-thingy, a different screen would pop up with the skizzle data."

And if the team had guessed correctly, just such a screen might be available. Even if the team hadn't anticipated her need for skizzle data, the Facilitator could easily continue the discussion about that need and why it should appear at that moment or in that flow.

But the conversation could easily go in a completely different (and less useful) direction:

Stakeholder ⟨*brow furrowed*⟩: "It just doesn't seem right…"

Facilitator: "What is it that doesn't seem right?"

S: "The button. It's just not in the right place, or maybe it shouldn't be a button. I'm not sure why it's over here rather than next to these other ones. Can we move it next to the other ones?"

The best solution for the Facilitator is to appease the stakeholder and absolutely agree to move the button, since it seems to be getting in the way of the underlying conversation. Again, the Facilitator must extinguish this sort of focus at the same time. He may need to remind the stakeholder the artifact is really not refined, and what would be helpful, in terms of getting the stakeholder a better system or outcome, is to focus on the intention behind the button.

Facilitator: "Of course!" ⟨*motioning to the Designer*⟩ "While Frederick is changing that up, let's chat for a moment about that button. What about that button, other than its location or association with the other buttons, is relevant to the sembiguent processes we were just discussing?"

If we were interested in the button itself, we'd pursue a different line of investigation, digging deeper into the stakeholder's concerns about the button. The Facilitator might ask, "While Frederick fixes this up, tell me a little more about the importance of that button and its relationship to the others, especially as it relates to the sembiguent processes we were just discussing." This is a different way to guide the stakeholder back to the assumptions and objectives while focusing on whatever caused the distraction.

In both the "rough edge" and "distraction" pitfalls, the outcome is the same: By latching onto something in the artifact, the stakeholder has shifted her focus from her work to the artifact itself. In both cases, the Facilitator *must* correct the situation with diplomacy and creativity as quickly as possible.

On the other hand, if a particular element elicits distracted behavior in more than one stakeholder, that is an interesting data point to think about further. Is there something going on the team should be paying attention to? Alternatively, is the artifact rendered in too distracting a way, calling attention to itself inappropriately? Either way, the next sessions may need to be adjusted—either the script (to accommodate the new possible insights) or the artifact (to extinguish the conversation before it begins).

Difficult Conversations (Uncooperative Stakeholders)

This pitfall is part of any field research manual: What do we do when we encounter stakeholders who just aren't prepared to play? Sometimes we just have to stop the interview and thank them for their time. While it is never desirable to lose an opportunity to work directly with a stakeholder, it is far worse to create an environment of hostility. Clearly there had been miscommunication along the way, otherwise why would they have agreed to participate in the first place?

We have witnessed many Engagement Sessions in which the stakeholders *hadn't* been properly introduced to the protocol. Perhaps we weren't allowed access to them before the date of the session. Perhaps they had claimed to understand what we were proposing but in the moment became completely confused. Perhaps they really hadn't reviewed all of the prework and introductory material we had sent in advance. In other cases, well-meaning individuals find themselves under a lot of pressure and couldn't really afford the time but didn't feel comfortable reneging.

Presumptive Design
DESIGN PROVOCATIONS FOR INNOVATION

Mike found himself the center of attention, with his boss and co-workers watching him perform. This is not the desired dynamic!

See Appendix A: The Case of the Reticent Respondent

Whatever the cause, we might find ourselves in front of a stakeholder who cannot have a back-and-forth conversation with us. In The Case of the Reticent Respondent, for example, Mike found himself the center of attention, with his boss and team in the room while he was asked to "perform." This sacrificial lamb creates an awful dynamic for stakeholders, especially for junior team members like Mike. Thankfully, Mike was up to the task. We pressed forward with the session and were rewarded by a completely surprising outcome.

The Discussion Strays from the Objectives

Which brings us to the last pitfall of Losing Our Audience: The stakeholder drifts from the objectives.

As with an uncooperative stakeholder, this pitfall is a challenge in any user research engagement. Good Facilitators are comfortable with providing the right degree of freedom for the conversation, whether to build rapport or to allow a stakeholder to explore the question. There is no hard and fast rule about what constitutes straying. A good Facilitator knows it when he hears it.

In Chapter 12 we discussed the importance of solid objectives. Before we can declare the stakeholder is straying from an objective we must agree on the objective. It's possible, in spite of our best efforts, the artifact we created inspires rich conversations that aren't in service of our objectives. Here again, the team must decide: Is the problem with the objectives, the artifact, or the facilitation? If the conversations are really interesting, and highlight an intriguing set of problems, perhaps that's the direction the team needs to go. If, however, the artifact is continuing to drive trivial and distracting conversations, it likely needs to be revised. And, finally, it may come down to proper facilitation. Assuming the stakeholder is moving away from the session's objectives, the Facilitator must step in and gently guide the conversation back on track. In Chapter 14 we offer a deep dive into facilitation techniques suited to PrD and artifacts.

Summary

PrD is fundamentally about stories, storytelling, and conversing with our stakeholders. In these, it shares many characteristics of other social science research techniques. But by offering a concrete artifact, PrD focuses stakeholders' attention, fundamentally shaping the stories they will tell.

Because of its reliance on a messy, but concrete, artifact, PrD requires expert facilitation. The Facilitator keeps the focus on the stories, not the artifact. Yet the artifact is necessarily ambiguous and messy. As a result, stakeholders will get distracted by irrelevant details, irrelevant to our objectives, to the problem space, and to their mental model.

- Specifically, the artifact may distract users by its rough edges, causing stakeholders to drift from the desired path.

- Some amount of confusion is appropriate, but a messy artifact may create low-value confusion.

- Stakeholders may not be prepared to deal with the artifact or the approach during the interview.

- Everything we do is in service of our objectives, but the artifact we created may inspire rich stories that have little to do with our objectives, requiring us to reconsider the objectives, the artifact, or our facilitation.

Part 3: How-To Manual and Recipes

The three chapters in this part describe in detail *how* to do PrD.

Chapter 14 begins by focusing on facilitation, one of the key skills required to make the process a success.

Chapter 15 offers a step-by-step breakdown of the Creation Session, one of the two sessions comprising PrD.

Chapter 16 describes, in detail, how to approach the second of the two sessions, the Engagement Session, to make PrD successful.

Presumptive Design
DESIGN PROVOCATIONS FOR INNOVATION

Many a treasure besides Ali Baba's is unlocked with a verbal key.
—Henry Van Dyke

Overview Over the years we've observed both Creation and Engagement Sessions (discussed in detail in the chapters that follow) that have not risen to their potential. In the prior chapters we discuss many of the reasons for their falling short, and in the next chapters we provide recipes for improving their successful outcome. In this chapter we focus on a key element of PrD without which it will fail: expert facilitation. We characterize an expert Facilitator as one who prompts participants to keep exploring, without leading, and who keeps participants on track with respect to the session's objectives. An expert's engagement maximizes the interviewee's engagement and minimizes confounding their responses.

Interviewing people is an art: Journalism, psychology, and ethnography, among dozens of other disciplines, all demand a nuanced and sophisticated form of facilitation. We don't believe PrD requires anything less of a Facilitator than these other forms of engagement. But in our workshops, Creation Sessions, and Engagement Sessions, attendees remind us PrD facilitation differs substantively from other forms of interviewing.

Facilitation occurs in both the Creation and Engagement Sessions, but each context differs significantly in its needs and demands. Chapter 15 covers Creation Session facilitation. We cover facilitation within the Engagement Session in this chapter. We offer additional examples of good facilitation in the context of the Engagement Session itself in Chapter 16.

This chapter is divided into two sections. In the first section, we review facilitation techniques applicable in any research context. If you are already comfortable as an interviewer/facilitator, feel free to skim over this first section. We tailor these techniques to PrD. These include:

- Offering the Artifact, Not the Design
- The Present Tense
- Judicious Prompting
- Honoring Silence
- The Five Whys

The second section describes facilitation specific to PrD. These prescriptions differentiate facilitation in PrD from facilitation used in other contexts:

- The Artifact
- Losing the Script
- Ignoring Usability
- Forgetting Quantification
- No Requirements
- No Opinions
- Light-touch Subjunctivity

In Chapter 11 we discussed the hazard of believing our own story to the extent we lead the stakeholder. There we discussed *pitching* the design, *explaining* the design, and, in the worst case, *arguing with stakeholders*. Here we reinforce this prohibition: Facilitation is not a demo.

There's always the danger of a Pygmalion or Rosenthal effect wherein we set up and run a session in such a way that it amounts to a self-fulfilling prophecy. As Portigal[1]

Fundamental Facilitation Techniques

Offering the Artifact, Not the Design

stresses, we've got to check our worldview at the door. We're not looking to find anything *in particular*. We're just there to learn. Portigal discusses another danger: establishing a dynamic in which the stakeholder avoids being critical of our work.

Consider the following scenario: The Facilitator sits down with a stakeholder and says, "Here's a design we've been working on." With that simple sentence, the stakeholder may be less likely to share critical feedback. He believes it is *the* idea. Contrast that statement with one Portigal suggests as an alternative: "Here are some early ideas we've been asked to share with you." This small change in wording alters the message. A "design" sounds like the result of a committed team. "Early ideas" are wisps no one is devoted to. This lets the stakeholder know no one will be offended by blunt, honest reaction.

The Facilitator must remain neutral: neutral in her presentation of herself, neutral in her presentation of the artifact, and neutral in her reactions to the stakeholder's responses. Being neutral doesn't mean being cold. The Facilitator is neutral, inviting, warm, and sincerely interested in the stakeholder's point of view, but without telegraphing her own agenda, interests, or expectations.

Since we're interested in the external stakeholder's interpretation, explaining the design is a form of leading. Since we simply hand over the artifact without explanation, the stakeholder will likely struggle with the task we give him. This creates a challenge for the Facilitator: Watching someone struggle is uncomfortable. An expert facilitator resists the temptation to help, letting the stakeholder figure things out for himself. An expert knows if she breaks this rule (e.g., if she explains the team's ideas), she implants that knowledge into the stakeholder's brain. There's no way the participant can unlearn it. That's the hindsight bias.[2] The jury can't unhear what's been "stricken from the record" (Figure 14.1).

Interrupting by being helpful has further consequences. Under the best of circumstances, the interruption delays the session as the stakeholder reengages with the artifact on his terms. At worst, he won't explore alternative path that may otherwise have been explored. Similarly, he'll fail to raise key questions that shed light on his mental model.

Figure 14.1 "It's too late to correct it: when you've once said a thing, that fixes it, and you must take the consequences"

Being in the here and now is challenging and tiring, yet expert Facilitators are active listeners. The act of being present means being in the room, with the stakeholder, listening to his words, tone, and body language. It is about guiding the conversation and mirroring back the stakeholder's own words.

Staying Present in the Present Tense

Use Their Words

The Facilitator adopts the stakeholder's vocabulary. When a Facilitator mirrors back the stakeholder's words, verbatim, there is no opportunity for misunderstanding. When the Facilitator uses any word other than the stakeholder's, the stakeholder faces confusion. It also risks wrecking the dynamic: The Facilitator should never correct the stakeholder. It changes their relationship, (as discussed in Section "Actively Listening without Judgment"). It also influences the stakeholder's behavior by providing clues to the team's intent behind the artifact. Snyder[3] gives the following example: Suppose the stakeholder keeps referring to the company logo sketched at the top left of a page as "the beach ball." The Facilitator should also refer to it as "the beach ball." If, instead, she refers to it as the "home page link," the stakeholder could alter his natural response.

Being Present

Being in the here and now is consistent with playing pretend. We keep the stakeholder imagining the artifact is here in their hands, now, even though it is a gift from the future. We have the stakeholder perform his current work using the artifact. This is why we conduct Engagement Sessions in the context of the stakeholder's real work. As the team and stakeholder coexplore and possibly rework the artifact, everyone's focus remains on the stakeholder's actual, real work (Figure 14.2).

We're not interested in what the stakeholder might do with the design idea "if" (more on that further along in this chapter). We keep the stakeholder in the present by focusing him on his job, his tasks, and his goals. We ask for real examples from the recent past. Recall is more reliable than speculation. When the stakeholder drifts from the here and now, the Facilitator redirects.

Keeping it Real

Peyrichoux[4] stresses maximizing the usefulness of users' verbal comments by keeping the stakeholder focused on his own, real experience. Don't let him speak for others. He is an expert on his own experience, not on the experiences of others. If the stakeholder says, "Well, the average user might find this difficult," or, "For someone who does this type of work, I think this would be good," the expert Facilitator is polite, and redirects.

Experienced Facilitators are comfortable with redirection because they do it frequently. The prompts are simple and respectful. For example, when the stakeholder brings up "the average user," we simply ask, "But what about for you?" If the stakeholder says, "Oh, it's very complicated but I guess for people who know the field it would be ok," then restate, "You said it's very complicated. Tell me more."[5] Peyrichoux[6] states such a stakeholder is self-censoring, toning down his feedback. He's trying to be nice, or he has a

Figure 14.2 Working with stakeholders in their context improves their ability to play pretend in the here and now

mixed reaction to the artifact. The Facilitator needs to unpack his concerns. What he's censoring is precisely what we're interested in, so the Facilitator digs in.

In a successful Engagement Session the stakeholder becomes engrossed using the artifact. He plays pretend and starts telling stories. The Facilitator needs to be in the moment: not a

207

cold, scientific observer but actively facilitating the abductive process and getting the stakeholder to tell his story.

Maintaining Engagement

Expert facilitators aren't aloof. Facilitation is an active engagement with the stakeholder, a combination of observation and gentle inquiry to add dimension to what the team is seeing and hearing. Observable behavior doesn't have inherent meaning: We make sense of the behavior we observe by *interpreting* it. But without any insight into the user's thought process and mental model, we're interpreting blind. Thus, we need to pair observation with interview.

Judicious Prompting

The Facilitator's main responsibility is to keep the stakeholder talking. The stakeholder, in short, does most of the talking. The Facilitator *facilitates*, nothing more. The Facilitator does less than 3% of the talking. ("Listen," as the old saw goes, has the same letters as "silent." We can't really listen unless we are quiet ourselves.)

A good facilitator acts like a psychic (Figure 14.3). Think about how psychics

Figure 14.3 Master facilitation is much like a psychic reading

208

operate. They engage in a form of facilitation dubbed "cold reading." A psychic amazes us by the information she reveals about us she couldn't possibly have known. What is really going on? The psychic says very little! She certainly didn't *provide* any of the information. She listened. She asked short questions. She got us to follow up. She inconspicuously prompted *us* to share and then merely restated what we said. She had us validate and elaborate. She kept *us* talking. A Facilitator has much to learn from a psychic!

Prompting doesn't require more than a few words—they just need to be the right words. The Facilitator follows up comments with clarifying questions, revisiting things the stakeholder said earlier. This helps us dive deeper and communicates we're listening and interested. We cover specific ways of prompting further along in this chapter.

Building Rapport

As with responsive interviewing[7] (in which interview data are used to reframe the problem being explored as the team learns more and more), building rapport with the interviewee is crucial. Different people require the Facilitator to build rapport differently. An interview is both a research method and a relationship, and each relationship is individually crafted.[8] As The Case of the Reticent Respondent highlights, Ivan, who the team didn't think was listening, turned out to be its best source of information, largely due to expert facilitation.

Seidman, borrowing from philosopher Martin Buber, distinguishes between "We" and "I–Thou" relationships.[9] Seidman stresses *I–Thou* relationships are preferred in qualitative research. In a *We* relationship, both the stakeholder and the Facilitator are equal participants.[10] The result is a conversation, not an interview. In an *I–Thou* relationship, the stakeholder has the floor. The Facilitator

Ivan, ostensibly ignoring the entire process, in fact provided key information to the team's understanding of its proposal.

See Appendix A: The Case of the Reticent Respondent

gives him as much space as possible to respond to prompts independently.

To maintain the proper dynamic, Seidman cautions against going too far in building rapport with the stakeholder. Crossing a line risks altering the transaction into a full *We* relationship.[11] Proper rapport building for qualitative research, including PrD, is a balancing act. The Facilitator wants the session to be friendly, but it's not a friendship. Going too far in pursuing familiarity distorts the results.

Consider the following scenario: The Facilitator shares a few of her own stories during the session to make the stakeholder comfortable. The stakeholder will consciously or unconsciously anchor on the Facilitator's stories. In what directions would the stakeholder have gone if not so influenced? The team will never know. And "faking" friendship to build rapport is disastrous. We approach the interview with authenticity and err on the side of formality.[12] The stakeholder is coming to the session unclear about what is going to happen, what is expected of him, or why he's there. The Facilitator answers his questions respectfully and transparently, remembering *he's* doing *us* the favor.

Actively Listening Without Judgment

If the stakeholder says something that doesn't make sense or appears incorrect, the Facilitator doesn't mark the event. As Portigal[13] stresses, we avoid correcting the stakeholder. Correcting shifts the power balance of the session: The stakeholder is the *expert*; we are the apprentices. In such a relationship the apprentice never corrects the expert. Correcting the stakeholder in the interview, even regarding a mispronunciation, alters this dynamic, dampening the stakeholder's eagerness to share. Our goal is to understand the stakeholder's worldview, his vocabulary, and his mental model.[14]

The Facilitator doesn't just avoid correcting a stakeholder's perceived error; she doesn't presume there was an error at all! The Facilitator trusts the stakeholder knows what he's talking about. Any seeming difference of opinion is due to the Facilitator's faulty interpretation of what's being said. In philosophy this is known as the "principle of charity."[15] Since the stakeholder is the presumed expert, if there was a misunderstanding, it must be on the part of the Facilitator.

Prompt, but Don't Lead

An expert Facilitator prompts without leading. Leading invalidates stakeholder feedback since it contaminates results by introducing *confounds*. As we've described throughout the book, there are dozens of ways to introduce confounds: by being too "helpful," pitching the design, explaining the design, or telegraphing our expectations through poorly worded questions or through our body language.

A leading question suggests the very information the Facilitator is hoping to elicit, invalidating the response. Say the Facilitator hands over the artifact and gives the first task. The external stakeholder struggles somewhat. After a pause of 10 seconds the Facilitator asks, "How might this play into your work?" This is a perfectly acceptable prompt. Imagine instead the Facilitator asks, "Don't you see how this interactive financial display might be used to do your billing?."[16] The Facilitator just sold the farm! She not only revealed the intended purpose of what she's showing, she also (rudely!) implied the stakeholder *should* find this intuitive, and if he doesn't, there's something wrong with him. Or consider this question: "Is that feature useful?" Not only is this a poorly worded question, it leads: Perhaps *utility* isn't of interest to the stakeholder at all!

Distinct from leading are "loaded" questions. Leading directs stakeholders to a certain type of response. Loaded questions also bias to desired responses, but do so by inserting assumptions within the questions. They often take the form of a question that presents a "reason" for doing something included in the question.[17] Asking whether users would use a solution or a feature is bad enough (they can't accurately predict whether they would or wouldn't). This would be made even worse with a loaded question: "Do you think you would use this to help ensure data was made more transparent, thereby helping out your colleagues?"

Leading Through Body Language

Clever Hans was a horse who became famous throughout Germany for his alleged ability to answer questions by tapping his hoof. In 1904, *The New York Times* reported on Hans' ability to perform feats of arithmetic, spell names, and recognize musical tones. The paper quoted Prof. Moebius, the "eminent zoologist," as saying, "He possesses the ability to see sharply, to distinguish mental impressions from each other, to retain them in his memory, and to utter them by his hoof language."[18] Psychologist Oskar Pfungst conducted a series of experiments, concluding the horse could only answer questions correctly when he could see people who knew the answers. In other words, the horse wasn't doing arithmetic; he *was reading* people's body language (Figure 14.4).

The Clever Hans phenomenon has been compared with leading users during testing.[19]

Figure 14.4 Clever Hans, a famous body language-reading horse

Imagine if we frown every time the stakeholder begins a certain type of action and then smile and nod whenever the stakeholder begins some other action. It's pretty obvious what we want the stakeholder to do. This effect is equally likely to happen verbally. Imagine we say "Excellent" or "Great" every time the stakeholder uses the artifact one way but merely say "Hmm" whenever the stakeholder uses it some other way. Our words of encouragement inadvertently reveal our expectations to the stakeholder. Specific words such as "Good," or "Excellent," telegraph what we want to hear but they also sound judgmental. They imply one response is good while another is bad. Because of this, it's better to rely on "valence-free" responses, ones without a value judgment attached, such as "Got it," "I understand," or "Could you elaborate?"[20]

Not leading means not guiding the stakeholder and not answering his questions. Remember, we're doing PrD because we don't know the answer! After a few interviews, we *will* be asking questions we're certain we know the answers to (because we've heard them before from other interviews). Portigal stresses to set that feeling aside.[21] He offers two rationales. First, we learn things we weren't expecting. We may have heard a question answered several times in the past, but we never asked it of *this* stakeholder. Second, when we ask "obvious" questions, humbly, we convey we're the apprentice seeking the stakeholder's help. This assists in getting him talking. Asking a few obvious questions up front, even silly ones, is a good "ice breaker," getting the stakeholder comfortable with talking and sharing. Of course, there is a point of diminishing returns in asking questions we really have heard the same answer to, as we discussed in Chapter 11.

The Five Prompts and How to Avoid Three of Them

Expert Facilitators keep a stakeholder talking by offering *prompts*. Remember, the stakeholder should be doing 97% of the talking, which means the Facilitator's prompts should be

Presumptive Design

1. Go do X.
2. You seem hesitant. Is there a problem?
3. How might you start doing X on Y?
4. We thought Y might be a useful place to start X.
5. Great. Now let's pretend you had pressed Y. So go ahead and press Y.

Figure 14.5 Five levels of prompts

limited to 3% of the dialog. Not just any old utterance will do: The specific words the Facilitator says makes or breaks an Engagement Session. We have adapted a list of prompt types[22] into a five-level hierarchy (Figure 14.5). Each level increases the intensity of intervention.

PrD facilitation remains at Level 1 or 2.

At Level 1, the Facilitator hands over the artifact, gives the stakeholder the first task, and watches him attempt it. That's it. At Level 2, the Facilitator prompts the stakeholder to share his thoughts. That's it. The Facilitator is still not leading. The team's still safe. The Facilitator asks brief, nonleading questions as necessary (and should be asking "Why?" a lot). Other than this, the Facilitator (and the rest of the team) isn't saying much of anything.

At Level 3 a shift happens. At Level 3 the Facilitator starts being "helpful." She starts guiding the stakeholder and the Engagement Session in the process. This level of prompting is necessary *in the context of a usability test*; in PrD it violates the entire purpose. An Engagement Session is not a guided tour.

Stated plainly, at Levels 3, 4 and 5, the Facilitator is no longer doing PrD. We prompt and redirect, but we don't lead (Figure 14.6).

At Level 3, *X* is a task the team wants the stakeholder to perform and *Y* is some element of the artifact. In the context of usability testing we want to learn how efficiently and effectively a user can perform a specific task using a specific interface. In the context of PrD, this prompt guides the stakeholder, contaminating the results. The Facilitator guides the stakeholder's attention to the part of the artifact the team wants him to look at. That's what the *team* wants. But is that what the stakeholder wants? We would never know after a Level 3 prompt.

As a corollary, expert facilitators don't explain stakeholders' behaviors.[23] Asking, "Is the reason you didn't do *X* because of *Y*?" is a poor prompt on several levels: It's a closed-ended question, but more critically, it suggests its own answer. In revealing our hypothesized rationale for the stakeholder's behavior, we fail to test the validity of our hypothesis. Instead, the Facilitator might say, "I'm curious about that last thing you did. Can you tell me a little more about that?" In this way, the stakeholder is invited to offer up his own understanding of "that last thing" and "more about that."

At Level 4 the leading is more obvious and at Level 5 the stakeholder is being flat out told what to do. Again, in the context of usability testing, this can be necessary to keep the test going. In PrD, though, the team has accomplished nothing.

The five levels are guideposts. In an actual session the Facilitator often won't say any of them verbatim. In practice, leading is subtle and simultaneously *seems* innocent. When people lead, they don't realize it. Figure 14.7 lists a variety of stakeholder prompts.

1. Go do X.
2. You seem hesitant. Is there a problem?
3. How might you start doing X on Y?
4. We thought Y might be a useful place to start X.
5. Great. Now let's pretend you had pressed Y. So go ahead and press Y.

Figure 14.6 Good prompts and bad prompts

'How do you see that playing into your work?'

'What are you seeing?'

'Is this what you expected?'

'Say more.'

'Ok. So you see this as a timeline. Show me how you'd proceed if this was in fact a timeline.'

'How might you do this task using the advanced search here?'

'Would you use this?'

'Go here. Ok. How does this work for you?'

'Well, we'd thought you would do it this way.'

'Do you like these features? What features would you like?'

Figure 14.7 Which prompts are good, and which are bad?

Presumptive Design
DESIGN PROVOCATIONS FOR INNOVATION

Good	Bad
'How do you see that playing into your work?'	'How might you do this task using the advanced search here?'
'What are you seeing?'	'Would you use this?'
'Is this what you expected?'	'Go here. Ok. How does this work for you?'
'Say more.'	'Well, we'd thought you would do it this way.'
'Ok. So you see this as a timeline. Show me how you'd proceed if this was in fact a timeline.'	'Do you like these features? What features would you like?'

Figure 14.8 Good and bad prompts

Read through them. Are they leading? What levels do they fall under?

As Figure 14.8 illustrates, the prompts on the left-hand side are innocuous. They prompt the stakeholder to share his true uncontaminated reactions to the artifact, the design, and the team's assumptions. The prompts on the right-hand side are not innocuous. They're noxious. They tip the stakeholder off as to how we *want* him to perform the task. They preempt the stakeholder's honest reactions by contaminating his thinking with ours.

The Facilitator rarely asks "would" questions (see the Section "The Perils of Subjunctivity"): "Would you use this?" "What would you do if this was located here?" "Show me how you would work this." The first two are questions the stakeholder can't accurately answer. The third is potentially patronizing and contributes nothing to the storytelling process. The "good" prompts on the left-hand side of Figure 14.8 are open-ended, as opposed to the "bad" prompts on the right-hand side. Open-ended questions are preferred. They get stakeholders to say more than closed-ended questions. "How do you see this playing into your work?" is an effective prompt. It keeps the storytelling about the present. "What are you seeing?" is perfect.

These are not the literal prompts the Facilitator uses, since prompts are made off-the-cuff and in-the-moment. The Facilitator may rely on a list of "safe" prompts she can glance at if in a bind.[24] PrD facilitation, however, is an improv session; scripted prompts are a safety net, used only in an emergency. Facilitation always involves a certain amount of ad-libbing. An expert Facilitator is comfortable responding extemporaneously with follow-ups and prompts unique to each session. The directions in which stakeholders go will vary from session to session. As the Facilitator follows along, encouraging the stakeholder to dive deeper, each session branches out and evolves in unique ways.

There is a "script," created during the Creation Session, but the script doesn't tell the Facilitator *how* to facilitate. The script consists of tasks the stakeholder will be asked to perform in each Engagement Session. In addition, the script has a standard set of questions the team would like to ask of each stakeholder. It does not specify everything the Facilitator should say in every session. The two things that remain the same are the artifact and the task list: Each stakeholder is given the same artifact and tasks, worded in the same way.

The team needs to keep quiet, 97% of the time. Insight stems from the right combination of watching and listening. Keeping quiet is especially important after the Facilitator asks a question. As Portigal puts it, "Silence defeats awkwardness." The stakeholder in the Engagement Session is likely a stranger to the team. The Facilitator won't know the intricacies of the stakeholder's conversational rhythm, how receptive he is to this process, or the types of cues he'll give when considering how to respond.[25] During these moments, what the Facilitator *doesn't* say is just as important as what she does. She has to be very careful about each.

But not everyone on the team is the Facilitator, and we want other team members at the Engagement Session. Team members with less discipline but a lot of enthusiasm

Honoring Silence

may not realize they are interrupting or engaging with the stakeholder, and they often won't realize when they are leading. If anyone on the team feels uncomfortable and starts offering suggestions or help, the session is at risk. If the stakeholder is at a loss about his next steps, he will latch onto whatever suggestions he's offered. Why? Because it's easier.

The Facilitator must be comfortable with silences. Good Facilitators have nerves of steel. If the stakeholder stops talking, the expert Facilitator waits. She doesn't interrupt the stakeholder's thinking. He might not be finished with what he was saying; he might be mentally formulating what to say next. If interrupted, this could block an important insight. We often start a mental count up to 10, focusing our thoughts on the next possible questions, reviewing the information we've received before, perhaps filling in notes we couldn't get to during the rush of words coming from our stakeholder. All of these provide enough distraction to let the silence continue.

It's amazingly uncomfortable for the team, but consider that the adrenaline levels are not symmetrical. The team is probably far more hyped up than the stakeholder, and to him, it looks like everyone is buzzing, while to them it looks like he's completely forgotten the prompt!

The Five Whys

The Facilitator should be comfortable using "The Five Whys," a practice originally developed at Toyota.[26] The root cause of a defect is often identified by the fifth iteration of asking "Why?" Following up a why question with another gets people to drill down. The response to the first "Why?" will likely be too high level. The goal is to get the stakeholder to dig deeper, to become more specific, and then more specific still. In reviewing videotaped sessions of our own team members learning the PrD approach, the most glaring gap in the team's interviewing process was their failure to simply ask the stakeholder "Why?"

A typical example of what we heard might go something like the following:

Stakeholder: "This button just doesn't make sense. I'd never find a use for that!"

Facilitator: "Hmmm. Okay. So, what else do you see?"

But what we would have hoped the team did was the following:

Stakeholder: "This button just doesn't make sense. I'd never find a use for that!"

Facilitator: "So, the button labeled 'Incursion' doesn't make sense. Why?"

After the next answer we will likely have to ask "Why?" again, until the conversation has entered existential philosophy. This is very similar to the interview technique of "laddering." Hawley states laddering was developed by clinical psychologists and later adapted to market research; although, he argues, it is equally applicable to UX.[27] Stakeholders will initially respond to questions by discussing surface-level attributes. The Facilitator guides the stakeholder deeper, from discussing attributes to their consequences. Ultimately, the Facilitator helps the stakeholder to reveal his core values, the reasons *why* the consequences of attributes really matter.

Laddering from initial comments about design attributes down to the level of the external stakeholder's core values gets us to what will guide our strategy and design decisions.[28] The stakeholder doesn't like an attribute of the design. The Facilitator can't leave it there: "Why don't you like it?" "What does it mean to you?" etc. Laddering across sessions allows us to identify patterns of values across the stakeholders we engage with. Of course, asking "Why?" repeatedly becomes annoying. As part of stakeholder orientation, before the artifact is presented, the Facilitator explains how she will be asking a lot of questions, at times coming across as a three-year-old.

Sometimes stakeholders won't be able to answer a why question. That's fine. Make a note of it. Maybe the stakeholder will return to the issue later on his own. If not, the Facilitator can always bring it back up later in the session. One approach is to turn trouble questions around. If the stakeholder can't offer a response, ask him "Why not?" This might get him unstuck.

Facilitation Unique to PrD

Expert facilitation is the hallmark of many research activities. The preceding section provides a few of the basic facilitation techniques useful to PrD. In addition, PrD requires practitioners to let go of many interviewing techniques they may have previously mastered.

People are trained in facilitation and interviewing in a variety of contexts: psychological counseling and human resources, social science research (ethnographers, anthropologists, and the like), market research (focus group facilitation, for example), usability engineering, business analysis, and design. Psychologists, human resources professionals, and social science researchers (accustomed to working without preset scripts) will easily adapt to PrD's approach. Market researchers and designers may be uncomfortable working without a comprehensive script and may need to refocus their attention from product features to the assumptions behind those features. Usability practitioners will need to rethink their usual questions since PrD isn't about the artifact itself but the overall problem space. Analysts, accustomed to capturing requirements, may need substantial reorientation as few of the outcomes from PrD result in hard "requirements."

As mentioned in the overview, PrD facilitation differs from facilitation used in other contexts in the following ways:

- The Artifact
- Losing the Script
- Ignoring Usability
- Forgetting Quantification
- No Requirements
- No Opinions
- Light-touch Subjunctivity

As discussed in the Section "Offering the Artifact, Not the Design," the Facilitator offers the artifact without presenting the design. Here we describe the artifact itself as the central differentiating aspect of PrD from other qualitative research interviews. This is an important difference. The very presence of the artifact in the session changes the entire dynamic of the interaction. It allows the session participants to focus on something *other than each other*.

The Artifact Is the Thing

Social Objects

In PrD, the artifact crafted in the Creation Session and handed to the stakeholder in the Engagement Session is a "social object." In her book, *The Participatory Museum*, Simon explores the importance of artifacts as social objects, noting their ability to allow two people to become instantly conjoint and collaborative as they focus their attention on a third thing.[29] The social object (the artifact) triangulates those joined to it *through* their different connections. It creates, as Simon states, a transference of attention from person-to-person to person-to-object-to-person. She uses her dog as an example: When she goes on walks, she says, lots of people end up having interactions with her, but not because they engage with her directly; they interact with her through their interest in her dog.

With a social object, those who created the artifact and those who will critique and use it are instantly affiliated with each other through their variant interests. Cointerest in the object produces and supports social interaction, resulting in an emergent social "network." Simon cites sociologist Jyri Engeström,[30] who notes we mustn't think social networks are composed only of people. They're not. They're typically composed of people affiliated via their shared interest in some specific social object. Without the social object, the social network collapses. Of course, not all objects are social. Simon defines a social object as one that connects those who create, own, use, critique, or consume it. In PrD, the artifact handed over by the internal team to the external stakeholder constitutes just such a social object, which softens and relaxes the exchange. She lists four attributes of social objects: personal, active, provocative, and/or relational.[31]

A Personal Object

A personal object is one to which someone has a personal connection. A personal connection triggers associated stories and natural sharing. In PrD, artifacts are personal objects *of the team*, offered to the stakeholder early on in the session. The stakeholder is not blind to this. He knows he's being handed something the team has invested time in. By transferring it to the stakeholder, the team is putting him in a position of trust, which the Facilitator recognizes and enables. The stakeholder might not be prepared to accept this responsibility, no matter how unspoken or implied. Adding to the importance of the transference, the Facilitator has let the stakeholder know that the team has done this *for him*. This makes the artifact personal to the stakeholder as well because it is *intended to* relate to some aspect of the stakeholder's life. Whether the artifact was envisioned as a productivity tool or to improve the quality of the stakeholder's life, the team has clearly taken time and effort to make it personal. The stakeholder might laugh when presented the artifact because of the contradiction this creates: Here is this social object, something dear to the team, handed with gravitas and trust to the him—and yet it looks like junk. It is a comical juxtaposition.

An Active Object

Active objects physically insert themselves in the space between strangers, like a pool table in a bar. In PrD, the artifact is a personal object the Facilitator physically hands to the stakeholder, along with a task. With the object contextualized in the task, the stakeholder's attention is drawn to active exploration of the object through the lens of the task. By offering the artifact as an active

Figure 14.9 The Engagement Session is about telling engaging stories

object, the Facilitator focuses the stakeholder's attention on *it* and not so much on the team. The artifact thereby becomes like a campfire. There might be several people gathered but their attention is all on the fire. The transference of attention from person-to-person to person-to-object-to-person not only makes the object a social object but also reduces the challenge of rapport building (Figure 14.9).

A Provocative Object

Provocative objects surprise or even shock people, sparking a reaction, comment, and conversation. A PrD artifact is provocative for a variety of reasons: It is crudely built, provoking humor and deprecation; it is from the future, suggesting outlandish functionality or intention; it violates

223

Sometimes the artifact's provocative nature eclipses its personal nature.

See Appendix A: The Case of the Business Case

stakeholder's expectations about its use. Balance such an object with the personal object described earlier: The Facilitator needs to have empathy for the tension created by such an artifact. In The Case of the Business Case, the entire presumption about the business model was so foreign (read: revolutionary) that stakeholders didn't recognize it as relevant to their current working model. It took several minutes for some stakeholders to grasp the team's intention; for a few they couldn't make the bridge without a lot of facilitation. For these stakeholders, the provocation outweighed the "personalness" of the object.

A Relational Object

Relational objects invite interpersonal use. In the context of PrD, *interpersonal* does not mean between the Facilitator (or team) and the stakeholder. More typically, it is between two stakeholders. With the increasing interconnected nature of products and services, artifacts need to address collaboration. We've hosted numerous workshops in which stakeholders were asked to use an artifact others in the ecosystem were also using behind the scenes. In these Engagement Sessions, stakeholders might be working with a display that suddenly changes based on work others are doing in the system. Here again, the Facilitator needs to anticipate stakeholder surprise or tension.

Improvisation Is Key

In a conversation with Nathan Shedroff, Chair of Design Strategy at California College of the Arts, he suggested PrD "requires a fair amount of improvisation on the part of the Facilitator. That's not for everyone." Throughout, we've underscored that point. Because the artifact is necessarily "wrong," and because we really don't know what the stakeholder's problems, concerns, or pain points are, the Facilitator must be skilled in improvisation.

In this context, we define improvisation as "performing without much preparation." The Facilitator must actively listen, follow trains of thoughts down rabbit holes, backtrack to prior branches in the conversation, pause, keep quiet, and use subtle prompts to keep the conversation on track. Certainly these comprise the usual list of facilitation skills, but in the case of PrD, the Facilitator is mostly operating without a script. The Facilitator is focused on the *assumptions behind the* artifact as a stimulus for the conversation. Even Facilitators comfortable with ethnographic interviews can trip up.

On the surface it feels like a typical usability study: We offer a stakeholder an artifact and ask him to perform a task. As he works through the task, he thinks aloud. We take notes of his questions, concerns, and confusions. These are all typical parts of evaluative usability studies. Below the surface are major differences between the two approaches.

Why PrD Isn't Usability

Performing a Task

In a usability test, the investigator measures task performance. How long did it take to complete? How many errors did the user suffer? Was the task successfully completed? In usability, the task is key since the very nature of usability is about performance *on the task*. In PrD, the task is just as likely to be wrong as the artifact. Remember, we don't know a thing about the stakeholder and are only guessing at the task. We've likely proposed a task he doesn't understand or ever performs. In a usability test that would be problematic, but in PrD it is perfectly okay; in fact, it's desirable.

In PrD, the artifact is conceptually vague by design; it hasn't been designed to definitively support a prespecified set of tasks. Pick a task, hand over the artifact, and invite the stakeholder to go for it. The friction he experiences should lead to learning and exploration. The task may actually be irrelevant to the stakeholder. This is itself an excellent opportunity for engagement: Does the stakeholder perform this or similar tasks? How? Why? Such exploration uncovers valuable information about the stakeholders, the work they do, and how they really do it.

If the task is inappropriate, the artifact is still "usable" to elicit further conversation: The Facilitator asks the stakeholder to perform a more relevant task. Just understanding what makes this new task relevant may be new information for the team. Regardless of the proposed or revised task, the stakeholder is still asked to use the artifact to complete it.

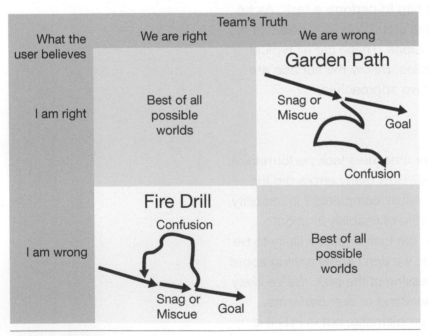

Figure 14.10 Whether team goals and user goals align, PrD works equally well

User Goals

Consider the framework given in Figure 14.10 put forward by David Stubbs in the context of testing user interfaces (UI).[32] In Figure 14.10, Stubbs is looking for any glitches in the labeling or pathfinding elements in the UI.

The "best of all possible worlds" is when both the team's notions of the goals and the user's notions of the goals align. Stubbs' dysfunctional outcomes, "Garden Path," and "Fire Drill," point out where users' behaviors differ from the team's expectations. In "Garden Path," the user is attracted away from the desired vector, away from the goal, to end up in some other "place." In usability, this would be an indication of a problem.

The "right" choice (the choice desired by the designers) was not clear enough. For example, the system may have presented a set of buttons or interface elements with ambiguous labels. The system, as designed, failed to support the desired end goal by not definitively orchestrating the user's choice.

In "Fire Drill," the user loops back because something is unclear in the design. In this instance, the user backtracks to reconsider his prior step because his reading of the current presentation is different from his expectations. Again, in usability this behavior indicates a problem with the design as the user was unable to successfully complete the task.

Stubbs' framework focuses on the screen elements, but it applies equally well in PrD. In PrD, Garden Paths and Fire Drills occur when the stakeholder encounters team assumptions that differ from his own expectations. These are beneficial outcomes. The stakeholder has led us to an interesting place, offering us insights into his thinking.

Stubbs offers a second 2 × 2 table (Figure 14.11). In what he calls "Operational/ Functional traps," Stubbs describes design errors the team would never find without usability sessions. These errors are the result of unintentional typos, a misreading of the specification, or an usual case that hadn't been considered. He calls these errors the "Black Hole," and the "Rabbit Hole."

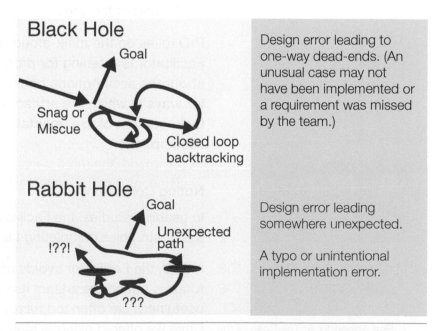

Black Hole

Goal

Snag or Miscue

Closed loop backtracking

Design error leading to one-way dead-ends. (An unusual case may not have been implemented or a requirement was missed by the team.)

Rabbit Hole

Goal

Unexpected path

!??!

???

Design error leading somewhere unexpected.

A typo or unintentional implementation error.

Figure 14.11 When users pursue their goals, they bring the team on a journey of discovery

Stubbs refers to these as "errors in the design or execution." In PrD we would consider these "errors in the team's assumptions," likely indicating the team's presumptive "goal" was incorrect. These outcomes are as rich an opportunity for discussion and discovery (or perhaps more so) as those when the stakeholder "successfully" completes the task.

Thinking Aloud

Experienced Facilitators are familiar with the "think-aloud protocol," in which stakeholders are asked to say what they are thinking, doing, and feeling as they go about the tasks given to them in a usability study. The think-aloud protocol is the mainstay of many usability interviews. In usability, these thoughts are used to identify potential problems with the design in service of improving the experience: poor language and labeling, poor help or instructional text, inappropriate use of color or visual design or anything causing confusion on the part of the user.

PrD relies on the think-aloud protocol as well, but the Facilitator is listening for problems with or questions about the assumptions behind the artifact. We are listening for ways in which the artifact violates the stakeholders' task, context of use, mental models, or operating assumptions.

Noting Confusions

In usability studies, the Facilitator focuses attention on the user's struggles completing tasks.

> In PrD, the focus is on the stakeholder, not on the artifact.
>
> See Appendix A: The Case of the Business Case

In PrD, the Facilitator avoids usability-centric language. The focus is not on the artifact itself. Even questions about its usefulness are often too narrow. In The Case of the Business Case we offered external stakeholders an extremely crude paper prototype of a screen representing the essence of the business proposition (Figure 14.12). During a dry run, our pilot stakeholder expressed confusion about many of the elements he saw on the screen. The Facilitator paused appropriately, and prompted with, "What would be more useful to you?"

Notice how this constrains the stakeholder's response into talking about the artifact, blocking conversation that could produce broader insights: Community, relationships, purchasing power, any number of things could be important to the individual as they are provoked by an ambiguous artifact. Framing the question around any one dimension may mask key insights into the user's mental model.

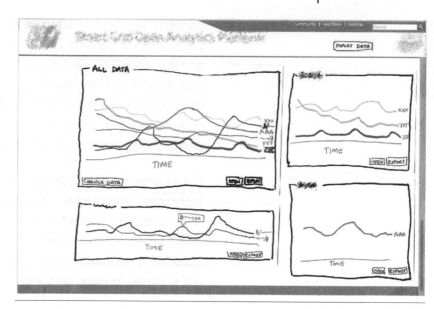

Figure 14.12 A crude artifact to provoke conversation about data displays

We guided the Facilitator to consider mirroring with lightweight subjunctivity: "You mentioned they were just squiggles. What do you suppose those squiggles mean?" or simply, "You mentioned you were confused by those squiggles. Tell me more about your confusion." As discussed throughout this chapter, the stakeholder will have problems interacting with the artifact. In PrD it's a desired outcome. Unlike with usability testing, confusion around the artifact is considered a good thing: It's the catalyst to insight.

Capturing Quantitative Data

In many usability studies it is important to capture quantitative data, such as time on task, its error rate, and so on. Such data are not pertinent to PrD. Further, in either usability testing or PrD, it would be a mistake to try and capture such data by requiring users to estimate (guess) the answer. Their answers to such questions are likely wrong, and they're typically not useful given PrD's goals. Remember the purpose of the Engagement Sessions: to capture stakeholder reactions to the team's *assumptions*, not to capture frequency and quantitative estimates.

For example, when our team members were just learning the technique, they turned to questions inspired by Six Sigma: "How often do you do that?" "When do you do that?" "How many times do you need access to that data?" PrD (like any qualitative research technique based on small numbers) is not suitable to capture these data.

There are limited occasions in which quantitative information is important to understand, specifically in its relationship to key assumptions. Important insights sometimes emerge as the stakeholder attempts to navigate the artifact. For example, the stakeholder might say, "This would be silly. I couldn't possibly use this given how much information I usually need to see." If the team was unaware of the amount of data, this could be a good time for them to learn more about that, perhaps by having the participant switch to a real system to demonstrate the kinds of data they work with. But this isn't *asking* about quantities, it's recognizing the need to observe the quantity directly.

With the search for quantitative data, as in the other pitfalls, the team is missing its true purpose: to hear the external stakeholder's stories. This isn't a Lean Six Sigma go to Gemba session in which the team is trying to eliminate waste. The purpose of the Engagement Session is to understand the external stakeholder's point of view. If quantitative details turn out to be important *to the stakeholder*, the team is obliged to go there.

Quantitative questions can be answered *directly* using data sources available to the organization. Use other research techniques and data sources, such as direct observation or data mining of logs, to uncover frequency or other quantitative data.

Relevance

Even in those cases where the stakeholder provides accurate estimates, the data are irrelevant; they have little to do with the purpose of PrD.

Asking stakeholders to quantify their behaviors negatively impacts PrD results by turning the session away from the objectives. We have a limited amount of time with each participant. Every sentence becomes precious; every question we ask is a balance between the objectives and our curiosity. Focusing on unreliable and unsubstantiated information means less time for capturing information germane to our objectives.

Ultimately, we have to ask ourselves: What would we do with the information (even assuming it was accurate)? Will it have a major impact on our objectives, design, or strategy?

Collecting Requirements

In many product development processes, and certainly in waterfall-type approaches, a project begins with "requirements." A "product manager," often a marketing role, is responsible for assembling all of the requirements, whether they are technical, business, or experiential. Analysts, specifically "business analysts," play a supporting role in gathering requirements, usually where business processes and technologies meet. Consider a fairly typical example: A business is updating its content management process and systems. One of the business requirements is the ability to publish in several different languages across several different media. A business analyst would offer requirements mapping the processes

231

and technologies necessary to support that business objective.

PrD is an awful method to use for this purpose. It will fail in this context of use (recall the Cynefin Framework discussed in Chapter 3). The types of conversations PrD enables rarely get into the specifics of technologies, processes, or the like. General discussions of these topics naturally occur, but PrD isn't the place to get into the specific, stepwise deconstruction of a stakeholder's engagement with a process or technology. Similar to the points made in the Section "Capturing Quantitative Data," asking stakeholders to self-report their experiences with technology or processes (when the data are often available through internal logs and other data repositories) not only risks wasting valuable time but also isn't reliable or actionable.

When product managers, business analysts, or system architects are in a facilitating role, special care and practice must be exercised to help them distinguish the objectives of PrD from the focus of the interviews with which they are more familiar or comfortable. If the team truly needs hard requirements, PrD isn't the right choice of method.

Refining the Design
Here we highlight the fine lines between exploring the stakeholder's mental model and refining the artifact.

In the "dreamcatcher" artifact mentioned in Chapter 9, when presented with the device, the participant looked confused (Figure 14.13). This was a signal to the Facilitator to explore further. Two primary paths could have been pursued.

Refining

In the refining path, the team explores the specific attributes of the over-the-ear device that caused the stakeholder's hesitation. The team asks: "Should it be adjustable?" "Is it not clear where you're supposed to wear it?" These, and dozens of other similar prompts, drive the conversation about the form factor of the artifact itself. This is not the purpose of PrD in the predecision phase; postdecision, the team will drill down into these concerns using suitable artifacts (see Chapter 2 for the definition of these terms in the context of the Double Diamond diagram).

Figure 14.13 The stakeholder is confused by the artifact

Exploring

In the exploring path, the Facilitator simply asks: "I noticed you looked concerned. Tell us about that." At this point the responses are about the stakeholder, not the artifact. It's possible the participant wasn't concerned at all. Perhaps the artifact reminded him of an unpleasant experience with an ear bud. Perhaps he was perplexed why he should be wearing anything at all. In any case, the exploratory question raises the chances of learning more about the participant's mental model.

Alternatively, the Facilitator allows the stakeholder to simply explore the artifact without any interruption. Allowing stakeholders to explore the artifact in service of completing a task requires them to play pretend. As they encounter surprises or misunderstanding, they will offer up something (interpretations, functionality, capabilities) completely at odds with what the team expected or intended. This is exactly what the team is looking for, and so the expert Facilitator plays along—it's improv after all.

This is the process of discovery. It requires the Facilitator and the team to mentally regroup (quickly), improvise, and find a way to pretend the prototype actually does what the stakeholder is suggesting. Because we're asking him to play pretend with crude artifacts, we must maintain *our* belief in the artifact. We must be confident the artifact serves the stakeholder's purpose even when the stakeholder is uncertain. Through this belief in the artifact's suitability, we allow the stakeholder to discover how the artifact behaves as he imagines it should.

Do You Like It?

Leo's general reaction when he hears someone asking stakeholders, "Do you like it?" (or variants on it), is to roll his eyes and ask, "Who cares?" What difference does it make if somebody likes the design, concept, or assumptions? Or if they hate it? PrD isn't a survey, it isn't a popularity contest, and it certainly isn't a means of validating the team's designs so they can return to the sponsors and declare how much stakeholders love it. When we believe our own story, we want to know if others believe it too. But that's not what PrD is about. We want to hear the stakeholders' perceptions of their work, and if we're really lucky, or after a few iterations into the process, we'll hear words that sound like *our* story coming from *them*. The most amazing times are when the stakeholder states what he would expect to see or do with the artifact, without any prompting from the team, and *it is exactly what the team had hoped*.

"I hate that." This could be one of the best things the team hears from stakeholders. It means something struck a nerve and provides a fantastic opportunity for further digging. If the stakeholder ignores entire aspects of the artifact, that too is a data point to make note of. It may require further prompting by the Facilitator, especially if a key assumption is being ignored. In either of these cases, the team may learn their assumption just didn't matter, was irrelevant, or was perhaps mIsguided. Whether stakeholders love, hate, or are indifferent to an artifact (or its underlying assumptions), their sentiments are merely signals for the team to perk up its ears. They are not data points to tally up.

That is not to suggest the team isn't capturing sentiment along with everything else. Sentiment is captured by observation and used for color or depth in retelling the stakeholder's story. Are stakeholders engaged? Are they using the artifact? Are they talking? Are they cocreating? These are the indications they are "getting it," that the assumptions are resonating.

Do they like it? Maybe, but that's not the point.

There is no greater testament to the relevance of the team's assumptions than if the stakeholder is taking the idea and simply using it, without noticing it. There's no detectable sentiment whatsoever and we've found an answer we were looking for: Our assumptions are obviously, transparently, acceptable.

The Perils of Subjunctivity

"In English, the subjunctive mood is used to explore conditional or imaginary situations."[33] In PrD, we live in the subjunctive mood because the artifact is intentionally provoking imaginary scenarios. Subjunctive phrasing must be used with care, since the conversations quickly spiral into extended flights of conjecture, and worse, opinion, on the part of the stakeholder. Consider the following interaction typically occurring in a PrD Engagement Session:

Facilitator: "So, what do you do next?"

Stakeholder: "I would likely press that button, there." ⟨Presses button⟩

235

F: "Cool. Now we haven't mocked that part of the experience up. Tell us what you would expect to happen after pressing the button."

S: ⟨Stakeholder begins to describe expectations for results from pressing the button.⟩

This example is the ideal use of subjunctivity. In this scenario, the request is around "expectations," not designing a screen or evaluating an interface that isn't visible. When stakeholders offer their "expectations," the Facilitator discusses those expectations, offering an important window into their thinking.

This use of "would" differs subtly from our discussion regarding prompting in the Section "The Five Prompts and How to Avoid Three of Them." There we proscribe using "would" to prompt the user to do something: "How would you use this?" Here we are asking them to reveal their expectations on the system's response: "What would happen next?"

Consider the following example:

Facilitator: "Tell me what you would do next." (*Here we're using subjunctivity inappropriately. A better prompt is "Go ahead, please continue."*)

Stakeholder: "I'm a little confused. I would expect a button to press, somewhere."

F: "Okay. And what would you expect that button to do?" (*This is exactly wrong because we're asking the user to imagine an element that isn't there at all, and then imagine how it would behave. A better prompt is to direct the stakeholder to something on the interface: "Ah. We had imagined that button there would have served that purpose. Tell us about that." We're now focusing on the button as a trigger for further conversation.*)

S: "Oh. I didn't see that." ⟨Presses button⟩

F: "So, we haven't mocked that screen up. We thought it might … ⟨describes a variation⟩." (*And the session has entered complete fantasyland. Rather than asking the stakeholder to describe (or draw) their expectations, we overlay our own. This is a failure.*)

We use the subjunctive mood sparingly to prime the stakeholders' imagination. We quickly find a way to make their thoughts and insights concrete. Returning to the first, ideal use of subjunctivity, consider this alternative interchange:

F: "… would you expect to happen after pressing the button?"

S: ⟨Describes expectations⟩

F: "Very cool, we're not familiar with some of the things you've mentioned. Could you help us better understand what you've said by ⟨drawing out/explaining⟩ how that might work?"

Here the key is asking the stakeholder to use a physical means to "explain how that might work." We ask the stakeholder to draw his expectations for the screen. We rely on Participatory Design principles[34] and proceed to look for the "why" behind the stakeholder's needs.

A concrete artifact from the stakeholder's experience works as well. We ask him to draw a diagram of his workflow, or he pulls out a document to explain his thinking. In The Case of the Pushy Pillboxes, the residents grabbed their own pillboxes to explain their points of view. A concrete artifact (whether created or found) anchors the conversation in reality. An analysis of the different artifacts collected from several stakeholders reveals their mental models.

Subjunctivity is challenging and difficult to facilitate. We don't avoid the words "would," "should," or "could;" we are careful

Whether the artifact is found or crafted, the key is to anchor the stakeholders' reactions with a concrete object.

See Appendix A: The Case of the Pushy Pillboxes

in how we use them. The key is to use the mood sparingly. We focus the stakeholder's imagination on his expectations for something we haven't provided and quickly move back to the concrete.

Summary

This chapter contains a lot about facilitation, and for good reason: PrD rests on expert facilitation, and specifically, highly improvisational facilitation. The team has sketched an artifact, hopefully representative of its assumptions, and it is now counting on external stakeholders to reflect on them. The problem is the artifact won't be sufficient to move the conversation along; stakeholders will be confused or distracted by it. They will need gentle prompting to reveal their mental models.

- Facilitation in PrD is walking a tightrope: Too much emphasis on the artifact and stakeholders will parrot back what they think the team wants to hear; too little and they won't engage deeply enough to provide valuable insights.

- In addition to many tried and true facilitation techniques (e.g., honoring silence, judicious prompting), PrD relies on several unusual aspects of facilitation:

  - Social objects

  - Improvisation

  - Mental models, not requirements

  - Keeping things real about an imaginary future

When the Facilitator focuses attention on the artifact (and the assumptions behind it), not as a means of refining its design, but as a topic of conversation, the team learns amazing things about the stakeholder, his unmet needs, and potential opportunities for innovation.

Chapter 15: The Creation Session

Presumptive Design
DESIGN PROVOCATIONS FOR INNOVATION

Objects are a form of knowledge about how to satisfy certain requirements, about how to perform certain tasks.
—Nigel Cross

Overview The extraordinary detail we cover in this book belies one of PrD's greatest advantages: the speed by which research can be completed to gain key insights. PrD shouldn't take a book to understand and implement, and we believe it really doesn't. The information we provided in the first chapter is probably sufficient for experienced researchers and designers to be successful in applying the approach. For everyone else who is interested in using PrD, we recognize the importance of laying out the details. In the prior chapter we focused on the need for expert facilitation. In this chapter we offer the details around setting up and running Creation Sessions to enable the best possible outcome. As with any performance art, there is no one right way to execute PrD; we don't want to suggest the recipes we provide are the only way to be successful. Instead, we believe all successful sessions share common attributes that we offer in this chapter and the next.

The importance of the Creation Session to PrD cannot be overstated: The Creation Session drives team coherency, articulates assumptions, socializes the approach to sponsors, and, of course, generates artifacts. Although there may be more than one Creation Session for any PrD, there is always only one "first" Creation Session. Since PrD is designed to reduce the amount of time and effort to insight, making the first Creation Session as successful as possible reduces the need for and number of subsequent sessions. Attendees from highly successful Creation Sessions report similar results: "They made it look so easy." "I've been to hundreds of company-sponsored trainings … this was by far the most impactful." "The session stayed on time, we accomplished everything on the agenda and we discovered breakthrough ideas."

Some Creation Sessions are like stage performances: You need props, support crew, a great program, an entertaining experience, and more than a little magic. Others are literally grabbing a few folks out of their seats and whiteboarding. The remainder of the chapter dives into details about all aspects of a Creation Session, whether it is formal or *ad hoc*, including:

- Complexity
- Staffing
- Budget
- Preparing for the session
- Running the session

How Big, How Complicated?

Creation Sessions come in three sizes:

- *Ad hoc*
- Single team
- Multiteam

and three lengths:

- Half a day
- Single day
- Multiday

We've found the two attributes, size and length, are related: With a couple of exceptions, the relationship between size and length is implied, not hard and set. Figure 15.1 shows the most likely size and length for a Creation Session.

Of course, the longer the duration and the greater the number of attendees, the more complicated the logistics. The key thing we keep in mind is that PrD scales (it doesn't matter whether we are doing it for an hour with three people,

	Ad hoc	Single Team	Multi-team
1/2 day	Usual	Usual	Rare
Single day	Possible	Usual	Possible
Multi-day	Never	Possible	Usual

Figure 15.1 Length and size of session

or five days with 120 people); the same techniques are used and the same outcomes are possible. Some organizations would never dream of taking 120 people through a five-day workshop. Others couldn't imagine placing bets on their future using only three people for a few hours. Clearly the reason to scale one direction or the other has nothing to do with the process; it has to do with the business objectives and the project's level of risk, among other factors we cover in this chapter.

Before proceeding to the details, be forewarned, we spend most of our attention on the most complex Creation Sessions because they are the most challenging to execute, having the most "moving parts." We hope this doesn't scare folks away. As stated in the opening remarks to this chapter, a Creation Session *can* be as simple as grabbing several people and doing some whiteboarding for half a day. The scale of the Creation Session has to do with the team's objectives.

If you are quickly testing a team's assumptions and only a few people are needed for a few hours, scan this chapter for tips and tricks. Alternatively, if you are forging a multiyear strategy disrupting existing products and services, read the following sections in detail to understand the potential complexity of the sessions.

Staffing

Chapter 10 covers in detail the types of individuals needed in a Creation Session, ranging from Designers to Builders. In that chapter we also touched on how many individuals should be at the session. In this chapter we explore in greater depth the question: What is the right size for a Creation Session? Of course, the answer is as always, "It depends." It depends on the team's business objectives first and foremost, it depends on how much investment the organization is planning to make, and it depends most of all on the amount of risk the organization faces and the capacity for that risk. We offer several examples of prospective candidates for PrD to illustrate the different scales of Creation Sessions.

Consider an organization trying to retool one of the products in their line. It's been a fine moneymaker for many years, but it's getting a little "long in the tooth." Some sponsors think all it needs is a simple refresh. Others believe it won't be worth any investment without addressing its fundamental flaws. In this case, having a single team with only a couple of the sponsors may not be enough to truly get everyone's assumptions out on the table.

Example 1: Product Line Refresh

In another case, a product manager thinks a web app needs a quick refresh and poses a variety of ideas for how it can be updated. In the past, his assumptions have been all that's needed to identify a way forward, but he doesn't have a broad picture of his end-users' experience. Having a single team working a quick PrD can save months of potential conflict, heartache, and disappointment, especially if visitors don't share the product manager's assumptions.

Example 2: Product Refresh

A start-up has a radical idea for entering a market. There are only a handful of people in the entire company, all playing multiple roles. The start-up is determined to hit the market with a hybrid product and service differentiating it from the competition. Everyone knows their offering has to be compelling to their prospective customers. They can't afford to mess up.

Example 3: New Product Introduction

So, the first questions to get straight include the following: How many people, and how many teams? And to answer those we need to answer a few more:

- Who is the primary sponsor for the project?

- How many people will be impacted by a change to the *status quo*?

- What is the budget for running the session?

With respect to the sponsor, we are as concerned about the highest-paid-person's opinion (HiPPO) as we are with their "footprint." In many organizations, the higher up the chain of command, the more people are involved with any given decision; as a result a greater number of people need to be brought along with the decision. Many higher-ups prefer to provide input throughout the decision-making process; receiving a "nicely wrapped present" is less desirable (and less likely to win their support) than a work in progress.

With respect to the number of people impacted: The more people affected, the greater the inertia, drag, friction, and in some cases, backlash to the decision. The Creation Session is an opportunity to win these people's support as they see their contributions baked into the project's strategy from the outset.

We cover the third bullet, budgeting, in the next section.

Let's look at these questions in the context of the three examples we introduced on the prior page.

For the product line considering a product refresh, there could easily be 100 people impacted by a change in direction: from hardware and software engineers to analysts, tech comms, program and project managers, and product marketing and sales teams. PrD doesn't require everyone to participate in the Creation Session, but with these many people impacted, managers and leads at a minimum must be aligned on the value of the change. We especially want to include the strongly opinionated leaders, who are certain about their assumptions. Often these individuals have good reasons to strongly defend their points of view, whether due to years of experience in the domain, their strategic position in the organization, or their long-standing engagement with external customers.

If these individuals (and their assumptions) are not included in a Creation Session, we run the risk they will put up roadblocks to the outcomes. Conversely, when their assumptions are included, and external stakeholders strike down those assumptions, these leaders become the most vocal champions of the outcomes. Highly confident, influential leaders are the first to admit their error, as long as the data supports the result. These same individuals are more likely to accept the data when it comes from the very customers they are trying to serve. These leaders know getting it wrong at their level will have major negative impacts on the company.

In the second example, the app refresh, there may be 30 people impacted and the revenue to the company is a small fraction of total sales. Here, the product manager needs to ensure the key individuals responsible for the refresh are on board from the start. There may be great collaboration, trust, and camaraderie in the small team. There could also be differences of opinion, potentially scuttling the execution downstream. Getting everyone's assumptions out on the table right away (and having them tested by the end-user) settles matters of opinion. In the end, it's the end-users' and customers' reactions to our assumptions we're striving to capture.

For the start-up example, everyone is virtually a sponsor, including, of course, the financial backers. These individuals' assumptions matter. Even though there are few people, everyone is impacted. Of greater concern is how few people there are: There may be too few to have at the Creation Session. The team may need to find trusted partners and advisors who can participate.

There is no good rule of thumb here for any of the examples. How many people to include is as much political as it is situational. Even within the same organization, one PrD requires several teams for an engagement while another needs to assemble a single, *ad hoc* team. If unsure, we recommend soliciting opinions from key sponsors. At a minimum, make sure the most opinionated voices that matter are invited to the Creation Session.

Presumptive Design
DESIGN PROVOCATIONS FOR INNOVATION

Budget

We have run moderately sized Creation Sessions (~30 participants, two days) on a shoestring (<$10 per person) and larger sessions (>50 participants, three plus days) with a healthy budget (>$150/person). Do the outcomes differ materially? Not in terms of the artifacts created or the conversations elicited. But the sessions' successes aren't measured solely in terms of the material outcomes. The success of a Creation Session is based on its *goals*. If the point of the session is to get artifacts built and get ready to talk to customers, then it can be run with a bare-bones budget: enough to buy some materials and maybe get some snacks on the tables. If, however, the goals include disseminating the PrD process across multiple organizations, getting buy-in from sponsors, building cohesive teams, and otherwise preparing the vision for a multiyear program, the budget needs to expand accordingly. Establishing goals with the sponsors paves the way for budgeting; obversely, if the project is budget driven, the goals will shrink to fit.

Environment

Location

Depending on the goals, the environment becomes a key consideration. When pulling a few folks into a room, we make sure the room has enough whiteboards. Securing a conference room for the duration is all we need. Cost: $0. (That is, assuming you have access to a conference room; a library is a good inexpensive alternative.)

If hosting >50 people for multiple days, a conference *center* that can accommodate everyone will be needed. If the team is part of a company with these kinds of facilities, it's a matter of reserving the room. If not, hotels are the likely choice. There are other resources available: community rooms at libraries, city halls, schools, and other institutions. Even if the team is hosting a few handfuls of people, we recommend going "off-site." Creation Sessions require team members' uninterrupted attention. When leaders participate, they need to be present and uninterrupted (to model the desired behavior). Hosting the event off-site significantly reduces the likelihood of interruption. Cost: $500/day and up.

Size and Setup

The room size also depends on the goals. If the Creation Session is an information transfer *and* artifact creation event, the room requires enough space to present material both on paper and using a projector. In addition to floor space, the room needs wall space. If projecting, the team will need a projector as well as a screen (Figures 15.2 and 15.3).

For artifact creation, we use "cafe seating," generally eight-person "rounds" roughly four feet in diameter, one per team, with adjacent rectangular "supply" tables to hold the artifact raw materials. Leave space on the cafe tables for snacks and munchies. If we are providing other meals, we allot additional space for food, whether for a separate buffet table, carts, or takeout boxes. It is essential to have teams eating meals together,

Figure 15.2 Example layout and room size for large-scale Creation Session

Figure 15.3 Materials for "junk prototyping"

247

especially in multiday visioning sessions. Breaking for lunch, leaving the facilities, and trying to regroup people back on time are ineffective. The session loses time while the team is eating, and it loses time getting people back into the swing of things on their return. There is insufficient time as it is; participants will appreciate using the time during lunch to work on their artifact.

Some exercises require wall space, a lot of it. We calculate each team needs about six to eight feet of wall, eight feet high on which to place their sticky notes, flipcharts, and the like. Count on using the windows in the room, if there are any (Figure 15.4).

Figure 15.4 A team member using windows to organize sticky notes

If we are grabbing a few folks into a nearby room, we need whiteboards, flipcharts, and maybe a projector; the room layout becomes immaterial.

Food

Amenities

Food is always essential, but never more so than during Creation Sessions. Brainstorming requires serious thinking. Munching on snacks as people work and play keeps them immersed in the session. We provide nutritious snacks catering to a broad set of food tastes. Snacks are a "must-have" at each table for anything but the most informal *ad hoc* sessions; even then, we've seen snacks work magic (Figure 15.5).

When our session goes for a full day, we bring in lunch. Conference facilities often include allowances in the room charges for food purchased from their catering department. In other cases, we've selected a local restaurant, electing the Facilitator to take responsibility for ordering food and getting it delivered. In addition, we provide a continental breakfast with coffee and tea service. This improves on-time arrivals to get the day started promptly.

For multiday events, two additional meals help achieve team cohesion and general camaraderie: A cocktail or happy hour after the first day lets people blow off steam and get to know one another in a less formal context. This

Figure 15.5 Snacks at the table and lunch served in the room are essential for all-day events

is especially important if all attendees don't know each other or if many are coming in from out of town. For large groups (>50) we've organized "locals' night out," in which local team members guide groups to a favorite hangout.

The second meal is a proper breakfast on the second day, more substantial than pastries and coffee. We've found for larger engagements, participants are tired after the first day. To help entice them to be on time and to shorten their morning schedule, we include breakfast. It also affords team members another opportunity to mix.

A Printed Program

For any Creation Sessions with greater than 20 attendees, whether single or multiday, we budget for a formal, printed program. Even in this digital age, with concerns about carbon footprints and dead trees, a printed program helps attendees stay on track with the agenda. In addition to providing a copy of the agenda, a printed program provides written instructions for unfamiliar exercises, additional research material, technical information, directions to off-site locations (if off-site trips are part of the session), and other reference material (Figure 15.6). We always include ample blank

Figure 15.6 A printed and bound program helps people stay on track

pages in the program for attendees to take notes during any presentations or during the exercises. Not only is the program an aide to keeping people on track during the Creation Session, it also acts as a reminder for them when they write their trip reports after the fact.

Because the UX team is often driving the Creation Session, it usually has the resources to produce the program. Printing and binding is done most economically by quick print services, a local print shop, or a company's internal printing department.

Even if the Creation Session (or budget) doesn't warrant a formal, multipage, printed and bound program, offering a simple stapled set of pages helps keep people on track, allows note-taking, and gives the participants a firmer impression of the session.

Prepping for the Session

As the number of people, the risk, and the potential impact of the work increase, so too do the lead time and preparation time. Six teams of eight people spending eight hours in a Creation Session represents nearly 400 hours of "lost" productivity. The time they spend in the Creation Session must be equal to, or preferably far more valuable than, the time they would otherwise spend doing their "day jobs." Prepping for a session that size is far different from gathering a few key individuals together for a quick *ad hoc* session (although even an *ad hoc* session requires some prep).

Invitations, Calendaring, and Prework

Unless the session is rapid and *ad hoc* with a few folks in the office, people require advance notice to put the event on their calendars. In large organizations with team members in multiple locations, we plan on at least four weeks' to (more commonly) six weeks' notice to let invitees know we are hosting the event. Even if we don't have details about

251

location or agenda, we give a quick sketch of what attendees can expect and why they should attend.

So too for the venue. Becoming friendly with an administrative assistant may make magic happen, but we don't count on getting a suitable room only two weeks before the day. Reservations for high-demand rooms may require a two-month notice. Conference centers and hotels may have more options and better lead times.

We plan on inviting at least 10% more people than the Creation Session can handle. We get last-minute cancellations, last-minute write-ins, and constant churn at the edges, even on the day. Better to have a few more people wait-listed than too few attending.

About three weeks prior, we provide more details— location and timing—so travelers can get their itineraries squared away. About two weeks in advance, we provide notice of prework requirements. For any large-scale multiday session, prework will be a necessity, even if it is only a few minutes of the attendees' time. We get people thinking about the problem in advance, starting the assumptions bubbling in their unconscious. (See Appendix B for more details on the logistics and value of prework.)

A simple prework exercise we use has attendees provide the top three challenges facing the organization, the product, service, or whatever the focus of the session is going to be. Entry to the session requires they complete and send the prework back several days before the session. Keeping to this requirement telegraphs the seriousness of the session and informs invitees their input will be a part of the overall effort. As we discuss in Appendix B, this information forms the basis for one of several exercises during the session.

No matter how small or how elaborate, a Creation Session must have an agenda. When we tap a few folks on the shoulder and interrupt their work, we still need to offer them a reason to go into the other room. Similarly, if perhaps more formally, when we ask people to reserve several days of their work life in support of some crazy visioning activities, we need to assure them their time will, at a minimum, be well organized.

Publishing an agenda for larger-scale Creation Sessions is required. In large organizations, many prospective participants won't even consider attending an event if there isn't a published agenda. Regardless of the scale of the Creation Session, the agenda remains roughly the same, whether it's formal and published, or informal and in the background. One might think the larger the event, the more there will be to do, suggesting the agenda increases accordingly, but we've found that's not been the case. We will go into the agenda items in a little more detail in the next section. In addition, we provide in-depth discussion of several of these activities in Appendix B.

The agenda includes the following items:

- Meet and greet/Team building

- Introduce workshop goals and agenda

- Teamwork/Presentations (optional)

- Craft tasks and Engagement Session objectives

- Artifact creation

- Engagement Session prep (optional)

- Engagement Session (optional)

- Report Out

- Debrief/Closure

When Creation Sessions extend over multiple days, we will do multiple presentations, teamwork exercises, a round of

Agenda

253

Figure 15.7 A typical scene from a Creation Session

Engagement Sessions, and post-Engagement Session rework and debrief. For Sessions lasting less than one day, we abbreviate the didactic presentations, ask attendees to do more prework, do the Engagement Sessions separately, and reconvene after the Engagement Sessions for any rework. One important tip to keep in mind: The more teams there are, the longer the Creation Session, simply because each team needs time to share its insights and lessons learned during reporting out and debriefing (Figure 15.7).

In the case of just grabbing a few folks, the agenda forgoes team building or presentations and dives directly into creative exercises and artifact creation. We make sure team members are sufficiently prepped to be in a creative mood, are relaxed, and have the minimum amount of technical and/or market information they'll need to start expressing their assumptions. In these *ad hoc* Creation Sessions, we don't include Engagement Session preparation, letting the Facilitator/Researcher and Designer tackle that effort in a separate meeting.

We discuss the alternatives of including an Engagement Session within the Creation Session further on in the chapter.

Establishing a Theme   For multiday Creation Sessions with multiple teams, the focus is usually on something big, for example, a kickoff of a new product or product line. The business has already identified key value propositions, markets of interest, and perhaps an initial strategy. To give the session a coherency, consider creating a theme. The theme pervades the session, from the initial emails to the agenda, to the name badges to table tent cards identifying the teams. Wherever a participant turns, the theme will be evident, branding the session and making it memorable.

Again, assuming the UX team is driving much of this work, they can assist in crafting the visual design elements to create a theme. See Appendix B for more details on theming at the session level and at the team level.

Running a Creation Session

Kicking Off with a Bang

Regardless of how much time there might be, attendees are likely to be impatient and want to get down to business as soon as possible. They may view the Creation Session with some skepticism in spite of cherishing a few hours away from their usual work. This will certainly be the case if it's their first such session.

Most meetings start with a slide presentation describing the agenda, the objectives, and so forth. Although we eventually put up such a deck, we don't begin the session that way. Instead, we find a way to get people on their feet, energized and laughing. It sets the stage for the Creation Session, and it offers a glimpse of the rest of the day. Again, we offer specific exercises in Appendix B.

Even if they've been through similar workshops in the past, what is important in *this* session is to get them out of their usual way of thinking as quickly as possible. If we are part of a coherent team, we don't emphasize *team* building as much as *creativity* building within the team. Until PrD becomes a standard practice in the organization, even team members who work well together under normal circumstances may not be familiar or comfortable working together in a Creation Session.

If the attendees are not part of an existing team, we spend time in team building exercises. In large organizations, with multiple sponsors and dozens of attendees, not everyone knows each other. The team building exercise accomplishes multiple objectives: getting people to know one another individually, clustering individuals into teams, bringing immediacy to the workshop (by starting an activity right at the start), and telegraphing novel (perhaps) mental processes the session will require of them. See Appendix B for many different types of exercises we use throughout the sessions, including meet and greet, team building, and creative blockbusters.

Pacing the Session

In the prior chapter we focused on the role of the Facilitator in the context of the Engagement Session. The Facilitator's main job during the Creation Session is to set the right pace. For example, after the big warm-up there is a natural lull while people are settling into their tables, grabbing another cup of coffee, and sharing last-minute delights from the initial exercise.

The Facilitator uses this time to introduce the agenda, ground rules, and other administrivia. This is an instance when the Facilitator needs to assert herself: Attendees are likely to be chattering excitedly, riled up by the introductory exercises. In our Creation Sessions we alternate quiet with active exercises, getting participants' energy levels up when the mood is sagging. We are careful to schedule intensely creative time in the morning, when people are still buzzing from their caffeine and not suffering afternoon lethargy from lunch.

But scheduling passive presentations in the afternoon can be equally problematic, so we make sure we've got the most charismatic presenters scheduled for after lunch. In any event, we try to balance active and passive, creative and analytical, biasing the deep thinking and creativity for the morning with more kinesthetic and active exercises in the afternoon.

By the late afternoon, we know we've been successful with our pacing if we still have active engagement by all participants and if we're seeing exhaustion on their faces. The Facilitator drives that sort of engagement by making sure every exercise, every activity, is about 15 minutes shorter than feels right. Throughout the session, the Facilitator needs to keep everyone apprised of the clock, letting them pace themselves. The clock forces the teams to get stuff done. We provide more details about the Facilitator's role in the Creation Session a little further on.

Introducing the Goals

Introducing the goals is key to the Creation Session. We recall sessions in which we spent considerable time (perhaps as much as 15 minutes) going over the goals, answering questions, and confirming everyone was on board, only to learn at the end of the session several attendees were still confused by the goals. For the session to be a success, everyone must be aligned with why they are there, what is expected of them, and what "success" looks like. We invite the individual responsible for the effort to introduce the goals, whether that is a VP, a Director, or a Program Manager. When the goals come from the top, people listen.

Level Setting on Existing Data

Everyone brings their individual understanding of the problem space to the Creation Session. In addition to prework, we introduce the teams to background information we believe will be useful for them to craft an artifact.

We don't spend a lot of time preparing for this part of the Creation Session. We identify potential experts, we

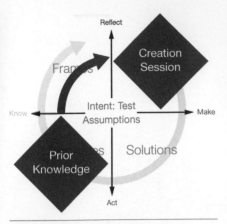

Figure 15.8 PrD starts in the "Concepts" quadrant and assumes team members bring prior knowledge to the discussion

Using creative immersive exercises during the Creation Session aligns participants to elements important to their stakeholders.

See Appendix A: The Case of the Pushy Pillboxes

collect existing data as easily as possible, and we create appropriate visual aids in as quick a manner as possible. We spend perhaps as little as one day (eight hours) putting together existing information; otherwise we risk emphasizing the "Discovery" quadrant over the "Concept" quadrant (Figure 15.8).

Presentations

For casual sessions, presentations aren't necessary, with the exception of aligning participants with an important technical or contextual element. For larger complex projects, presentations are a must-have to familiarize all team members with various aspects of the problem space.

For example, during The Case of the Pushy Pillboxes, the teams were introduced to several aspects of aging: difficulty with small and large mobility, changes in vision, hearing, and cognition. An expert facilitated an immersive exercise in simulated arthritis (Figure 15.9).

In one particularly complex Creation Session, we invited experts to present topics ranging from data analytics to game design. In every case, we find ways to quickly supplement participants' existing understandings of their stakeholders' world. We spend less than 20% of the Creation Session on background information.

Information Kiosks

We balance passive presentations with other forms of knowledge sharing to make sure we pace the session appropriately. In one Creation Session we facilitated, the UX team had an enormous amount of data to share about the users, their context, and other previously completed field research. While we avoid lengthy knowledge transfers in general, in this case so much information had already been collected, we would have been delinquent by holding it back.

Much of this information was new to the teams. If we had presented the information using slides, everyone would have had to sit for several hours.

Instead, the UX team hosted separate information "kiosks" positioned around the room. Team members got up from their seats and moved from kiosk to kiosk at their own pace. This highly interactive approach allowed team members to ask penetrating questions, dig into the material, and focus on the areas that interested them most.

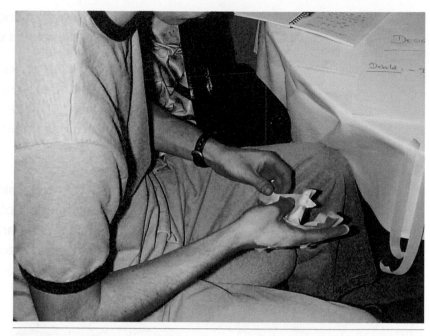

Figure 15.9 An exercise simulating arthritis as part of the Creation Session

Using kiosks has several advantages, not the least of which is getting people in front of the information of greatest interest to them. Still, the Facilitator must make sure to move people along so that all teams visit all kiosks within the time available.

Walking the Walls

Another common technique to get people out of their chairs and engaged with existing data is to have the information on the wall for participants to inspect. This is a less formal method than kiosks and is useful when the information is self-evident or doesn't require extensive curation. With this approach, the Facilitator may need to float from poster to poster, either answering questions (if she knows the answer) or finding individuals in the room who can.

Presumptive Design
DESIGN PROVOCATIONS FOR INNOVATION

Engagement Session Tasks and Objectives	Before teams can begin crafting an artifact, they must decide on what external stakeholders will *do* with it: the tasks.
	As with the artifact itself, tasks represent the team's tacit assumptions about the external stakeholders. As discussed at length in Chapter 12, the teams must define clear objectives for the Engagement Session.
Artifact Creation	The bulk of the Creation Session is dedicated to creating the artifact. In preceding chapters we've written extensively about the importance of the artifact, how artifacts are used, and the hazards of poor artifact creation.

Figure 15.10 Materials laid out for junk prototyping

In our experience, teams rarely are comfortable building artifacts. With the exception of Designers, most participants stopped playing with paper and glue in elementary school. Crafting "junk" prototypes is at best foreign, and in some cases dismissed as useless (Figure 15.10). That's why we make sure to have at least one Designer, and perhaps more, at each table. In a Creation Session Leo and an associate facilitated for a team of game developers (not Designers) they were pleasantly surprised to see a couple of engineers leap out of their chairs to begin crafting objects to express their ideas. That was a delightful exception; usually team members are hesitant to take the first step into the "Concept" or "Solution" quadrant.

To help the teams get over that hump, we start them with a smaller exercise to give them a practice run at creating a junk prototype, get more familiar with the materials, and ease into the notion of making stuff up. If the Creation Session is less than a full day, we may skip this introductory exercise in service of getting to a usable artifact.

The primary outcome of the Creation Session is to create at least one artifact (i.e., one per team) to be used in the Engagement Session. Without an artifact, the session is a failure. We offer more details about artifact creation in Appendix B.

The Engagement Session is covered in depth in the next chapter, but we want to address an important option: including the Engagement Session within the Creation Session.

Engagement Session Prep and Execution

Engagement Sessions in the Creation Session

In this book we discuss the two sessions as separate efforts: The Creation Session is where teams craft their artifacts and prepare for the Engagement Session. The Engagement Session is where teams interact with external stakeholders to test the team's assumptions. In practice, if we have a large group already setting aside several days for the Creation Session, we take time in the agenda to actually run through several Engagement Sessions with external stakeholders as a part of the Creation Session.

This approach has significant advantages:

- It leverages everyone's time efficiently.
- It demonstrates the full cycle of PrD to the teams.
- It permits the teams to rework their artifacts based on what they've learned.

This approach works for only those external stakeholders who are in the same geographical location as the Creation Session. When it makes sense as a part of a multiday Creation Session, we make an effort to complete at least one set of Engagement Sessions; regardless we'll set up additional Engagement Sessions afterwards to work with other stakeholders.

Reporting Out

When the Creation Session has more than one team, we reserve time for the teams to present their findings, solutions, exercise results, and artifacts to each other. The Report Out process provides:

- Opportunities to learn from other teams and expand everyone's points of view

- Practice in the art of "critique," in which teams reflect on others' work

- Opportunities to cross-fertilize ideas for other teams to take advantage of

Generally Creation Sessions are not competitive, although the Facilitator may make some exercises mildly competitive to increase divergent thinking. The race is against the clock, but if teams need a little incentive to get more ideas going, competition can be used sparingly. Results of these competitions can be included as part of the Report Out process. If there's time, the results can be treated like a variation on the tabletop game *Boggle*, in which unique results are counted separately from results shared by two or more teams.

Critique

For some Creation Session exercises, especially for those in which the majority of participants are unfamiliar with design thinking, we run the Report Out process as a mini-design critique. Critique is a process deeply ingrained in the design studio and design education, but is not a common process in most other disciplines. The "design review" (the process used by engineering teams to review individual contributor solutions on paper before they're implemented) is a close relative.

Critique begins with a designated team member (usually the Designer) presenting *the team's starting assumptions* and then walking listeners through the solution as it relates to those assumptions. The listeners are expected to ask questions and challenge the Designer on any number of fronts: the starting assumptions (why those, why not others) and each expression of those assumptions. Challenges to the team include whether the artifact truly expressed the assumptions (just because the Designer *says* it's so doesn't mean others see it that way) and whether the artifact is coherent (the Designer may have addressed each assumption beautifully while the overall solution is incomprehensible).

Critique can be brutal for people who've not experienced it before. It requires a letting go of ego and of investment in the solution. It also presumes the presenter is truly interested in critical feedback. For those teams that will be working together over an extended period of time, Critique can be an excellent team *building* exercise, but it requires nuanced and expert facilitation to make sure everyone follows the rules, everyone understands the point, and hurt feelings are prevented.

Rewards

Capping the end of a Creation Session with a ceremony, perhaps in which awards are offered, is an effective technique. Whether to have a ceremony, recognition, or awards depends on the goals of the Creation Session. If the session includes goals for:

- Team building
- Sponsor buy-in
- Broader organization buy-in
- Socialization of the PrD technique

then consider using awards, recognition, and ceremony.

In the following subsections are a few ideas in which we make these elements work to our advantage.

Judging

We've used judging to great effect. Of foremost importance is to find the "right" judges. Reach out to thought leaders in the organization who will be recognized by at least a majority of the attendees. Selecting these individuals adds credence and gravitas to the Creation Session, especially for those attendees who are completely new to the process. It also affords attendees the opportunity to inform the judges of creative ideas coming from the group. Including thought leaders as judges sets the seeds for more engagements in the future.

Figure 15.11 Esteemed judges reviewing candidate artifacts

We look to leaders both inside and outside the teams' organization. Of course, logistically, bringing in a famous thought leader for a half-hour judging activity may be prohibitive, but if it can be scheduled with other purposes and opportunities, why not? (At a PrD workshop during an international conference in which global thought leaders were attending, we were able to swing a few of them into the room for an hour at the end of the day (Figure 15.11).

Orienting the Judges

Regardless of how you source them, it is important you provide a solid orientation to judges both prior to their agreement and on the day. Because the artifacts from the Creation Session are not really meant to be juried by anyone other than stakeholders, the judges are really there to provide incentives to the teams and seriousness to the proceedings. With that said, the judges need to bring a strong sense of playfulness, lightheartedness, and fun to their office. They, as with everyone else, need to understand the purpose of the artifacts, and, it follows, the purpose of their judging. As an "expert critique" session, they are there to help participants think about the artifacts in terms of their stated assumptions. Did the participants actually build something to elicit the right kinds of conversations?

We reinforce a sense of playfulness by enlisting the judges in determining the rewards:

1. Provide predesignated award categories (e.g., "Best use of popcorn in an artifact").

2. Provide suggested criteria for consideration (e.g., "Most eclectic use of materials").

3. Provide the prizes and have them come up with their own categories.

4. Have them make up everything after they've heard the presentations.

Regardless of how the categories are determined, one thing is absolutely necessary: Every team wins a prize. The point is not the prize, or the recognition, just the fact that someone who matters is listening.

Running the Judging

Here's a recipe for successful judging:

1. Each team has a limited amount of time to present, five minutes tops, especially if there are several teams. The Facilitator, as usual, can play timecop. Remember, time must be set aside during the session for the teams to prepare for the judging session. Usually 30 minutes is necessary for them to get their five minute spiel down pat.

2. Optionally, provide a two-minute Q&A for the judges to get clarifications.

3. After all teams present, the judges are given 10 minutes for consideration. (Figure one or two minutes per team. So again, allot time according to the size of the group.)

4. The judges then provide their determination. Usually a judge provides a brief narrative about Team X's contribution, the key attributes they found compelling, and perhaps a constructive remark about what they could do to enhance or improve the artifact in service of their assumptions. And they offer the award, with whatever name it might have.

Under the best of circumstances, judges are as challenged to provide creative feedback as the team was challenged to offer creative insights. It can be daunting to be a judge!

Awards

Clearly if every team is a winner, every team member must be a winner as well. Who doesn't appreciate a small gift after going to an all-day (or multiday) workshop, having worked hard and been away from one's family?

Budgeting becomes a concern immediately, of course, so we've kept our awards to $5 or less. It's surprising the kinds of gifts we find in that price range, whether online, in a box store, or at a local thrift shop. It does take preparation, so if judging and awards are part of our session, we prepare in advance. We make sure to get a few extra.

Of secondary concern, but sometimes as important, we keep in mind attendees may be flying commercial airlines, perhaps internationally. Any gift should be suitable for airline security.

We find gifts associated with the theme—for example, if the theme was "Mining for Gold," a miner's light (from a big-box hardware store) is an inexpensive and practical gift reinforcing the session's theme.

Debrief and Closure   For *ad hoc* Creation Sessions, at a minimum the team decides next steps. These might include assigning responsibilities for scheduling the Engagement Session, polishing the artifact, or writing the script prompts.

There are actually two debrief sessions in which we engage our teams: debrief about the Creation Session and debrief about the Engagement Session. When the two sessions are combined, the Facilitator needs to distinguish between them. In general, when the Engagement Session is part of the Creation Session, the Creation Session is self-evaluating: The success of the session is measured by the engagement with external stakeholders. We offer details about Engagement Debrief and Closure in the next chapter.

There are always ways to improve a Creation Session, and it is critical for the Facilitator to solicit feedback about the event from the participants.

Debrief

For Creation Sessions longer than half a day, the Facilitator leads a 10- to 15-minute "plus/delta" activity at the end of each day. During the "plus" portion of the activity, participants shout out the first things that come to mind that went well. A scribe writes these down as quickly as possible (you may need more than one scribe). During the "delta" portion, attendees shout out what could be improved either the next day or in future sessions. As the comments duplicate, the Facilitator prompts for ideas from anyone who hasn't spoken until everyone who has something to offer has contributed. Some people may not be comfortable initiating a comment, but will offer one if invited (Figure 15.12).

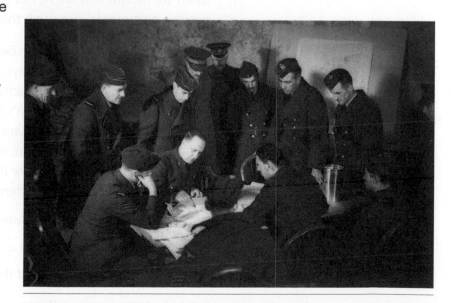

Figure 15.12 Senior officers debriefing with King George VI

267

Presumptive Design
DESIGN PROVOCATIONS FOR INNOVATION

These closure sessions are essential for participants to offer comments they may have been harboring all day but not found an opportunity to voice. They also allow everyone to hear what others experienced during the day. Individuals will offer conflicting opinions about the value of any given activity: Some will call it out as an amazing experience, others as a complete waste of time (although usually people are more polite than that). It is also the time for the Facilitator to reflect on her work and how she could improve it for the following day, or in general.

During the debrief process, the Facilitator must remain absolutely neutral *and engaged*. Sometimes that is difficult to achieve if she is the target of desired improvements: if certain exercises didn't go well, or the session didn't stick to the agenda. Regardless, these are important issues to be aired. Participants are more likely to come back to another session in the future if they believe the organizers have listened to their concerns and are committed to act on them.

We expect the "deltas" to outnumber the "pluses." In fact, when we facilitate, if we're not getting more critical than positive comments, we push the group to dig a little deeper.

At the very end of the Creation Session (for multiday events, this would occur on the last day), we offer written evaluations for participants to fill out. By allowing anonymous feedback from everyone, those who didn't feel comfortable shouting comments out in public are given an opportunity to contribute. It's not unusual to receive far more frank comments (and more of them) when participants offer their critique privately and anonymously. We limit the written evaluation to three questions:

- What were the top takeaways from the session?

- What would you tell an associate about the session?

- Would you recommend this to your associates?

In this last case, we craft it as a Net Promoter Score.[1]

Closure

If the session has lasted more than half of a day, the participants will likely be exhausted and still filled with adrenaline. Attendees may wish to decompress and chat, while others are eager to get on with their evening.

At a minimum, we discuss next steps, responsibilities, and a game plan for the artifacts.

If there hasn't been judging as a part of the session, we have a closing ceremony in which we offer gifts to the attendees and collect their written evaluations.

Outcomes

The most important outcome of the Creation Session is each team has created an artifact and a script. The artifact is the physical thing handed over to the stakeholder in the Engagement Session.

The Script

The script is the protocol for the upcoming Engagement Sessions. It needs to specify exactly how the session will be run, how the Facilitator will set the stage with each external stakeholder, and how the internal team says "Hello" and introduces itself and the session. In short it is the preamble, explaining why the team is doing the session, what it is, and how it will proceed. The script also identifies the objectives for the Engagement Session and the tasks the internal team wants the external stakeholder to perform with the artifact. For example, "In our conversations we've learned you might want to" (then present that task). "Let's pretend this piece of cardboard is a tool to help you track your sales. Please claim one of your deals as a win." The script may include questions for the stakeholder, but for the most part the interview aspect of the Engagement Session involves unscripted prompting (as discussed in the preceding and following chapters). Although hopefully the Facilitator is great at improv, the script can include good prompts or replies as a reminder.

The Artifact

The artifact as we suggested in the Section "Artifact Creation," is often constructed out of junk. It might be a piece of cardboard with sticky notes and pipe cleaners and doodles on it. It might be a sketch. It could even conceivably be a wireframe. What it must be is a physical representation of the internal team's first, best guess as to what the external stakeholders need. The point, as discussed in Chapter 4, is to get your ideas out into the world as quickly as possible, to see, firsthand, how the stakeholders play pretend with them. And through playing pretend and interacting with the artifact, they expose and vet the team's assumptions. We offer more details on artifact creation and possibilities in Appendix B.

Facilitation

We finish this chapter by returning to the subject of facilitation. As we have written repeatedly throughout the book, facilitation is key to a successful outcome in PrD, in the Engagement Session for certain, but equally so in the Creation Session. The Facilitator must be intimately familiar with the agenda, the business objectives, and the goals for the Creation Session. The Facilitator should be generally familiar with the problem space the attendees are exploring but doesn't need to be an expert.

Timing

The Facilitator keeps careful watch on the time. Optimally, the Facilitator should have had an opportunity to influence the agenda. An experienced Facilitator can estimate how long things will take to complete. When an activity runs over, the Facilitator needs to decide how to make up the lost time: shorten another activity, delay something to the next day (if that's available), or eliminate an activity altogether. Holding people later than the allotted time is not good form, is viewed as unprofessional by some audiences, and should be the last resort. Ending early is usually received much better, so the agenda should have enough slack time built in to account for activities taking longer than estimated.

Respect

The Facilitator needs to earn the respect of the attendees. She does this by comporting herself professionally, modulating her voice so everyone can hear, and by articulating her words. All attendees may not speak the native language in the room, so the Facilitator should accommodate and compensate for foreign speakers who may need her to speak more slowly.

When the Facilitator needs to move a group along, whether because they are taking too long to move through an exercise, arguing about a detail, or fixating on something that ultimately doesn't add value, she has several options:

- She can speak to the entire group, not just the problematic team, to remind everyone of the key issues she's noticed—it's possible she's noticed several around the room—without singling out any one team.

- She can quietly sit with a team for a few minutes and listen to their process before making some suggestions. In this case it's important for her to actually sit down, rather than bend down from a standing position, showing her respect for the team.

- If, after several attempts, she's been unsuccessful in getting a team to move forward, she may ask the team to take a break (or wait for a regularly scheduled break as appropriate) so she can point out the issues she's been observing. In this case, she needs to help them understand the importance of moving quickly and/or identifying concerns they have that are holding them back.

- Finally, and as a complete last resort, she may have to ask the team to switch one or two members out with another team. Before resorting to this ultimate solution, she should consult with the key sponsor, indicate what she sees happening, and ask for any other suggestion. It's possible the sponsor could intervene, helping the team understand how important it is they get through the session.

Improvisation

The Facilitator should be an improv artist, whether formally trained or a natural. During the session, regardless of how well the agenda has been crafted and how well the teams are doing, there are constant course corrections requiring her attention. These could include a reluctant participant in a creative exercise, a lack of refreshments, or poor temperature in the room.

She is a consummate "hostess," making everyone feel welcome, keeping things light but focused, playful but with serious intent. If she has a great sense of humor, that can't hurt, but equally important is her sense of confidence and assuredness about the process, the agenda, the exercises, and the ultimate goals for the day (Figure 15.13).

Figure 15.13 Facilitating a Creation Session (and modeling prizes for the attendees)

Even in very lightweight sessions, gathered *ad hoc*, the Facilitator makes or breaks the mood. She needs to get people excited, energetic, and focused on the problem. She needs to get people articulating, brainstorming, and sketching. Because many workshops are stuffy, passive

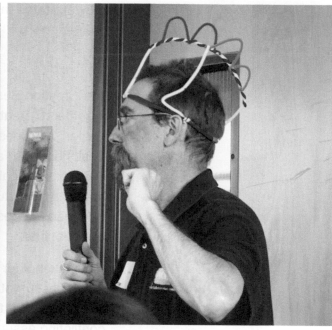

Figure 15.14 The authors facilitating a session

affairs, we work hard to make Creation Sessions active, lighthearted, and silly. This is about exercising the right side of the brain, and it craves play. As the teams construct junk artifacts, the Facilitator should be at ease putting on a funny pipe cleaner hat, a mustachioed pair of glasses, or whatever flotsam or jetsam appears in her path as she floats through the room (Figure 15.14).

Reflection

As discussed in the Section "Debrief and Closure," each Creation Session should end with a debrief. The Facilitator should be actively seeking reflection about the day, about the process, the environment, and her own facilitation. In a multiday session, getting this feedback during the first day and acting on it for the remainder of the session dramatically improves the group's productivity and loyalty to the process. When every participant knows everyone in the room is dedicated to making this the best possible session, including the Facilitator, they will work harder for the sake of the greater good.

Summary

The Creation Session is when one or more teams come together to create an artifact. It relies on Participatory Design, a process of cocreation between stakeholders and Designers, with a simple twist: The stakeholders aren't end-users or external; they are internal. Internal stakeholders have the opportunity, during the Creation Session, to influence the design of the product, through articulating their assumptions.

Any stakeholder invited to the Creation Session is expected to offer assumptions and ideas for expressing those assumptions. If there are wildly different assumptions, or conflicting assumptions, the Creation Session is the context in which teams can discuss and ultimately resolve their differences.

The Creation Session scales up or down based on:

- Its goals
- Budget
- Number of participants

The Creation Session sinks or swims because of the Facilitator. Keeping the agenda moving, keeping teams on task, and keeping the atmosphere light and playful all contribute to successful Creation Sessions.

In the end, Creation Sessions succeed when:

- Teams craft at least one artifact suitable for Engagement Sessions.
- Team members align on their assumptions.

Presumptive Design
DESIGN PROVOCATIONS FOR INNOVATION

The proper function of a critic is to save the tale from the artist who created it.
—D.H. Lawrence

Overview

The team has completed a Creation Session and has an artifact, ready to engage with external stakeholders. Team members are cautiously hopeful their assumptions will resonate. The relative informality of the Creation Session contrasts sharply with the discipline of the Engagement Session. The external stakeholders—whether customers, clients, employees, or otherwise—have their own time pressures, commitments, and priorities. We schedule Engagement Sessions around their needs.

This chapter covers the following details about running Engagement Sessions:

- Prepping for Engagement Sessions, including sampling, calendaring, and logistics

- Trade-offs between remote and collocated sessions

- Number of stakeholders

- Facilitating the session

- What to do after the session

Simply put, the Engagement Session is a conversation: an intimate, geeky conversation about the meaning of an object. But that description belies the intricacies of the Engagement Session. The simplicity of the Creation Session is opposite to the Engagement Session: The Creation Session is complicated to set up; getting people in the room is relatively easy. Facilitation is at the group level: encouraging, energetic, and task oriented. Contrast this with the Engagement Sessions: Setup is simple; getting the stakeholder in the room is the challenge. Facilitation is intimate, intense, and improvisational.

As we discussed in Chapter 14, this is improvisation at its finest. The Facilitator monitors in real time whether a reaction is leading to new insights or is a distraction. Because the Engagement Session is about a *conversation*, it looks a lot like other forms of interviews: usability tests, field research, and requirements gathering. The key difference is the artifact. The artifact both initiates and anchors the conversation. As a social object it forges the relationship between the stakeholder and the team's assumptions.

Throughout the book, we've emphasized the need to be in the same room, whether during the Creation Session or during the Engagement Session. As with the Creation Session, it is *possible* to successfully run remote Engagement Sessions. The trade-offs of running remote Engagement Sessions are significant. With reduced cost comes reduced information. We discuss these trade-offs in this chapter.

PrD is a "small numbers" research effort. There's nothing remotely interesting about the results in a statistical sense. With only a handful of interviews, perhaps dozens of key insights each, the outcome is a set of stories or themes. The search isn't for averages, confidence intervals, or the like. The focus is on themes, ideas, turns of phrases, analogies, and metaphors. We analyze the results by steeping ourselves in the reactions from stakeholders: a torrent of words, feelings, and beliefs.

We can't talk to every potential stakeholder. We're only going to talk to a few people, altogether. How do we decide whom to talk to? How do we know the stories we're hearing apply across the entire population? We delve into the principles of sampling to improve our outcomes (Figure 16.1).

Users

The Engagement Sessions are with people who would use the product or service the internal team intends to build.

Prepping for the Engagement Session

Sampling

Figure 16.1 Sampling: finding only the chocolate coconut–flavored jelly beans

Presumptive Design
Design Provocations for Innovation

In *using* the PowerPoint deck the team had created, the VP revealed his level of discomfort with its content.

See Appendix A: The Case of the PowerPoint Play

External stakeholders are actual, intended users, because we're aiming to learn *about the users*, not the artifact. The artifact is merely an embodiment of the team's assumptions. But it is designed to be used, because through its use, the stakeholder reveals her reactions to those assumptions. As The Case of the PowerPoint Play illustrates, the *product* was a PowerPoint deck, a deck the VP was expected to use. In using it, he revealed his level of discomfort with its content.

Sample Size

Our sample starts with actual, intended users of the product/solution. But how many? It's natural to want some convenient rule, such as usability's famous "five-user assumption"[1] (a rule that has only limited validity). As of this writing there is no such rule of thumb for PrD. It's also natural to desire some rigorous quantitative assessment. In inferential statistics there are ways to quantitatively assess the likely sample size needed for certain comparisons. Such measures don't exist in PrD. "Gut feel" is typically the criterion used.

Such an approach is common. Qualitative researchers explore a problem and understand its context. They dive into meaning and uncover variables of interest.[2] The aim is deep understanding, not estimating confidence intervals or calculating statistical significance. Still, sampling is about representativeness and inference: studying a small portion of the population to infer about the larger group. PrD, like any study relying on sampling, makes inferences. Why bother learning about someone's needs, goals, and frustrations if they have nothing to do with the goals and needs of the larger group? In PrD, the key attribute defining the sample is *use*: PrD requires us to engage with actual, intended end-users.

Saturation

The problem with representativeness in qualitative methods (e.g., interviewing) is the data from a session speaks to only that particular interaction.[3] In qualitative research, representativeness is expressed as data "saturation." Saturation tells us we keep increasing our sample size, keep interviewing, until we're not capturing enough new insights to warrant going further. So it is with PrD.

There is no hard and fast rule for when we achieve saturation. It's a matter of diminishing returns. Diminishing returns applies to insights about a stakeholder's mental model, goals, and frustrations. It applies to how much an artifact continues to reveal her real work and her real needs. The more Engagement Sessions we run, the less novelty emerges about the problem space. How many sessions are needed to achieve saturation? As few as three are sufficient.

How is that possible? If talking to a few folks sheds light on some ideas, how do we know talking to a few other stakeholders won't paint a completely different picture? By sampling. We test hypotheses and minimize the risk of unrepresentative sessions via *purposive* sampling. We select specific external stakeholders based on purposely selected characteristics. The art is in choosing the right characteristics: ones we think are important to our assumptions.

For example, we believe a new offering will resonate more with loyal buyers (people who have been buying from us for over 10 years) than for recent customers (those who just came on board in the past two months). We can create a purposive (or "theoretical") sample based on longevity of tenure as a customer. We can pick a handful of folks from each length of tenure and have them engage with the artifact in exactly the same way. To prevent confounds, we would carefully conduct ourselves the same with each group, regardless of tenure.

Based on our assumptions, we'd expect to have very different Engagement Sessions. If that was the case, we'd be more confident there was a difference. If there wasn't any appreciable difference in their engagements, we'd have to rethink our assumptions. By "appreciable difference," we mean a clear distinction in the way stakeholders approached and worked with the artifact, the questions they raised, and confusions it may have created for them.

The key assumption here—length of customer tenure would affect stakeholder engagement—should be immediately obvious. If the two populations behave similarly, we should feel confident our assumptions were wrong, at least for the two groups in our Engagement Sessions. (By "similarly" we mean so close to the same that a third party reading the transcripts wouldn't be able to tell the difference.) If the PrD was quick and dirty, the expedient thing to do would be to abandon the assumption and try something else. If this assumption was key to a major project, we'd likely run a quantitative study to be more certain.

We reduce arbitrariness and maximize representativeness by purposely seeking stakeholder qualities in which we're most interested. We don't create a sample by picking people arbitrarily (or even pseudorandomly) but instead by an up-front conscious definition of how we're going to populate the sample. There are several types of purposive samples used in qualitative research:[4]

- *Extreme or Deviant Case*: Learning from highly unusual manifestations of the phenomenon of interest, such as outstanding success/notable failures, top of the class/dropouts, exotic events, and crises.

- *Intensity*: Information-rich cases that manifest the phenomenon intensely, but not extremely, such as good students/poor students and above average/below average.

- *Maximum Variation*: Purposefully picking a wide range of variation on dimensions of interest. It documents unique or diverse variations that have emerged in adapting to different conditions. Identifies important common patterns that cut across variations.

- *Homogeneous*: Focuses, reduces variation, simplifies analysis, and facilitates group interviewing.

- *Typical Case*: Illustrates or highlights what is typical, normal, and average.

- *Stratified Purposeful*: Illustrates characteristics of particular subgroups of interest; facilitates comparisons.

- *Critical Case*: Permits logical generalization and maximum application of information to other cases, because if it's true of this one case, it's likely to be true of all other cases.

- *Snowball or Chain*: Identifies cases of interest from people who know people who know people who know what cases are information-rich, that is, good examples for study and good interview subjects.

- *Criterion*: Picking all cases that meet some criterion, such as all children abused in a treatment facility. Quality assurance.

- *Theory-Based or Operational Construct*: Finding manifestations of a theoretical construct of interest so as to elaborate and examine the construct.

- *Confirming or Disconfirming*: Elaborating and deepening initial analysis, seeking exceptions, and testing variation.

- *Opportunistic*: Following new leads during fieldwork, and taking advantage of the unexpected.

- *Random Purposeful* (still small sample size): Adds credibility to sample when potential purposeful sample is larger than one can handle. Reduces judgment within a purposeful category. (Not for generalizations or representativeness.)

- *Politically Important Cases*: Attracts attention to the study (or avoids attracting undesired attention by purposefully eliminating from the sample politically sensitive cases).

- *Convenience*: Saves time, money, and effort. Poorest rational and lowest credibility. Yields information-poor cases.
- *Combination or Mixed Purposeful*: Triangulation, flexibility, and meets multiple interests and needs.

Any one of these can be considered a way to select which stakeholders to work with. Typically, however, we work with a *maximum variation* purposive sample. That is, we try to include individuals with widely varying differences in the attributes of interest. In such a sample, if they all respond identically to the Engagement Sessions, we have increased our confidence those variables don't really matter by identifying "important common patterns that cut across variations."

Some of the other extreme purposive samples make sense in particular situations, such as finding only experts in the domain or, obversely, only newbies. It just depends on our assumptions. We avoid a purposive sample of "convenience." Convenience in this case is only in creating the sample, but the sample wastes time. With such a purposive sample, at the end of the Engagement Sessions we really don't know whether we've learned anything about our population. We just know how the people we could get ahold of easiest reacted to our assumptions.

For us to create a maximum variation purposive sample, we decide what the dimensions are—geography, industry, and type of Web browser—whatever they might be. We decide what specific variables we need within the dimensions (the United States, Japan, France for geography, for example). Then we go about getting at least three individuals for each variable. For example, if we are interested in six different dimensions with three variables each, we'd need to engage with $3 \times 3 \times 6 = 54$ people. In fact, we can reduce the total number of people based on how many characteristics an individual may have. In the most absurdly reductionist case, we might find nine people all of whom share the same variables across the six dimensions. Possible, but highly unlikely.

We create a small table of the characteristics and through a quick evaluation of the stakeholders (a simple email, phone call, or perhaps database/log files can tell us the answers we need), we fill in the cells. An example is given in Figure 16.2.

	Region			Persona			Experience with Offering	Domain Experience	Function			Industry		
	Region 1	Region 2	Region 3	Persona 1	Persona 2	Persona 3			Function 1	Function 2	Function 3	Industry 1	Industry 2	Industry 3
Individual 1														
Individual 2														
Individual 3														
Individual 4														
Individual 5														

Figure 16.2 Characteristics table

In practice this takes a few hours at most, assuming we have a good handle on our stakeholders. If we don't, then PrD itself isn't slowing us down. In fact, any user-centered technique would run into the same hurdle: figuring out who our stakeholders are and how to reach out to them.

Recruitment

Though time consuming, recruiting for PrD is pretty simple, once we've figured out who our candidate pool is. The easiest method is to pull from a customer list, usually owned by the sales and marketing group, public relations group, or the product line. Sometimes the list has many of the dimensions the team is already interested in. For those that are missing, we can craft a quick "screener."[5]

In the sections that follow we describe situations typical in "B2B" engagements. In some ways the process is easier working from one business to another than working with consumers. Businesses have clear policies for employee engagement; facilities are available, and the stakeholders understand conceptually what the team is trying to do.

Presumptive Design
DESIGN PROVOCATIONS FOR INNOVATION

Still, everything we discuss in the following sections applies equally well in the consumer context, even if the particulars shift. For example, where a consumer may not require security clearance from the team, she may expect to meet us in a public location for her own peace of mind. Similarly, just as working in factories requires specific preparation, so too does working with minors or at-risk populations.

Using Sales Teams

In general, we rely on our sales people to refer us to potential candidates. When working with sales, we are careful to specify who we are looking to interview, since they may have other reasons for us to talk to customers. When our reasons align, great! But we don't accept names willy-nilly; we work with them using the purposive sample. The internal team may have names of prospects from prior engagements or relationships they've established. Regardless, the team should get approval from the sales teams before talking to customers. Even if we have an established relationship with customers, we let the sales team know we're intending to reach out to them.

While emailing is easy, it isn't as effective as a direct phone call. In a few minutes, assuming they'll take the call at all, we can quickly establish:

- The purpose of the call (no, we're not selling anything—we're really and truly trying to make life better).

- Whether this is the right person (based on the purposive sample) and if not, who might be.

- If it is the right person, getting her agreement to work with us. This requires additional effort, best done by phone. (NDAs need to be in place if they aren't already; we may need to overcome objections about implicit endorsements of products and so forth.)

User Groups

An organization's sponsored user groups (assuming it has some) or social communities can be another great way to find prospective stakeholders of products and services. Broadcasting a general offer to the group will at least get the word out quickly and efficiently. PrD's unusual requirements will require more detailed conversations once a prospect responds. Be advised, user groups, or interest groups on social network sites, are populated by all sorts of denizens— some are professional "respondents." Others may be competition. Broadcasting an invitation to participate has some risk. Wording should be considered carefully.

Panels of Experts

Some companies invite customers to opt-in to ongoing market research efforts. In some cases, these become go-to panels against which marketing bounces key ideas. As long as these individuals fit the purposive sample they should be fine, with one exception. Any customer who has been participating frequently may no longer be representative of the broader population. One of the characteristics we use in our samples is how recently the individual was contacted.

Support Call Center

Another source of recruitment is the support call center. While customers may have explicitly opted out of any *marketing* contacts, *product research* participation is often not as carefully articulated. Work with the support center and see if they can offer an opportunity to callers who meet certain criteria (the purposive sample chart) and confirm they'd be okay with a follow-up call from someone on the UX team.

Web or Social Media

Sometimes a pop-up survey on a website or a tweet to a community of interest finds suitable candidates. The annoyance and spam factors need to be balanced against the benefit of breadth.

Third Parties

Recruiting can be tedious, time consuming, and a challenge. But in our experience, outsourcing recruiting to a third party has not been effective. We've tried third-party market research recruiters and internal admins, but neither have worked well. From the perspective of market research, PrD is strange. Recruiting companies have amazing technologies to rapidly screen candidates, but they may not have the right characteristics in their call lists. Getting the script right and training the call center staff takes time. Perhaps more time than if we just found a few handfuls of people ourselves.

Internal staff, such as an admin or a project manager, will need to be trained on the process to assist with recruiting. If not properly trained, when the prospective stakeholder says they're not interested, the assistant may accept the answer without probing further. Perhaps the prospects don't understand the process; perhaps they think we're selling them something. Unless the recruiter understands the PrD process, it is difficult for them to overcome objections.

If we are eventually able to work with reluctant stakeholders, they become our greatest "inside salespeople." After going through a session, they see how valuable and fun the experience is. Whenever possible, we use these recent "believers" to help find others they know in the organization. We balance such "snowball" sampling against our purposive sampling chart.

Calendaring, Communication, Setting Expectations

We don't expect to schedule our first stakeholders sooner than two weeks after our first contact with them. Naturally this depends on stakeholder availability, so we really can't predict. If time is of the essence, we don't wait. Once we know the date for the Creation Session, we schedule Engagement Sessions to follow immediately afterward.

We start with a brief phone call confirming they're interested and identifying a specific time and date. After we hang up, we send a brief email describing what we're planning on doing. The email is redundant: It covers everything we discussed in the phone call. People are busy; the process is new to them; some details are important for them to know. It both is courteous and reduces misunderstandings to provide a *brief* overview of what they can expect during the session.

A day or so before the meeting we confirm they've completed any outstanding tasks required of them (such as scheduling a conference room, or having access to a particular area in their workplace). This final reminder primes them for the session, especially helpful if it had been scheduled weeks before. If there is more than one individual participating, whether together or separately, we schedule a collective orientation session. We don't ask stakeholders to do prework or prepare for the Engagement Session, but this reminder helps if they need to prepare the environment for the sessions.

If the artifact is to be used under "normal" working conditions, we'll want to make sure the stakeholder has planned for the team's access to the usual and customary environment in which he works. The stakeholder may need to get special security clearances or may need to notify peers the group is arriving. Of greatest concern is the normal work of interest that is actually going to occur *while the team is there*. In such situations, PrD begins to share some common characteristics with contextual design.[6] Usage is highly affected by context: whether the stakeholder works on the factory floor or in a cubicle, etc. When the stakeholder is distracted by normal interruptions, external validity of the team's observations is increased.

During our conversations, we stress our interest in seeing the stakeholder doing actual work. Even so, we often arrive and are ushered into a conference room where the stakeholder is happy to engage with us. If the Engagement Session's success depends on the stakeholder using the artifact under usual circumstances, we may start the session in the conference room. Soon after the orientation is over, we ask to move to the location where the stakeholder would normally perform the desired activity.

Special Preparation

The team may need to prepare for the Engagement Session beyond the artifact and script. The stakeholder may require the team to get security clearances, prepare specific identification documents, don special clothing, or comply with other prerequisites so the team can participate. We have had some embarrassing moments when team members failed to have the proper IDs and had to stay in the lobby while the rest of us proceeded with the session.

Nondisclosure Agreements

One mutual prerequisite most companies require is an NDA. For some organizations this is practically an automated process; for others it is a "one-off" every time. Because the team will be discussing the stakeholder's work (or play), and the stakeholder will have an opportunity to explore the team's thinking, everyone must agree to the confidentiality of the conversations. For some stakeholders this requirement cannot be overcome and they may need to defer their participation. For others, they may require additional people in the session with whom they can consult if the conversation enters prohibited territory.

Regardless of the level of restriction, it is up to the Facilitator to continue to reinforce a key point: The team isn't interested in secret information. In almost all cases, stakeholders can discuss their work, demonstrate how they would use the artifact, or provide use cases without revealing company secrets, trade secrets, specific personal information, or other harmful information. Although PrD expects a certain level of specificity, PrD's success doesn't require secret information.

Logistics: Traveling with an Artifact, Traveling with a Herd

The Engagement Sessions require very little infrastructure: a place to meet, preferably where the stakeholder does the activity of interest, and an undisturbed period of time, usually less than an hour.

Traveling with more than a couple of people does create some logistical issues: transportation, lodging, food, and any special needs. In larger organizations, an admin or PM can often take care of these details, but if you are on your own, you'll need to account for the additional effort of coordinating all of the little details. Sure, each individual can make their own travel plans but that is suboptimal: Much discussion and work is done in airport gates, in the car between meetings, and the like. The group in short, should expect to travel as a group. For some, food is essential. For others, a quick pickup at a convenience store or gas station and a cup of coffee is all they need (Figure 16.3).

To keep costs down, we schedule multiple stakeholders in the same region. We take the time to know team members' food preferences and align on meals in advance of the trip. Again, much work is done over meals: conversations, insights, and reviews of the sessions; it's essential to capture everyone's viewpoint.

Figure 16.3 A PrD fuel stop when the team is on the go

Presumptive Design
DESIGN PROVOCATIONS FOR INNOVATION

Consider the logistics of transporting the artifact to avoid special shipping and handling.

See Appendix A: The Case of the New Case

Usually we craft artifacts to fit in the overhead bin of an airplane, but not always. In The Case of the New Case, the boxes were large enough to require special shipping. As the team is crafting the artifact, they'll need to keep travel in mind; if travel is by air, either the budget needs to address shipping through or the artifact needs to be sized small enough to avoid shipping costs.

Crafting the artifact for travel will be a welcomed challenge for industrial designers or mechanical engineers on the team. We've seen artifacts designed to be "knocked down" for easy reassembly after arrival. But, as we discussed in Chapters 5 and 8, we must strike a balance among sophistication, complexity, value, speed, and overall investment. We bias our effort and investment toward the simplest possible artifact to drive the right conversations with stakeholders.

Remote or Collocated

With so much work being done digitally and so many relationships and interactions intermediated by screens, it seems quaint and outdated to actually meet face to face. Quaint, perhaps, but the information gleaned working side by side is substantially more valuable than through a 2D screen. At least three reasons compel us to meet with our stakeholders face to face: nonverbal information, context and simplicity.

Nonverbal

Hearing the nuance of confusion, annoyance, or joy in a stakeholder's voice is one of the key pieces of information we listen for as he attempts to work with the artifact. Tone of voice, however, can be more difficult to interpret without nonverbal cues to help. A sigh that sounds like frustration on the phone might be a reaction to something we can't see (Figure 16.4).

Body language, facial expressions, gestures, and other means of communicating are mostly lost through a phone line, whether supplemented with a video camera or not.

With multiple Observers in the room, additional points of view help confirm what a single Observer thought she saw.

Context

Expecting stakeholders to work under "normal" circumstances is unlikely if they are working with us by hosting a videoconference call, unless of course that is the context in which the team is interested. Working on the factory floor, walking through the halls from one room to another, or getting interrupted by coworkers as they try to use the artifact, these "distractions" from pristine laboratory conditions are often *the* data of interest. If the artifact must address the stakeholders' true context, how can we know we're getting the right information outside of that context?

Figure 16.4 Working directly with stakeholders improves information capture

PrD provides such a rich stream of information that we're baffled teams choose to throttle that stream by running the Engagement Sessions remotely. As we discussed in detail in Chapter 9, organizations cite several reasons for hosting sessions remotely, but they all boil down to perceived cost.

Simplicity of Engagement

Although traveling increases the complexity of logistics for *the team*, it makes life simple for the stakeholder. Asking stakeholders to set up remote technologies to share screens, observe their reactions on video and the like are not tasks they do frequently enough to be easy.

Even in high-tech companies in which employees rely on such technologies, we've had to abandon sessions because of system failures. Nothing beats sitting across from a stakeholder in terms of simplicity.

To Record   Recording the Engagement Session is a controversial decision. We are in the camp who believes recording is an essential tool; others think it's not worth the effort. Whether you record or not depends, once again, on your objectives. Figure 16.5 provides some of the key reasons to record or not.

To Record	Not To Record
Capture literal comments; ability to play back for others in analysis	Recording may be prohibited
Provide evidence to convince skeptics of process's efficacy	Saves considerable time on post-session activities
Provide material for highlight reels to disseminate the value of PrD to others	Reduces logistics and complexity of setting up and running sessions

Figure 16.5 Pros and cons of recording

We discuss each of the advantages to record, along with mitigations should the team decide not to record. Further, we discuss each of the downsides of recording, and appropriate mitigations should the team wish to record.

Capturing Words, Gestures, and Behaviors Literally

When we are trying to identify metaphorical thinking on the part of our stakeholders, we must capture their exact words and phrases. Recording captures everything, whether using a smartphone's recording capability, a special pen (e.g., Livescribe™), or a video camera. The team can relax and listen to the key things attracting its attention. There is no other way to capture a stakeholder's gestures, posture, or behaviors without recording them on video. Under certain circumstances, these become crucial data points for design decisions as well as communicating out to sponsors.

When working with no other Observers (a practice we don't recommend, as we discussed in Chapter 10), recording allows the Facilitator to relax without worrying about capturing every sentence.

If the sessions are not recorded, the team must find a way to capture gestures, literal turns of phrase, and the like. In our teams, one of us acts as the "scribe" (in general, one of the Observers), capturing everything she hears. While this approach gets the words straight, the team relies on everyone's memories (or notes—ideally more than one person should be taking notes) to reconstruct stakeholder gestures and behaviors. When we rely on taking notes, we:

- Include as many exact quotes as possible.

- Try not to paraphrase.

- Use the stakeholder's terminology.

- Avoid using the team's own jargon.

In short, when we take notes, we don't put words in the stakeholder's mouth. We clearly distinguish direct quotes and comments.

A master Facilitator *can* also act as the scribe, capturing stakeholder comments almost word for word. Under such circumstances, the Facilitator/scribe will miss important points in the stream of stakeholder responses. It's perfectly fine to ask the stakeholder to repeat whatever was missed, as long as such interactions occur infrequently. We block off time immediately following the session (while the interaction and discussion are still fresh) to review the notes and add in missed details and comments. Here again, however, merely transcribing *words* fails to capture stakeholder emotions, gestures and other non-verbal cues.

Providing Evidence to Skeptics

We need to make a case for Engagement Session results. This is especially true when stakeholder responses differ radically from the HiPPO (highest-paid-person's opinion).

Depending on the level of trust in the team's organization, a simple report out may suffice. In contrast, for some teams only one thing tells it like it is: hearing the results straight from the stakeholders' mouths.

The best approach is to bring the HiPP (the highest-paid person behind the HiPPO) with the team! She can hear the stakeholders' reactions, potentially probe (with the Facilitator's permission, of course!), and reflect with the team between sessions. Such opportunities are rare. When we need to convince a skeptical sponsor, we show them the evidence. Video tells the story without intermediation.

Replaying stakeholder videos doesn't guarantee we'll overcome skeptics. Regardless of what we use to convince skeptical sponsors, *there must be enough advocates* for the team's point of view. When a handful of people who've observed the results can present during the report out, the sheer numbers of impassioned voices is usually enough to counter the HiPP's skepticism.

Highlight Reels

When introducing PrD to a group, we like to tell stories about the process's effectiveness, the information captured, and how it differs from methods with which they may already be familiar. A highlight reel summarizing several Engagement Sessions (and perhaps the Creation Session that spawned them) is a powerful storytelling tool.

The downside is highlight reels take a huge amount of time. We estimate every minute of highlight requires an hour of postprocessing time: seeking, editing, compiling, producing, and finishing. For a team member skilled in the art of video work, it's just a matter of time. If the team lacks such skill, the effort becomes a major challenge, perhaps insurmountable.

Invasive

We are already asking a lot of our stakeholders: Meet with a handful of us, meet us in your home or workplace, and then use this crazy-ass thing we've brought along. Now, on top of all of that, would you mind if we just set this camera up over here and let the "unblinking eye" take everything in?

Oh, and could you sign this form please?

Everything about recording adds layers of invasiveness into the initial part of the session. So, yes, the initial portion of the session (as well as some prework around getting approval for recording) is hampered by the recording requirement. For some stakeholders there is no negotiating: No recording devices are permitted anywhere on the premises. In some cases we've even had to leave our cell phones at the security desk.

Now, with all that said, assuming we've received approval to record, something interesting happens shortly after the Engagement Session begins: Most stakeholders completely forget about the recording device, even if its red light is staring at them across the desk. The session is aptly named: It's meant to be *engaging*. Stakeholders become so engrossed in the work they're doing, in using the artifact, in the conversation, etc., they will remember the recording device only if they speak passionately about something (curse, emphasize a point with a strident tone, tell a "tale"). If it bothers them, the Facilitator reminds everyone the discussion is completely confidential and the device recedes into the background again.

With respect to security policies, except in extremely rare cases (even in cases where the policy is explicit), we've received approval for some kinds of recording, such as audio and photographs. We usually go up the chain of command for proper dispensation and/or we agree to specific restrictions.

Not to Record

In brief, if recording is important enough to do, it is possible to get it approved and the device has minimal impact on the stakeholders' willingness to share openly.

Postprocessing Time

If the team isn't prepared to add about an hour of listening for every hour of recording, they shouldn't bother recording audio. If they're not prepared to add at least 30 minutes of re-viewing for every hour of captured video, we recommend against videoing. These times assume no transcribing, noting, or other metadata capture, just reexperiencing the sessions. If the team is hoping to use the literal words in every session, consider hiring a transcription service or trying audio-to-text automation tools. Even with these alternatives, though, the team will spend considerable time editing and cleaning up garbled sections.

If the team has the budget and resources, this is an excellent summer intern job. We've had great success in getting video and audio snippets postprocessed, indexed, and keyworded by using a dedicated resource for several months. The database this created was useful for many years after the fact to help bring new sponsors up to speed quickly or to help ground new design efforts in the work already comprehended.

Running the Engagement Session

The time has arrived to actually engage with a stakeholder. In this section we dig into the many Engagement Session variables, ranging from how many people are in the room to interviewing techniques.

How Many Stakeholders, How Many Team Members?

As we've discussed throughout the book, an Engagement Session involves the internal team working with a single external stakeholder. We discussed how many team members should be included in Chapter 10. Here we discuss reasons to adjust those numbers.

How Many Stakeholders?

The majority of Engagement Sessions involve a single stakeholder working with the team, and for good reason: It is much easier. Keeping a single stakeholder focused on the objectives is challenging enough. With additional stakeholders the situational dynamics become very complex, in many instances too complex to handle. We don't consider dyads (two stakeholders) or triads (three stakeholders) without expert facilitation and a team disciplined in their behaviors and roles. We *never* have more than three stakeholders in the room. In The Case of the Reticent Respondent, the team had *four* stakeholders in the room, a major contributing factor to the key participant's discomfort. We found ourselves in that position because of miscommunications between the team and the group manager. The session only barely succeeded.

A Case for Two

There is one case in which having two (and rarely three) stakeholders in the Engagement Session makes sense: when the assumptions and objectives require individuals work *together*. The only way to observe stakeholder reaction to an artifact designed for collaborative work is to have multiple stakeholders perform the collaborative work! (It is possible to simulate the coworkers' actions through a Wizard of Oz approach. Such an approach requires the Wizard to be intimately familiar with the stakeholders' work. Alternatively, we've imagined cases in which the Wizard acts *presumptuously* to drive important conversations. That approach is a subcase of a single stakeholder working with a team that is simulating the collaborative behavior.)

Consider the case in which there are two stakeholders, each performing different aspects of collaborative activities. The team has oriented them (together to save time), and the Engagement Session has begun. Each is offered an artifact, or the two are offered a single artifact. In any event,

With his boss and co-workers watching him perform, Mike was extremely uncomfortable using the artifacts.

See Appendix A: The Case of the Reticent Respondent

Wizard of Oz

PrD is similar to the Wizard of Oz technique, a term coined by J.F. Kelley around 1980. In a Wizard of Oz experiment, the participant/user/stakeholder interacts with an interface while, unbeknownst to her, it is in part being controlled by a hidden human agent.[7]

during the Creation Session the team will have designed one or more artifacts to enable stakeholder collaboration. One thing the team likely *won't* do is have the two artifacts communicating with each other in real time. This implies the team has fielded an operational prototype. As we suggest throughout, such an engagement may be necessary, but it doesn't leverage PrD to its best advantage.

The artifacts *have* likely been designed to work together in some clever way, and they may very well communicate with each other. Think of it as a game of *Battleship*. The two players can't see each other's layout, but through a series of moves each affects the other's, even if those moves are expressed verbally. Using a Wizard of Oz approach, a team member could act as the "system," drafting up messages and delivering them between the stakeholders. The system could inject messages or state changes into the artifacts independently, as many systems would in the real world, as a means of moving the simulation forward. In one PrD workshop, teams crafted just such artifacts: When the stakeholder used an intelligent drinking glass, the team-member-as-system behaved autonomously, updating the glass's state with frequent messages.

Note: We are not suggesting having two or three stakeholders simply opining on the same artifact. That is getting close to focus group behaviors, and PrD has nothing to do with focus groups. If more than one stakeholder shows up for the same session when this was not the intent, the internal team apologizes for the error and reschedules. The results from multiple stakeholder participation (when the artifact was not designed for multistakeholder engagement) are so inferior that such sessions are not worth doing.

The Environment: The Room, the Table, the Proxemics

We prefer to have stakeholders engage with us in their natural habitat. Conversations are often triggered by the context in which they perform the activity of interest. If stakeholders spend their time in conference rooms, we'll set up the Engagement Session in the conference room; if it's at a restaurant or coffee shop, we'll do it there.

We want to experience what happens to stakeholders in their preferred context, the interruptions from others, and the stuff they reference in their cube or on the walls. These all help trigger interesting insights. If the activity is a specialized type of work, such as a process in a manufacturing line, observing it *in situ* is crucial to the team's understanding. Of course, the team must be flexible; working with the stakeholder in their native habitat isn't a hard or fast rule. The room may be too small, there may be security concerns, or the mere presence of the team will negatively affect the way the activity is performed. It is far better to engage than not at all, even if it means going to a lunch room or conference room.

Once we've determined the context, we turn our attention to arranging the group. The key relationship is among the stakeholder, the Facilitator, and the operator of the system (if there is one; it could be an Observer or the Designer). The first two must be near one another so the Facilitator maintains the right level of intimacy. The system operator must be close enough to the artifact to manipulate it as needed. If the three are standing, they create a U with the stakeholder at the bottom. If they are sitting at a rectangular conference table, the stakeholder should be at the head (which is generally an honored position anyway), with the Facilitator and operator on either side.

All others should be out of the way, but sufficiently close to observe what is going on (Figure 16.6). The team should consider having a floater who unobtrusively walks around as needed. Avoid having a lot of people standing *behind* the stakeholder for more than a few heartbeats. It's just creepy. While team members may be interested in

Presumptive Design
DESIGN PROVOCATIONS FOR INNOVATION

Figure 16.6 The team steps back from the stakeholder in Engagement Sessions

how the stakeholder is manipulating the artifact, her facial expressions and body language are equally important.

The Designer may be situated a little way away, with additional supplies in the event a quick design suggestion is called for. For example, the stakeholder may suggest a radical interpretation of the artifact the team hadn't imagined. (In fact, this very frequently happens.) If it is interesting enough to explore, and it requires the stakeholder to demonstrate, the Designer will need to mock up something quickly (within a minute) for the stakeholder to tear apart.

The Facilitator sits close enough to the stakeholder to observe what is going on and react accordingly. It is an intimate relationship, almost confidential: The stakeholder is revealing things going on in her head. The Facilitator is offering the social object while establishing a sense of security and camaraderie. The Facilitator needs to create the sense of a confidante who can keep the stakeholder's innermost thoughts safe and secure.

Facilitating the Session

We discussed specifics of PrD facilitation in Chapter 14. Here we offer vignettes of facilitating the Engagement Session.

The team—maybe an Observer, the Facilitator, and a Designer—sit in front of the external stakeholder, and the session begins (Figure 16.7). The Facilitator hands the artifact to the external stakeholder or sets it out on a table in front of her, simultaneously offering the first task. The Facilitator says, "I'd like you to pretend this piece of cardboard with sticky notes on it is a dashboard. For your first task, please check and see how likely it is you'll make your quota this quarter. As you do, please be sure to voice whatever is going through your mind. Say out loud what you're seeing, how you're interpreting the artifact, what your reactions are, as well as anything you find compelling or confusing."

Figure 16.7 Position the stakeholder at the head of the table

The stakeholder probably isn't going to dive right in. It's a slightly odd ask, given how crude the artifact is. It's unlikely she'll see how to perform the task right away. The stakeholder has to collect her thoughts; she needs to craft a narrative about performing a task with a somewhat nebulous artifact. It requires her to play pretend, to fill in gaps using tacit knowledge about her work. She must consider possible ways the artifact plays into her work. All of this takes some time, which the Facilitator knows. He remains quiet, knowing surprises will ensue as the stakeholder meanders through the exercise (Figure 16.8).

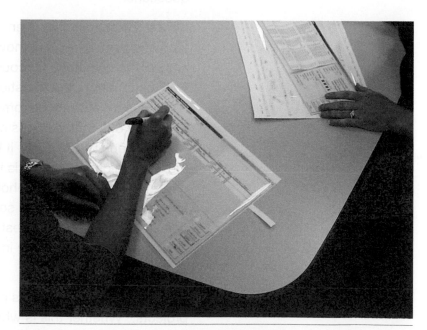

Figure 16.8 A stakeholder interacting with an artifact

301

The stakeholder may be hesitant, possibly requiring the Facilitator to ease her into the engagement. Perhaps the stakeholder points to one of the sticky notes and asks, "What is this meant to be?" The Facilitator, recognizing an opportunity to let the stakeholder answer her own question, mirrors it back. "What do *you* think it might be?" or, "When you look at it, what do you see?" or even, "You tell me." Maybe the stakeholder remains reticent, buying some time by being literal. She might say, "It's just a few lines and lots of little circles." The Facilitator takes this opportunity to redirect by reminding the stakeholder of the task, "Yes, and how might they help you see how likely it is you'll make your quota this quarter?"

The Facilitator, in short, *must be a pest*. He should be polite, respectful, and empathetic—and persistent. Offering good prompts and constantly redirecting the stakeholder means overcoming the urge to help. The Facilitator suppresses the human desire to step in to answer the stakeholder's questions.

Maybe the stakeholder then says, "Well, it could be some type of graph. What is it showing?" Should the Facilitator answer the question? Of course not! Once again, the Facilitator mirrors the question back. But using the same technique repetitively becomes irritating, so the Facilitator has a few different versions of redirection. He responds, "Play pretend. What might it be showing?" or, "You tell me. How might you use this to track progress toward your quota?" By now, the stakeholder has had enough time to think and sees the team is serious. She may laugh at the ridiculousness of the request, a good sign she is starting to play pretend, to engage in creative, abductive thinking.

She says, "Well … the dots here could represent my projects." Whether this is what your team was envisioning or not, the Facilitator says, "Ok. Tell me more." The stakeholder, giving it more thought, says, "Maybe the columns represent status, like pending, lost and cancelled, and then some of the columns let me assign which projects I'll likely claim as wins this quarter."

Here's an opportunity to dig a little deeper into the stakeholder's usual approach to project forecasting. Depending on the team's objectives, the Facilitator prompts the stakeholder to consider aspects of the artifact related to forecasting. The session's direction depends entirely on the objectives. In this case, the Facilitator says, "Ok. I see. You're seeing the columns as project statuses. How does that help you check on progress toward your quota?" The stakeholder responds, "I can see, at a glance, how many pending projects I have in my funnel. I can also see which I've assigned confidence ratings to. I can see how many wins I already have. All that helps me do my forecasting. Actually, if a display like this could be built, that would be really, really great. I would definitely like this."

These last comments by the stakeholder are valuable only in so far as they reveal something about the team's assumptions. If the team believed such a chart would be useful for doing forecasting, then the stakeholder has validated its assumption. If the team hadn't heard about confidence ratings before the session, this would be an excellent time to learn more. In any event, the endorsement or judgment about the artifact is completely irrelevant. It's not about how great the artifact is—it's sacrificial.

The Facilitator periodically says, "Ok. And what might be missing here?" The stakeholder states the display would need to show the percentage of projects she closes on, historically, to get a better sense of how many pending projects she needs to keep in her funnel. The stakeholder says the associated value of each project is missing. Here the Facilitator invites the stakeholder to add to it or edit it to provide that information. The stakeholder says, "You know, what would be really awesome is if this wasn't just a display, but something I could use to actually change my projects' statuses."

Once again, this could be an important idea the team hadn't thought of. Or maybe it was exactly what the team had in mind! Without hearing the team present its intended design, the stakeholder offered it up unprompted. When multiple Engagement Sessions result in similar outcomes, the team is assured they are on the right track. This is an example of how the conversation might go, with appropriate prompts and facilitating, and the insights that could follow, all spawned just from the first task.

PrD, like usability, is task-based testing, but as we've seen, the aim is not to refine the design. Unlike usability, we're really not interested in the stakeholder's ease of completing each task. In PrD, the artifact is vague and ambiguous; it's the merest wisp of something. As with the notion of cultural probes,[8] the point is to learn about the person. When the stakeholders tell us *how* we've failed, we gain insight into their way of thinking. We listen to the ways in which our team's assumptions are wrong; we listen to the stories the stakeholders tell and the ways in which the idea might be incorporated into their lives. This is the gold.

When is the Engagement Session Finished?

When the last objective has been met, the Engagement Session is over. The objectives are the guardrails within which the session operates. Even if we've achieved all of them in the first five minutes, we're done.

The objectives are only one measure of when the session is over. Sessions sometimes end before accomplishing all of the objectives. The session could be over sooner if the allotted time has run out. While it is perfectly acceptable to ask the stakeholder if she is available for more time, if the time is up, expect to be done. To minimize the chances of this happening, practice the session in advance, perhaps pilot it with a "friendly" and figure out how to pace it so it will complete in time.

When it comes to timing, Engagement Sessions are not any different from other field research engagements—the stakeholder is always in control. There are all sorts of reasons for the stakeholder to end a session before the objectives are met or the time is up. Perhaps she is being called out on an emergency; perhaps she no longer finds value in the session; perhaps she's just fatigued; perhaps a higher-up has messaged her and she has to drop what she's doing. Whatever the reason, if the stakeholder has decided the session is over, it's over.

After the Engagement Session

Postsession Dynamics

Immediately after the session is over, the team collects the artifact and the recording equipment. The last thing we shut down is the recording equipment, if we're recording at all. Even after we've officially closed the Engagement Session we will keep recording as long as people in the room are conversing. The last point is important: The people in the room are conversing. We don't follow people outside the room with our recording equipment; we're not the paparazzi. We don't risk capturing people who have not agreed to be recorded.

Much useful information is shared as soon as the stakeholder feels released from the session. Framed as casual conversation, the discussion after the "official" session is rich with insights. The stakeholder may review a piece of the session; she may offer her interpretation of what she did, or provide additional dimension to her thinking. Here, as in the official session, the team defers participation to the Facilitator. The Facilitator remains the primary point person unless the stakeholder specifically addresses another team member. In any event, we keep at least the audio recording going until we leave the room.

During an Engagement Session the stakeholder will have asked questions that can't be addressed during the session. We usually reserve a few minutes at the end to answer those questions, providing closure for the stakeholder. As the session winds down, the Facilitator takes a few minutes to allow the team to answer any outstanding questions.

Hot Wash Critique

We don't schedule sessions back-to-back. We leave 30 minutes minimum between them, assuming no travel time. During this gap, the team conducts a "hot wash critique"[9] of what each person heard. Find a quiet place out of the stakeholder's way where everyone can voice what they observed and what stood out to them. When there isn't enough time for a hot wash, we have team members annotate or circle their notes to help them remember top-of-mind points (Figure 16.9).

THE HAPPY DAY
Ball Bearing High Speed
WASHING MACHINE
SAVES
—Time
—Labor
—Nerves
—Clothes
—Strength
AND TRANSFORMS
"BLUE MONDAY"
INTO A BRIGHT AND
HAPPY DAY

Figure 16.9 The "hot wash" critique occurs immediately after the Engagement Session closes

Capturing impressions during the hot wash is important, especially if there are multiple sessions per day. Sessions start to blur into one another. As each person presents her top impressions, others listen for things they heard or saw. If there is a conflict, the Facilitator makes a note of it but doesn't stop the process. The team returns to these points after everyone has had their turn. After the first individual reports out, the next reports only things they witnessed that differed from the first. In the interest of time, repeating the same observations provides no value. Finally, after everyone has had a turn, the Facilitator returns to any points of conflict or controversy. The team discusses, as briefly as possible, nuances or differences of opinion. For Engagement Sessions lasting 30–60 minutes, the hot wash shouldn't take more than 15 minutes, even with a full contingent of team members.

Changing the Artifact

After the hot wash, the team needs to decide what, if any, changes need to be made to the artifact and/or the script. There are several reasons why the team would make a change:

1. The stakeholder was so confused by something in the artifact that the session was delayed significantly. Depending on the severity, the team may want to fix the artifact to avoid the same issue in following sessions.

2. The stakeholder made a change to the artifact during the session and it now represents a change to the assumptions. The team has a choice: Keep the change or keep it in mind for future sessions and restore the artifact to its original condition. Some changes open a new line of inquiry, exposing something exciting.

3. Saturation: The stakeholder identified nothing new (compared with any of the prior sessions). In this case, the stakeholder has trod the same ground as others, at least with respect to some aspect of the artifact or script. The team may change the artifact in service of additional assumptions or to approach the same objectives in a different way.

No changes should be made after the first session. The team doesn't have enough experience to know whether the first stakeholder's reaction is a common case or idiosyncratic. If after several sessions the same sticking points come up, it is time to consider a change. There's no value in covering familiar territory.

Changing the Script

If the team feels it hasn't heard enough consensus from prior stakeholders, there's no harm in leaving the artifact intact but

Changing the Artifact or the Script

shifting the script. When the controversial point comes up, we let the stakeholder pursue whatever direction he thinks he should go, and when he's finished, we offer an alternate consideration based on what we've heard others say and do. We frequently say, "Cool. There's an interesting difference of opinion going on and we're curious what your thoughts are. You've said the skaxis process would result in you knowing more about its operating conditions, but others have said the skaxis process isn't really the interesting part. For them, it's the loodoxle process that's likely to occur here. We don't know much about what you're doing, so it all sounds great to us. What do you think these other folks are talking about?" It's amazing what you learn. The stakeholder may provide all sorts of interpretations that are completely at odds with what he had first offered, which provides even more opportunity for conversation.

The Cold Wash After all sessions are complete for the day, the team should find a quiet place, perhaps a conference room in the hotel, sit back with a beverage, and go through the salient points of the day. Each team member will remember something slightly differently from the hot washes. Commonalities among the sessions will appear, as will key differences.

As the team collects these thoughts, they need to consider whether to take action on any of them the following day. Are there key points of confusion the next stakeholder could clear up? Should the artifact be changed or returned to its original form? Is the sequence causing a problem? Should the tasks be switched up? It's better to course correct in the middle than come back from a multiday research effort with impoverished results.

But Really, When is Enough Enough? As with each individual session, there comes a time when the team needs to decide whether it's worth proceeding with any more sessions at all. As we've said elsewhere, there are three reasons to stop any further Engagement Sessions:

1. The team has run out of time. Obviously, this doesn't apply if there are still sessions to complete. But if the team has finished a round of sessions and its deadline is looming, they'll have to stop wherever they are.

2. The team has run out of resources (money, stakeholders). In this case, the team can't afford to go back out to do further sessions due to budget or people constraints.

3. The team stopped learning new stuff. After the most recent session in a handful of sessions, the team heard nothing even remotely new. It's time to stop, reconnoiter, and figure out if changing the artifact, script, or types of stakeholders would drive more learning.

When the sample is purposively designed for maximum variation, patterns may not emerge for several iterations. Common themes *appear* to emerge within the first several sessions, but just as the artifact is presumptuous, so too are these initial thoughts and themes. We shouldn't believe them quite yet, even though we keep hearing them over and over. Test these thoughts and themes with the next stakeholders (if they don't mention them spontaneously). As with the conflicting interpretations mentioned in the Section "Changing the Script," it's perfectly acceptable to raise a previously heard common theme with a new stakeholder to understand it in her context. After we have heard a pattern three times across our sample, we reduce our skepticism; after five instances, we stop investing time in it and move on.

Summary

PrD comprises two parts: the Creation Session and the Engagement Sessions. Much like any other social science research involving interviewing people, the Engagement Session requires attention to detail.

- Create a "purposive sample;" specifically we recommend a "maximum variation" purposive sample. When the team's assumptions resonate with stakeholders having a wide variance of attributes, the team increases its confidence those attributes don't matter.

- Recruit stakeholders from a variety of sources, but remember each has its bias: Sales teams, support call centers, social media, and user groups may not overlap with the purposive sample characteristics.

- Although running sessions remotely sounds attractive, in our experience it is a siren call. The benefits of face-to-face engagements are far greater than the cost of travel.

- Almost all of our Engagement Sessions are with one stakeholder. Under some circumstances, we've benefited working with two stakeholders simultaneously.

- The session is over when we've achieved our objectives, time has run out, or the stakeholder says it's over.

- Capture themes, ideas, observations, and insights as soon as possible after the session in a "hot wash" critique. If there are many sessions in a day, allow for time between them to collect thoughts and set up for the next session.

- The artifact and the script are subject to change at any time it benefits the team to do so. If we've stopped learning, or we consistently run into trouble in the same place, we change things up to improve the likelihood of success in future sessions.

Challenging Research Protocols/ Social Innovation

PrD can be used to explore problem spaces in a wide variety of contexts and settings beyond product or service development. The cases in this section illustrate PrD's use for a wide range of goals: from social innovation in Englewood, Illinois, to rapidly capturing rich anthropological insights in Ghana. Two additional cases highlight PrD's flexibility: the design of a game to learn about Chicago residents and the design of workshops for teaching PrD.

The Case of Constricted Collective Conversation

The Resident Association of Greater Englewood (R.A.G.E.) had a challenge. The residents of this south Chicago neighborhood were not coming together as a community in ways that enabled them to tackle complex social problems as a whole: Crime rates were high, civic engagement was low, and neighbors didn't trust the city establishment (and oftentimes each other). R.A.G.E., a group of hypermotivated residents determined to change the dynamics of the neighborhood from the inside out, partnered with a team of six graduate student designers from the Institute of Design at the Illinois Institute of Technology to find more sustainable ways of reaching out to their neighbors and improving resident engagement. For six months, Maggee Bond, Diego Bernardo, Amanda Geppert, Alisa Weinstein, Helen Wills, and Janice Wong worked closely with Asiaha Butler and Latesha Dickerson of R.A.G.E. and other local organizations and businesses to explore opportunities.

R.A.G.E.'s process for convincing people to attend meetings—knocking on doors and putting out fliers—didn't scale. Meeting attendance remained confined to a small number of familiar faces and motivated neighbors. Together, the designers and their community partners posed the question, "Could design be used to engage a broader cross-section of the community?" How might design provide a more expansive set of tools or methods to improve R.A.G.E.'s outreach and engagement goals?

Adding to Englewood's intrinsic challenges of low engagement is its reputation for being one of the most dangerous neighborhoods in Chicago. As a high-profile community, it attracts a lot of well-intentioned offers of help. But historically such projects fail. This is because they fail to take the broader context into account.

The team wanted to stay contextual to the problem space. They figured if they and R.A.G.E. understood the problem space in a broader way, together they could identify better ways of improving neighborhood engagement. They also had a constricted time frame and decided PrD was right tool for the job. The team understood PrD (or "provotyping,"[1] as they had come to know the process) was a key method for staying in and rapidly exploring the problem space of the design challenge at hand.

PrD made sense in another way: The team was under time pressure with its academic schedule; they had to move fast. As Alisa said, "People spend their entire academic careers studying communities like Englewood. We couldn't do that. We just had to start." One of their initial ideas centered on this question: How can we create good news and spread that instead of always having bad news and negative rumors circulating about Englewood?

After collecting information and best known practices from a variety of sources, the team got started, forming their first assumption: People in Englewood weren't talking to each other. Because it was a highly territorial neighborhood (defined by the block on which one lived), neighbors had little trust of others. Although there were many platforms for information sharing in the community, it seemed these were not the best channels to facilitate engagement.

The team established a second assumption: Their approach had to be "real world," not digital. Only half of the residents had access to the Internet. This came with its own challenge. Englewood also had few physical spaces at the time, such as coffee shops or sit-down restaurants, to use to engage with people face-to-face in an everyday context.

These two operating assumptions, a lack of trust and a lack of physical space to bring people together, drove the first provotype. The team considered what sorts of artifacts they could introduce into Englewood to increase their understanding of neighbor's concerns and to learn more about the community.

Several other assumptions drove the team's consideration. They wanted to avoid the insider–outsider dynamics often present in an interview setting. Historically, previous researchers had used one-on-one or group interviews, but residents might have viewed those negatively. Such engagements might set up a power dynamic that could skew conversation. Recruiting participants through community groups or letting people self-select would likely run into the same problems R.A.G.E. had run into: The same activists would show up.

Their objectives were simple but challenging: What do the residents of Englewood consider positive engagement to be? What forms of engagement would they be interested in and willing to undertake?

The team relied on PrD's principles of Iterate, Iterate, Iterate! and The Faster We Go, the Sooner We Know. Alisa comments, "We got out there and started trying things. We deployed the artifacts in three phases." In the first phase, educators, students, parents, and residents were offered a "message board" on which they could leave anonymous sentiments. The sentiments shared on the walls and boards reflected optimism and hope. The team wondered, after analyzing the data, whether the context of the event affected the tone of the responses. How might a more public environment affect such sentiments?

For the second phase the team offered residents two types of artifacts. The first was a large Candy Chang–inspired prompt wall[2] they installed on a street corner at a busy intersection. At the top of the board it said, "I'd like others in Englewood to know …" (Figure A.1).

Figure A.1 Community member of Englewood using a presumptive chalkboard to engage in conversation

The second artifact was a set of paper books with the same statement on the cover, placed with local store owners and community spaces (Figure A.2).

While these two artifacts were, in many ways, *Participatory Design* elements, they became PrD by how they affected the team's understanding of the problem space. Each artifact generated very different responses. The chalkboard solicited bolder, less filtered statements, pleas to stop the violence, distrust of police, etc. The books elicited stories. People shared stories from their past, their hopes, and

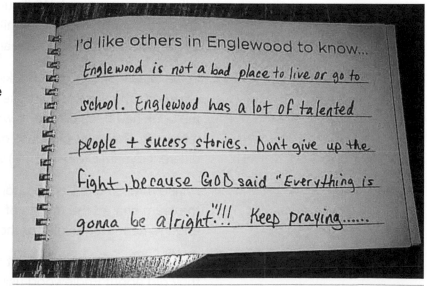

Figure A.2 A page from the paper book distributed throughout the community to elicit community conversation

315

their dreams. But the key reason these artifacts became PrD was how they affected the team's understanding of the community, *merely through the artifacts themselves* (not just from the content each elicited).

In the case of the chalkboard, each side was filled by the end of each day, requiring it be cleaned off nightly. While erasing the board afforded the team an opportunity to interact with curious neighbors who might have not participated, it generated significant *negative* reactions as well. Twice, a concerned resident rushed over demanding to know why the team was erasing what people had written. This demonstrated the community felt a sense of ownership over the board (one of the team's initial goals) and confirmed one key assumption: the community's distrust of researchers.

Alisa confesses, "While we had photographed the board before erasing, we hadn't posted the photographs immediately, ultimately posting them after the chalkboard had been torn down (perhaps by someone disenfranchised by the process). This lag was an oversight and significant failure of our protocol. While unintentional, the lag time shined a light on the community's deep concern about ownership and lack of transparency from outsiders."

In the case of the prompt books, a very different dynamic emerged. The store owners liked the books. One owner, seeing the book had been filled with writing, asked for another to replace it. The mere presence of the book began to drive a very different dynamic (albeit small) within the places it was located.

Phase three was a Participatory Design workshop in which the team shared the results of the prior PrDs and a potential engagement framework for the attendees to use.

Alisa states the team couldn't have learned as much as they did about Englewood using another method. R.A.G.E. continues to use some of these tools today, suggesting they made a real difference in helping neighborhood activists expand their outreach efforts, certainly a key goal of the effort. The artifacts, or provotypes, gave the team insights into the community that would have been awkward to tease out by simply talking with people. An artifact, after all, is not a set of eyes sitting across a room judging you.

Alisa concludes: "PrD is useful for social innovation in that these can be very sensitive projects that could easily go wrong. You could easily alienate people and lose their trust. Once that happens, that's pretty much the end of the project. PrD gave us a way to test our assumptions about citizen engagement and helped surface implicit attitudes and belief systems in a way direct conversation could not. With each iteration, the landscape of what we needed to understand to build the right set of tools became more and more clear. It also provided a means of involving a much larger cross-section of the community."

When Evan Hanover and Anne Schorr, as part of Conifer Research, went to Ghana on behalf of their client, they had two goals: contribute to the global fight against malaria and understand sub-Saharan market economics. Essentially they had one key question their client was keen to answer: What does a person need to know to build a sustainable business there?

Conifer discovered children, through schools and their older siblings, along with their early participation in work, are important conduits in the community. As a result, Conifer decided to do a session just with kids. They had no idea what they were going to learn.

Conifer focused on the kids' chores and responsibilities, such as hauling water. In some cases they have to travel a kilometer or so just to get water for their families. What did

The Case of the Black-Magic Batman

317

they think about these responsibilities? Conifer had them draw and talk about their favorite parts of the village. Because the researchers were a novelty, the kids were excited to talk to them. They were excited because Evan and Anne *wanted* to talk to them, to listen to them. The kids, Evan told us, were superengaged, happy and having fun with the exercises.

In the next part of its engagement, Conifer reflected with the kids about the things they do. "You go to school, fetch water, help with the food, help make bread, gather firewood, harvest grains and so on," Evan recalls. The researchers separated the kids into groups of four or five, turning their desks to face each other, and they handed out action figures to each of the groups. Evan continued, "We said, 'You guys do all this stuff and some of it's really hard, so let's imagine you're a super hero and you have a super power to change all that.'"

There was general confusion and discomfort. The feeling in the room shifted drastically. Where it had been fun and the kids were fully engaged with the notebooks and the drawing, there was now silence and avoidance. Not only was the American notion of superheroes completely foreign to these children they understood "super power" to mean black magic.

Naturally the kids shut down when faced with the prospect of wielding evil. Eventually, after the team realized their error, they reframed the exercise, asking instead, "What if you were President" or "What if you were the village chief?" When the kids heard these revised prompts, Evan said, "They were like, 'Oh, yeah, water should just be brought to people's houses.'"

Evan and the team had made some assumptions about the protocol they were using to work with the village children. Those assumptions were wrong in ways they couldn't begin to predict. But the key point is that in spite of a massively erroneous assumption, or perhaps because of it, the team learned wonderful things. As Evan put it, "We learned that, as much as modernization is taking place in West Africa—

you know everyone has relatives making profits off the natural gas boom or has seen international brands making it into the village—there are these traditional ideas that are still so ingrained in the children.

"It really drove home for us how much we needed to gauge the combination of tradition with the influx of the modern world. It helped frame up how to talk about aspirations and the future. What are the agents of change? Traditional healers and witches are possible loci of change. That was one of our big learnings and tenets that had been brought out by this failure, something that really wasn't exposed by speaking with the adults. Adult members of the community we had spent time with for two or three days never really addressed the spiritual side of things. There seemed to be a sensibility that Westerners wouldn't appreciate it, so we only got that insight from the kids. This was really important since we were wanting to influence their beliefs and practices having to do with healthcare. It changed how we looked for pitfalls."

This key failure with the team's research protocol led to deep insights into the way change is accommodated by village culture. It opened up pathways for establishing trust and authority. The deep integration of the supernatural in village life (exposed by the team's gaffe) gave the team ideas about how to introduce innovation and unfamiliar Western notions. Without acting on their assumption, and quickly identifying the results of their failure (i.e., without employing PrD), Conifer is convinced they would have missed key understandings, or taken much longer to realize them.

The city of Chicago was looking for help from its citizens to plan for the future of the city's arts and culture. Enter Jaime Rivera and his team (Lauren Braun, Kareem Hindi, Lee Lin, and Jose Mello), five graduate student designers from the Institute of Design at the Illinois Institute of Technology. Having learned

The Case of the Preoccupied Passersby

Presumptive Design
DESIGN PROVOCATIONS FOR INNOVATION

about provotyping from professor Anijo Mathew, they were ready to offer the method to the Chicago team. They began by building participatory games to capture people's behaviors and preferences for arts and culture (Figure A.3).

Within a week of fielding the low-fidelity games at Chicago City Hall, the team had learned that Chicago residents could be expected to spend only an average of 10 seconds at the installation before moving on. They also learned that participants liked to see the contributions of others before contributing themselves and that they preferred games requiring and rewarding self-expression. The primary benefit

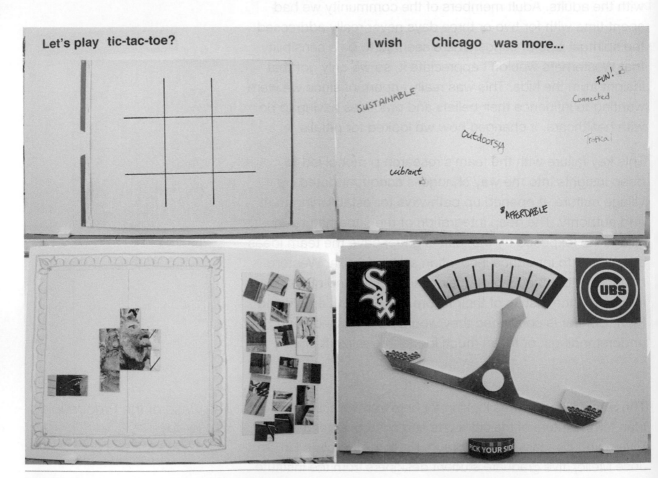

Figure A.3 Examples of participatory games designed to uncover time frames for engagement with Chicago residents

of running these quick provotypes was how *rapidly* the team gained these insights, all without building a complete installation. This enabled them to quickly set up the real installation, better positioned to succeed.

The outcome was "SkyWords," an interactive, dual-screen game set up in Chicago City Hall (Figure A.4). On one screen, passersby answered questions related to Chicago music, food, art, and community. For example, "Do you prefer Chicago have more hip hop, jazz or rock-and-roll?" Residents answered questions by inflating the digital balloon that contained the desired answer. To inflate the balloons they used a physical bicycle pump, pinwheel, or bellows. Once inflated, the digital

Figure A.4 SkyWords installation in Chicago City Hall

balloon with the selected answer floated up and off the first screen. It would then drift down on the opposing screen, where other stakeholders could take aim and pop the balloons to reveal fellow Chicagoans' answers and preferences.

The SkyWords installation engaged more than 2000 people who answered nearly 2500 questions in 10 days. The game was a complete success, creating awareness of and generating data for the 2012 Chicago Cultural Plan. The plan will direct the city's development of arts and culture for the next 10 to 20 years. By using PrD (in the form of provotypes) the team was able to quickly identify the key design criteria for the actual installation, greatly improving its chance for success.

The Case of the Pushy Pillboxes

On two related occasions, the CHI2004|ICSID Forum[3] and SEC05 (an in-house technical conference at Sun the following year), Leo first tested the notions of PrD.[4] In collaboration with his sister, Nancy Frishberg, and others, Leo explored a key question: To what extent would designers rely on PrD as a means of user engagement and research?

In the first instance, the team fielded a two-day workshop with 40 participants from different countries, industries, and roles: from human factors engineers to usability engineers to makers. The second instance was a single day, with attendees from outside of the usability or design professions. The overarching intention of both was to bring together professionals of all stripes to explore collaboration across disciplines. PrD was a method to ensure the attendees' engagement.

Both workshops were structured identically, becoming themselves prototypes for PrD as Leo fielded it in subsequent years: a Creation Session and an Engagement Session with real users. In both cases, the real users were elders in assisted living situations and the design problem was an "intelligent pill dispenser."

In the first occasion, PrD was not a requirement. Leo's hope was that the teams would get the hint: As they were crafting prototypes in advance of their user engagements, he had hoped they would take the prototypes along. He made no effort to force the issue, letting the situation act as a natural laboratory. What he and his collaborators observed was a fascinating difference among the attendees in their approach to solving the problem. The designers immediately began crafting artifacts, sketching, and exploring potential solutions to the brief (Figures A.5 and A.7). The usability

Figure A.5 Industrial designer crafting intelligent pillbox prototype from clay and sketches

Presumptive Design
DESIGN PROVOCATIONS FOR INNOVATION

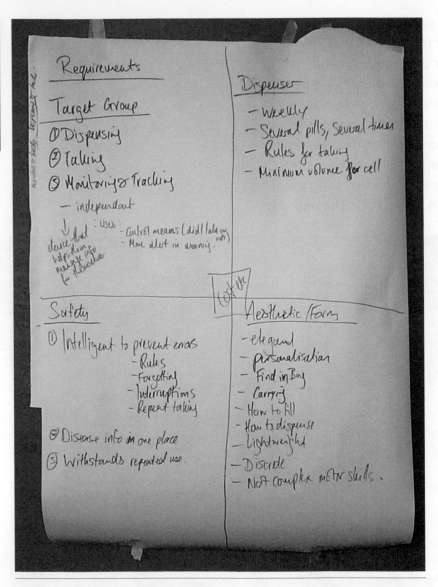

Figure A.6 Usability Researchers identifying qualities of the desired experience for an intelligent pillbox

professionals focused on decomposing the problem through whiteboarding, crafting matrices of attributes, and other analytic work products (Figure A.6). By the time all of the teams were loaded onto the bus to visit the assisted living facility ("Vienna Haus"), only one team had a physical artifact to offer the end-users.

In the second occasion, teams were required to use an artifact to elicit user reaction. Leo's intention was to learn to what extent teams would benefit from using the PrD process. In service of that objective, the organizers presented the process as part of the introductory material and facilitated the crafting of artifacts during the Creation Session.

The lessons learned from both engagements were strikingly similar: Even when they had an object to offer end-users, teams failed to offer it *for use*. Instead, teams treated the object as a prop for demonstration, explanation, or presentation. In fairness, the objective of the workshops was to build collaboration among the participants, not to focus on PrD as a method. As a result, teams relied on the processes they knew well, such as user interviews or the presenting of artifacts, in service of discovering users' needs.

Vienna Haus was striking in several ways. Imagine 40 professionals, of whom only a handful spoke German, arriving at an assisted living facility in which very few people spoke English. Imagine joining the residents (all women,

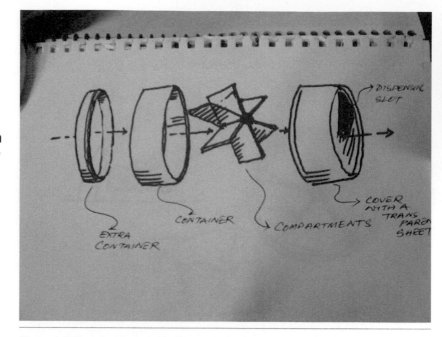

Figure A.7 Sketch ultimately leading to a physical prototype for a pillbox

none of the men wanted to play) in their community room—two of them with eight team members—and no one quite certain how to proceed. Almost all of the teams fell into typical user interview protocols, asking questions about the women's approach to medication, frequency of taking pills, and so on. Even in the case of the team with an artifact, they offered it for *presentation*. Imagine the teams' surprise and shock when the women dismissed most of their attempts and instead suggested everyone just get up and see for themselves what they did with their medication. Within 30 minutes, they were demonstrating their own pillboxes, explaining their comfort (or perceived comfort) with them and the attributes they held dear (Figure A.8). The session transitioned into a more ethnographic engagement: Residents told stories, demonstrated their artifacts, and offered tours of their context.

Presumptive Design
Design Provocations for Innovation

Figure A.8 Vienna Haus resident offering her pillbox (with remarkably similar attributes to prototype in Figure A.7)

In the SEC05 engagement, the results were more complicated. Because the teams weren't comfortable offering their artifacts for *use*, the end-users acted as clients responding to a design pitch. Since the end-users hadn't asked for a design pitch, they treated the engagement as an opportunity to critique the artifacts. The teams experienced several of PrD's risks that day: focus on the artifact instead of the assumptions, the need for expert facilitation, and, most importantly, a need for deeper interpretation of the users' critique.

In both cases, team members reacted differently to the end-user responses based on their profession. In general, designers were dispirited by what they heard while the usability professionals were delighted.

Because of the nature of the workshop format, teams were focused on designing a *solution* (as opposed to understanding the problem). They were on a mission to craft a design by the end of the second day, and the designers felt they had to start over. The usability folks were elated by capturing real-world needs and in-context data, but they too were concerned about how little time the teams would have to actually use the data in the design.

In the second case the designers focused on the critique of the artifact, using that feedback to reconsider their design, whereas the usability professionals interpreted the critique as insights into residents' needs.

For Leo, the results were revelationary: Nobody made the leap of crafting an artifact *in service of their research*! PrD was neither a commonly understood approach (as evidenced by the first case) nor intuitively obvious (or successfully applied), even when it was explicitly required (as evidenced by the second case). With the exception of the SEC05 results, in which usability professionals gleaned useful data from the residents' critique, none of the teams experienced PrD's primary advantages: using artifacts to provoke responses to their assumptions, teasing out end-user mental models, or inspiring visions of disruptive innovation through cocreation and engagement.

Indirect Artifacts

PrD relies on artifacts to elicit reactions from our stakeholders. But the artifacts do not need to be concrete expressions of a product or service, as several of the cases illustrate. This section includes two additional cases along these lines: artifacts that have nothing to do with a product or service *per se*. In the first of the two cases, the artifact is a series of provocative statements in a PowerPoint presentation. In the second, the artifact is a carton of plastic eggs!

The Case of the PowerPoint Play

From 2005 to 2008, when Steve Sato was part of HP's corporate design organization, he and his team were responsible for building the experience design capability across the company. In part, his mission was to help the Vice President of Corporate Design develop presentations to other executives.

The team utilized the presentations to perform PrD, using them to learn about the VP's attitudes and mental model of design, designers, and the role of design within the organization. In turn, through the VP's feedback, the team learned about other executives to whom the VP was presenting.

The process was straightforward and simple: They threw together draft presentations and worked with the VP in a weekly meeting. The team's objective was to assess how well their vision and aspiration for design would resonate with both the VP and the other executives he presented to. The specific "artifacts" were exploratory statements purposefully and strategically placed in presentations to gauge the VP's reaction to the slide. Through this ongoing process of provocation, the team learned how far the VP was willing to commit or what he was willing to show management.

No matter his reaction, the team would always ask him "Why?" Through this conscious process the team gained considerable understanding about his thinking on the positioning of design in the organization. By testing their assumptions first with the VP, Sato's team was able to reduce the risk of their vision being too outlandish for the rest of the company. They discovered, for example, the VP was uncomfortable suggesting to the Chief Marketing Officer (CMO) that they take over similar work previously done by other design teams in different business units. Instead, the VP thought it better to show executives what the issue was with the three design teams doing similar work, suggesting to them it was wasteful. If the VP got pushback when pitching the example to other executives, he could leave it at that. If they were receptive, he could go on to disclose more about his strategy for having corporate design take on the work.

Working with the VP in this way, the process revealed important information about the CMO's concerns and thinking. He was interested in the strategy but concerned the corporate design team's charter was becoming too broad too quickly, suggesting the CMO did not want to support further expansion of corporate design at the moment.

The team extended its use of PrD to almost all its engagements with executives to gauge attitudes and positions. For any specific initiative, the team would offer facts and a recommendation (as a provocation), keeping alternatives ready in their back pocket. If an executive pushed back, they would ask "Why?" and then bring out the alternatives.

The team used this provocative approach methodically. After each session, they plotted their understanding of key individuals' thinking using stakeholder position charts. By provoking their responses in methodical ways, the team was able to predict future interactions, improving their presentations and positioning with each subsequent iteration. As Steve says, "We were advancing design as one would in a political campaign. Say you have 40 people you need to influence. You need to know where in three to four different groups with similar needs each person stood. In our case, this PrD approach really helped with organization change."

In 2013, Leo and his team of designers were asked to improve collaborative work models for their employer's engineering teams. A major part of the effort was identifying and agreeing on the term "collaboration." Another significant part of the effort was understanding the current work models used by various teams. Once the basic workflows were captured and the team had an agreed-upon definition of collaboration, they turned their sights on designing

The Case of the Hard-Boiled Eggs

329

potential solutions. For several weeks, team members engaged in several rounds of PrD with end-users, teasing out assumptions, testing their understanding from the initial research, and trying to validate key concepts around collaboration.

At around this stage in the project, the system architects revealed where they were heading: The collaboration capabilities would be available as separate functions or components. Although this made a lot of sense from a system design perspective, it didn't necessarily align with the team's understanding of the work models, the results of the PrD engagements, or the working definition of collaboration that had been forming.

Still, the team was able to rapidly sketch several concepts, each assuming some kind of component-based collaboration framework—essentially diagrams with titles. But Leo could sense the team was getting ready to do a deep dive into design development. He estimated the effort would take at least a couple of weeks before they would have enough definition to really understand the differences among the initial concepts. He expressed his concerns to the team lead: "Why are you going to take any more time with design development, especially since we don't really understand what users would expect of such a componentized experience?"

"Well," the lead explained, "how are we going to get them to give us feedback if we don't have wireframes or some kind of design?"

"With a PrD," Leo recalls stating with a certain amount of smugness.

"Right," the lead retorted. "That's what we're trying to do. But we'll need to get wireframes together."

Leo threw down the gauntlet: "I could do that test with a carton of hardboiled eggs" (Figure A.9).

The lead recoiled in surprise, uncertain if Leo was pulling his leg or serious. "But…" he sputtered, realizing Leo was dead serious, "but won't they look at us as if we've grown a second head?"

It was at this point Leo figured out he might need to write a book, since the team lead hadn't really comprehended PrD, even after fielding several sessions in the prior few weeks.

Figure A.9 A carton of plastic eggs used to elicit reaction to a componentized experience

Leo went on: "The key thing here is we have a very strong operating assumption coming from our architects: that somehow componentized collaboration *is a good thing*. Are you convinced it's a good thing? Can you predict how our users will react to it? Will they even *understand* such a thing? Why bother crafting *anything* with a screen if we can't be confident in their grasp of such an approach?"

The team lead couldn't imagine how to proceed without further design effort. At this point the team's UX Researcher called Charles, who (unbeknownst to her) had already spoken with Leo about the exchange he'd had with the team.

After explaining the research problem she asked, "How would you research this?"

"I'd use hardboiled eggs," he said on the phone.

The researcher laughed and said, "Yeah, funny, but that's really not funny."

She was, however, intrigued by the seemingly absurd suggestion and took the challenge. Oddly, another of her team members had a whole box of plastic Easter eggs in his cubicle that he immediately offered her. (Leo denies knowing his team members kept such artifacts handy.)

Within three days the researcher returned with results, many of which were surprising.

As external stakeholders (users) played with the labeled plastic eggs (Figure A.10), some amazing things happened. The users *clustered* their components naturally, that is, without any prompting. The users gathered up the capabilities and began grouping them in the carton. Every one of the participants did this. In reviewing the protocol, including the script, there was nothing apparent that would have suggested the users were being *asked* to cluster the capabilities. They all just did it. The researcher hadn't predicted that would have been a desired or expected outcome when she went in. The team was focused on how a user would interpret an isolated, componentized capability.

Figure A.10 An Engagement Session with the eggs. Note how the individual selects specific eggs and sets them aside on the plate

Users also expected their cluster to behave, in sum, with greater capability than the individual components. In all cases, after participants put their clusters together, they spoke about them as if they were part of *one application*. Work done in one capability was expected to feed into, show up, or somehow be a part of another capability.

The point here is that with a minimum of preparation and artifacts, a single team member was able to complete the pilot the same day and complete six external stakeholder engagements within a couple of days. The results, some profound and others less so, had significant implications for the design of the experience (the team made several adjustments to their concepts as a result of the findings).

Further, the team was able to help prepare the architects for several elements in the system they may not have anticipated but which would be required for users to accept the solution. If they hadn't learned about the user expectation to interoperate among the capabilities or the need to cluster them in defined ways, the system may not have been robust enough to deliver on the users' expectations.

The fundamental aim with PrD is to expose and vet team assumptions to explore a project's problem space. In addition to several cases already offered, in which the problem space was ill-defined, the case in this section focuses on exposing and vetting *business* assumptions. This case reveals the benefits of PrD to align internal stakeholders on their assumptions about a business opportunity. Although it uses a direct artifact for a proposed service, the findings from the PrD sessions assisted the business team in understanding their intended market. Perhaps most dramatically, the process revealed deep divides in the team's operating assumptions, in spite of working together on the project for over a year.

PrD Serving Business Results

The Case of the Business Case

With the help of a market research firm, Leo's client had identified a compelling market ripe for a disruptive new business model. Part of the solution the team had sketched out included a technology "stack" involving cloud storage, data analytics, and a browser-based front end. At the point Leo engaged with them, the team had developed a "proof of concept" of the lower levels of the stack and was hoping to develop a prototype for the user interface.

Their intention was to continue exploring the business value of the idea by shopping the concept with prospective customers and partners at tradeshows. Time and money were short. After a couple of meetings with the team, Leo suggested they could make better use of their funds in the time they had to pursue a PrD rather than craft a UI prototype.

Leo offered three reasons to go with PrD:

- The team had dozens of assumptions about the business plan they hadn't had a chance to vet. Building a UI prototype would do little to address their *business* assumptions.

- The team had identified (but not developed in any detail) at least eight personas who would be key to their success. PrD could help the team build their personas, whereas building a UI would do nothing to better understand any of those personas' needs or influence on the business idea.

- They already had a PrD artifact: The market research team had crafted a PowerPoint deck illustrating the business concept. It was just a matter of getting it in front of the right stakeholders.

The entire process from the moment Leo first met with the team to the final report took less than three months. Leo facilitated a mini-Creation Session, bringing in designers to supplement the team. Because the client already had an artifact, Leo focused the team's attention on their objectives and tasks for the Engagement Sessions. They decided on two basic tasks: the persona's use of an out-of-box functionality and the persona's selection process for the equivalent of an "app store."

The PowerPoint deck was not appropriate for the team's purposes: It didn't permit users to actually work with the concept. Instead, the group crafted a paper prototype with an "out-of-box" display (Figure A.11) and an "app-store" display to support the two tasks. Within two weeks of the Creation Session, several team members (Leo, a Facilitator, the product manager, and the technical lead) were in front of end-users with the artifact.

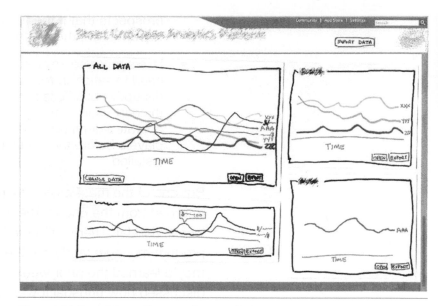

Figure A.11 One of the artifacts used to test the business case for a new service

The results astounded the team. Within a few hours, after working with only a few end-users, patterns began to emerge:

- The solution had to have an out-of-box experience that differed dramatically from what the team had assumed during the Creation Session. User expectations for that experience had significant impact on the technical stack. Additional systems and data needed to be integrated.

- The business idea was indeed revolutionary. Although this finding may have been trivial given the market research, it served to validate the direction the team was heading. But of greater consequence was the negative prospect of such a revolutionary idea. Users were completely befuddled by the business value proposition! The elements that made the idea revolutionary were so fundamentally foreign to the

335

prospects that if the team expected to deliver it in its current form, the venture would struggle.

- Users revealed key requirements the team would need to satisfy *in the sales process itself*. Even if the disruptive business model could be communicated to the end-users' satisfaction, the ecosystem in which they operated demanded the team engage with many other players before the solution could be purchased and installed.

But one of the most profound insights came after the team returned from the Engagement Sessions during a "cold wash" debrief. There, with the Facilitator, lead technologist, product manager, and Leo, the group reflected on what they'd learned the prior week. The product manager discussed how unusual it was for the users to not recognize an "app store" as an experience, given how pervasive app stores were. He also noted the users were unwilling to accept the apps' price points, which he assumed was based on their unfamiliarity with the proposed business model. It was at that point the lead technologist stepped in and expressed his own concerns about the business model, suggesting he had never intended to price or size the applications as the PrD had proposed!

What makes this so surprising and profound is that these two individuals had been working on this project, together, *for almost a year*. In addition, both were present and engaged at the Creation Session, in which these assumptions were clearly articulated and discussed. PrD revealed an unresolved tension between the product manager and the technologist. It was as if the process accelerated the time frame of product development, forcing them to confront a key business decision much earlier in the venture than they would have otherwise.

Although they had both been aware of the differences of opinion about the pricing model, PrD brought it to the table as a fundamental issue they needed to resolve.

Using Real Products as Artifacts

As discussed in Chapter 8, while iterating in the problem space of a project it's generally best to stay with low-fidelity, low-investment (in terms of time, effort, and money) artifacts, speeding time to insight and minimizing insight overhead. One of the least expensive artifacts is to use the stakeholders' existing products or services, illustrated in The Case of the Pushy Pillboxes (mentioned earlier in this Appendix). The cases in this section go the other route: crafting highly resolved prototypes. As these cases show, a high-fidelity, working system provides substantial benefits to the team beyond exploring end-user needs (e.g., understanding the system components or technical challenges). But these cases illustrate the basic tenet of PrD: Is the team's approach satisfying key issues in the problem space? In both cases, the teams realized the artifacts were far more resolved than required to uncover key problems faced by their stakeholders. In spite of this, one of the cases demonstrates that offering up a high-fidelity artifact *can* lead to rich insights of the problem space.

The Case of the Rx Reminder

Working with a large software vendor, Janna Kimel and her team focused on the problem of how best to remind seniors to take their medications. Twice as many people die each year due to nonadherence to prescription medications than die in car accidents. The key question her team intended to address was what could industry and technology do to help?

The team focused on the notion of "contextual reminders." They recruited 10 individuals in their 60s and 70s who agreed to try three different form factors, each for a week. The order of the form factors was counterbalanced. One was a smart pillbox with a visual reminder. It was magnetized so stakeholders could place it anywhere in their home or car. Another was a smart pillbox with a mobile audio reminder. The third was a smartwatch with audio and visual reminders (Figure A.12).

Figure A.12 A smartwatch as Rx reminder system

Aspects of this study were very much PrD, in that the team was testing their *assumptions* about these users' needs for medication reminders, the underlying drivers for *why* people fail to take their medication, and specific *beliefs* about technological approaches to the problem. The study, however, diverged from PrD in two key ways: The artifacts were functioning prototypes and the data collection protocol included indirect methods (personal diaries and data logs from the devices themselves).

The reliance on actual, functioning technology introduced significant complexity into the study. One of the first things the team learned was it couldn't expect the participants to understand all of the technology involved in the solution. The smart pillbox, for example, had to communicate to a laptop that was also placed in participants' homes. In one case, a participant loaned the laptop out to her son and the team stopped getting data. In another case involving the smart pillbox, one person didn't like how the activity beacon (used to track when the participant was moving around) looked on her wall. She hung a puzzle box cover over it so she could look at that instead, rendering the motion sensor useless for a period of time.

One of the biggest assumptions the team had made involved the seniors' mobility: They were much more mobile than the team had assumed. With the smart pillboxes, for example, the reminder was mobile but the pillbox itself wasn't. Just because stakeholders had the reminder with them didn't mean they were near the pillbox! One participant reported she'd completely forgotten to take her meds because she and her daughter had decided to take a long walk. Another apologized for missing an interview, saying, "I was on a raft." The team's big assumption was that the seniors would be sedentary enough to always be near a stationary pillbox. They weren't. The reminder and the pills needed to be together, as these people were highly mobile.

As the study was conducted in stakeholder's homes, it revealed much about their current practices for reminding themselves to take their pills.

One man had his pill bottles in a row. He would turn them all upside down. When he'd take a pill he'd turn that bottle right-side up, providing himself a visual indicator of which medications he'd already taken that day (Figure A.13). One stakeholder said, "At 11:00 we play Yahtzee. After Yahtzee I take my pills."

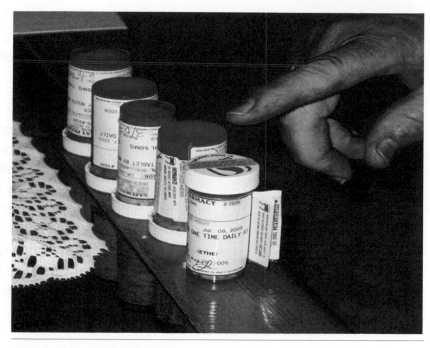

Figure A.13 Stakeholder demonstrating his system of remembering which pills he's taken

There was a woman who was taking care of her sister, trying to keep her in independent living. Her pills were arranged like an altar in front of a picture of her grandchild. Whether done consciously or not, the arrangement created an emotional connection: It's important to take this medication so she can be around to see her grandkid grow up.

Janna's team completed the study with a Participatory Design exercise in which participants were asked to craft their own vision of a reminder using Play-Doh. Even though they created artifacts looking like a much simplified version of the watch, it wasn't the form factor that mattered as much as the underlying assumptions it embodied. As Janna tells it, "When they described what they'd fashioned out of Play-Doh, it became apparent they'd only fashioned a watch because that's what they knew, what they were familiar with. They'd just had a smart watch in the study, but they hadn't really liked it. It was obtrusive and clunky. When they described what they were wanting it was clear it didn't need to be a watch, just something highly mobile, wearable and very easy to use."

The team's biggest takeaways dispelled their initial assumptions about a technological solution. The ultimate form factor would have to address the participants' needs for simplicity. No fancy buttons, settings, or the like. It just needed to work. In addition, it had to be highly mobile, maybe a button or pin that could be worn on a lapel, shirt, or blouse. Finally, it had to be unobtrusive and private. None of these were apparent going into the study, and while many of them may have been discoverable without functioning technology, the team's insights all resulted from real users using real artifacts.

The Case of the *Star Trek* Holodeck

Renowned ethnographer Steve Portigal and his team were working with a client on a futuristic smart TV. As Steve put it, "To call it a smart TV doesn't do it justice. It was a smart TV on steroids." At first blush, the engagement seemed straightforward: help the client through a feature prioritization exercise with consumers. But fairly soon after the team began, it realized its client may not have thought through their assumptions behind the device.

The complexity of the project added its own challenges. The client's concern about security and confidentiality prevented research team members from really understanding the technology, its features, capabilities, and intended experience before they were to engage with consumers. The client had created two very elaborate prototypes. The first, a high-fidelity simulation, required 12 hours for the client's team to unpack, install, and set up. "This was like something you'd normally only see at a tradeshow. It reminded me of the holodeck on

Star Trek: The Next Generation," Steve remarked. "We really didn't know what was 'real' and what was scripted." The second artifact was two full-sized mock-ups of screen displays mounted on foam core.

The research was split into two parts as well. In the first part, consumers would interact with the high-resolution simulation in the client's facility, with the expectation they would prioritize features. In the second part, a subset of these participants were enrolled to help understand how the device would fit in the context of their homes.

The client's goals for feature prioritization began to unravel during the engagement with the high-fidelity simulation. Users were confused by the mishmash of features. There was no perceivable narrative for the product, no underlying reason *why* it could it do all of these things. The users started offering up use cases the client had never thought of. "Oh, this is something that brings people together" or, "Oh, maybe this would be tabletop-like and we'd sit around it, interact digitally and share an experience."

After having seen and experienced the high-fidelity simulation, these participants were primed to consider the foam-core artifacts with a deeper understanding than simply, "Could it fit in this room?" The lower-fidelity mock-ups provoked rich conversations about the underlying value proposition of the product itself. Rather than focusing on the simpler aspects of how the device might fit in the users' homes, the team was able to probe into more interesting questions such as, "Now we've got this on your wall, let's talk about you owning one of these and how you'd live with it. What do you expect it to do?" When Steve and the team witnessed the challenges users were having and understood it was due to a lack of narrative, they took the research in a completely different direction. This was a surprise to both the team and the client, but exploring the narratives behind the device opened up a richer understanding of these users' needs, desires, and points of view. The responses enabled insights the client hadn't given much thought to or even realized were important to understand.

For example, users would hold up the low-fidelity mockups to their wall and say, "Oh, yeah, I'd walk up to it and do this ...." The client thought they were testing the solution, but the users' reactions made it clear to the team they were revealing the problem space. Because the screen was in their homes, users began to ponder how it might work with existing screens they already had, and what sorts of engagements it would enable based on its location, say, in the kitchen versus another room. The participants were reflecting back an experience: the bringing of friends and family together. For Steve and the team, that was huge. The client didn't have that kind of narrative; they had features. In looking for something to grab onto because the device hadn't been designed with a narrative in mind, users were offering up their own!

As discussed in Chapter 8, it's generally not a good idea to go high-fidelity, high-investment while in the problem space. Teams that end up here usually do so by accident, such as this team. It thought it knew what the solution was. The client's users informed it otherwise by asking, "Solution to what?" Still, as Portigal shared with us, the fact the client had produced such high-fidelity artifacts shifted the research in fascinating ways. It may not have been cost-effective, but it was still beneficial: If the client had followed conventional wisdom (starting with low fidelity and moving to higher fidelity only later), users would not have offered up as many insights or such rich understandings of the low-fidelity mockups in their homes. Without having experienced the touchscreen, moving data between devices using gestures, and other *Star Trek*–like behaviors, these users wouldn't have suspended their disbelief about the foam-core artifacts.

The client recognized business value in the results of the research team's effort, but Steve believed the process revealed a more valuable contribution: an opportunity to improve the client's product development *process*. The team suggested the client first establish a compelling narrative, test *that*, and then build features supporting the tested narrative. Without such a narrative, users provided one; when the client offered an ambiguous artifact (high-resolution but without a compelling narrative), the users were compelled to make one up.

This last point underscores the power of PrD: We will work hard to overcome gaps in our understanding of an artifact. The stories these people told illuminated their underlying values, desires, and, ultimately, the *business value* for the client's device.

Direct Artifacts

Most of the time, the artifacts we create in PrD sessions are a direct expression of a new product or service offering. The three cases in this section are a sample of the wide range of possibilities: a new form factor for a high-tech test instrument, a bicycle accessory, and a new approach to therapy.

The Case of the New Case

Leo was working for a product group with a serious problem: The entire product category it had originally created and subsequently been building, iterating, and engineering for over 15 years was under attack on numerous fronts. Competitors were shifting the focus away from the company's core competency, customers were grumbling about the product's usability, and key engineering advantages based on unique hardware designs were being eroded by ever-improving software. Of several initiatives launched to counteract the erosion, one was a simple refresh of the product packaging, updating it to a more contemporary look and feel. None of the features or functions (other than front panel knobs, ports, and other superficial physical attributes) would be touched.

This initiative was in flight when Leo came onto the scene. The group hoped to get feedback from sales teams about the proposed new look at an upcoming sales conference. The plan was to move some knobs and input ports from the back to the side of the box, and change its envelope dimensions as well as the color of its plastic housing. The engineering team had settled on an incremental shift in the current design. A newcomer (like Leo) looking at the old and new designs would have difficulty distinguishing much of a difference. The product manager explained the proposed changes were a response to several years of complaints about those specific issues. For the upcoming sales meeting, the team had decided to mock up three variations of these elements using foam-core models.

Leo realized that if ever there was an opportunity for PrD, this was it. He gathered together the core team of engineers for an hour, asking them to brainstorm all of the possible ways they could address the customer complaints—*without building a box* (Figure A.14). As Leo put it, "Once the constraint of incrementalism was removed, amazing things happened. Entire parts of the design were eliminated, functional elements such as the power supply or the disk drive, long considered 'anchors,' were reconsidered with completely different form factors. Even the screen, a key hot button for their users, became a target for reconsideration. At the end of a single hour we had generated four substantively different proposals, all of

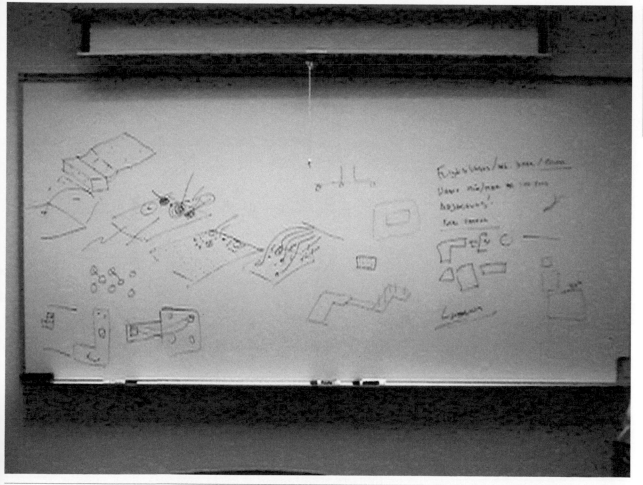

Figure A.14 The results of a brief Creation Session with key engineers

which we knew were problematic (both engineering- and usability-wise) (Figure A.15)."

The team crafted quick Photoshop mockups to use as artifacts. Given the enormous risk of the proposed designs, even creating 3D foam-core mockups of the ideas seemed an unnecessary level of investment. The team had gone in with the assumption that the product's form factor would remain unchanged. Leo prompted them to call out and question this assumption. What if they did change the form factor? Perhaps more importantly, what if changing the

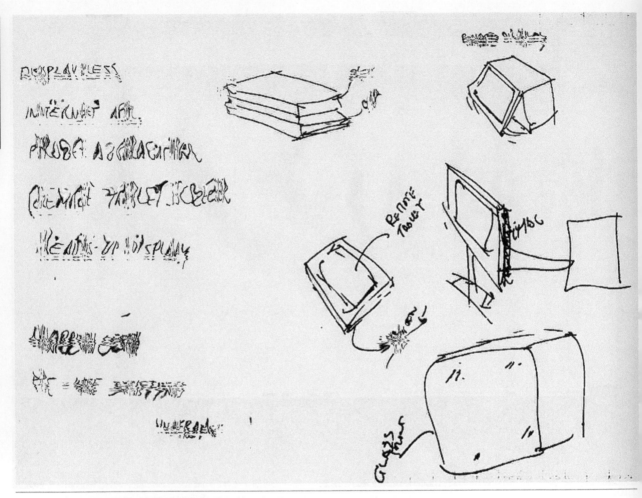

Figure A.15 The initial sketches of what would become high-res Photoshop images

form factor *didn't* address the perceived customer pain points? Would a radical change in form factor reveal true customer needs that might not need a changed form factor at all? Photoshopped screens as artifacts were more than adequate to test these notions.

Stakeholder reactions to the more radical proposals revealed important unaddressed needs, such as keeping certain parts together (little bits and pieces evaporate quickly in labs) while at the same time making the solution easily transportable.

The team learned about leveraging the compute power already existing at customer sites, whenever possible, while providing the top-notch accuracy afforded by the client's specially built hardware. In short, through PrD, the team gained a much richer understanding of the client's customers and of sales teams' needs, leading to a much broader set of possible offerings. These offerings were made possible only by calling out form factor as an assumption and directly questioning it.

Ohio State University graduate student David McKenzie had been drawn to the work of Liz Sanders, specifically in the area of research through making. As he began exploring the process of PrD he decided to focus on cyclists on campus and where their needs weren't being met.

The Case of the Balking Bicyclists

True to the principle of Create, Discover, Analyze, David and his team generated concepts based on an initial idea but without much supporting data. He and his team created a bicycle attachment allowing riders to use their smartphone as a rearview mirror (Figure A.16).

Figure A.16 The initial artifact: a 3D printed accessory

Once created, David introduced the design to a group of stakeholders for their reaction. David put it succinctly, "They completely trashed it." Recognizing the stakeholders might have other ideas for what made more sense, David engaged them in Participatory Design sessions in which they could craft their own artifact using a variety of

Figure A.17 A Participatory Design session with stakeholders in response to the initial artifact

Figure A.18 Participatory Design session generating stakeholder notions of a needed accessory

materials and tools (Figures A.17 and A.18).

In spite of the stakeholders' reaction to the initial concept, David and his team captured excellent information: what cyclists really wanted and the problems they have on or around campus and the Greater Columbus, Ohio, area. Out of several sessions, David created a "stakeholder map," a whiteboard with sticky notes (Figure A.19).

The results of this initial round revealed two areas completely different from the one assumed by his team at the start: security and infrastructure. Where his team had assumed cyclists would be concerned about lack of bicycle lanes and a desire for improved understanding of their surroundings, the underlying reactions to their artifact suggested a deep concern for security. For example, the more hardcore cyclists completely rejected the idea of using a smartphone as a resource. Although they complained about the clunkiness of the prototype, they also mentioned the risk of having their phone being exposed to theft.

The artifact generated stories about lights and even bikes being stolen on campus. Even their assumption about Columbus' lack of proper bicycle infrastructure was revealed to be unfounded. The team learned Columbus actually has a good cycling route and most cyclists don't use roads to move through the city.

With this new understanding, David and his design team considered a completely different artifact—a locking mechanism integrated into the bike itself (Figure A.20).

In a subsequent set of Engagement Sessions, David validated the need for security: Stakeholders were unconvinced this solution would be enough! As with the prior session, he welcomed the participants to craft their own ideas in response to the second iteration.

Figure A.19 Stakeholder map. Sticky notes placed in a two-dimensional graph. *X* is the scale of the problem and *Y* is the problem area of abstraction

David knew, in spite of the ongoing criticism of his ideas, that he was making forward progress. Using a process he calls "Trash and Praise" (in which respondents rate offerings on a

Presumptive Design
Design Provocations for Innovation

Figure A.20 An artifact revealing the need for security built into the bike

scale of 0 to 10, with Trash being 0 and Praise being 10), David had moved from low scores in the first iteration to middling scores in the second.

Shifting gears, so to speak, David's design team turned to social stigma as a way of reducing theft: Could the bike signal to a prospective thief a sense of shame? In the third round of Engagement Sessions they offered an artifact relying on this principle, to little fanfare. Security remained an important issue, but the group was unconvinced that stigma would be as effective a deterrent to theft as brute force (i.e., a strong lock).

David's case illustrates another principle of PrD: The Faster We Go, the Sooner We Know. All six sessions—three Creation Sessions and three Engagement Sessions—took only about two weeks of work to complete. In fact, David suggests, "It would have taken half the time if recruiting hadn't been such a stumbling block." He goes on, "The artifacts themselves take less than an hour to make. The turnaround of analysis and discussion are done in a single afternoon."

David has discovered many of the principles of PrD in the short engagement he's had with it. He told us some of his takeaways include the realization there's a big difference between sacrificial artifacts and refined prototypes. The creation of crude artifacts is a quick turnaround. In his first attempt, he used 3D printing; by the last he was using cardboard. The artifacts, he told us, create discussion entirely different from the purpose of the artifact. When these objects are in front of people, they project *onto* them. This led to valuable surprises and discoveries. That the artifact doesn't actually work, he told us, changes the dynamic with participants, generating a wider range of discussion. Steering the conversation toward the problem space by using the artifact led David to more interesting discussions with stakeholders, less about refining the artifact and more about the underlying problem it's trying to address.

And finally, David told us, getting going immediately has great value—even if you're dead wrong. Offering something that will be trashed, as David did in his first iteration, generated a strong reaction and response from stakeholders, revealing their passions around the real problems they faced.

Christopher Stapleton, with over 25 years under his belt in developing experiences and environments for companies such as Disney, Universal Studios, and Nickelodeon, had been sitting in on therapy sessions with People with Aphasia (PWAs). It occurred to him the work he'd become an expert in (immersive entertainment) would be a spectacular way to enable these patients and improve their lives.

The Case of the Transformed Treatment

He had a hunch his years of experience with alternative storytelling techniques could be a useful form of therapy. As Christopher told us, "I'm an entertainment story guy coming into a science world and working in their problem space. I'm a *novice* in their problem space. But I am an expert in what I do. They need help thinking outside the box. PrD is important because we have different perceptions of problem spaces and different solutions and processes. People with different backgrounds and expertise will see the problem spaces differently. They need to be able to play well together in order to come together and think outside the box.

"PWAs find their therapy emotionally overwhelming. They still have the cognitive abilities of all they've learned, their expertise. It's just that now they can't communicate it. It's like they're prisoners in their own minds. Traditional, evidence-based therapy for PWAs teaches language through drill and practice. Therapists focus on this relearning of language, and it can make therapy excruciating. It reminded me of having to go back to preschool as a 50-some-year old. Well, I thought, what if we question this approach? What if they don't focus on the language impairment but on something else? What if they focus on storytelling? PWAs have lost their ability to tell stories with words, but they can still *imagine* stories."

At Simiosys Real World Labs, Christopher and his research partner, Dr. Janet Whiteside (executive director), began with this assumption and started their work for the University of Central Florida's Aphasia House. UCF's Aphasia House follows the Life Participation Approach to Aphasia (LPAA), whose therapists want to improve communication through creatively building relationships. They are very open to trying new things, Christopher told us, which made this effort possible.

They offered clients an artifact they call the "Story Trove." "It's sort of like evidence to a detective or a hope chest. It's a box that tells a story by what's in it and how it's layered and how you unpackage it. It makes you jump to conclusions, intentionally. You use these objects to paint with your imagination. You put objects together as a story. Objects divert attention from being focused directly on the client. This depressurizes the situation and facilitates discovery. It pushes and challenges clients without making them want to give up."

Figure A.21 Story Troves reveal many stories beyond words through the juxtaposition of artifacts that paint with the audience's imagination

Christopher is referring to the Story Trove as a social object, a key aspect of PrD (Figure A.21).

By introducing the Story Trove, Christopher and his team were able to change the traditional therapist–client dynamic. With the Story Trove, everyone comes to the table: the client, the therapist, and the caregiver (Figure A.22). His operating assumption rested on the question, "Why should the PWAs have to do all the work?" By bringing everyone to the Story

Figure A.22 Through "Conversational Storytelling," group engagement with Therapist, Caregivers and PWAs rediscover the rich exchange of communication while using story to rediscover language skills

Trove, they introduced a notion of a "lifetime of therapy." The caregiver started to model the therapist and the therapist started to train the caregiver.

One day, due to events outside the team's control, client schedules got mashed up and two clients showed up for the same appointment. Much in the PrD spirit of improv, Christopher believes in leaving room for mistakes to happen, finding great value in the breakthroughs that can result. Rather than rescheduling one of the clients the team decided to proceed with both, to eye-opening results. Including both PWAs in the same appointment, the team discovered the two clients did much better talking to each other than talking to the others present. This was quite a discovery, suggesting another way to improve therapy with PWAs.

Simiosys Real World Labs has demonstrated a completely new way of thinking about therapy for PWAs, all through artifact building and experimentation. Their discoveries have made Christopher passionate about PrD.

In a recent keynote to the Aphasia Access Leadership Summit, Christopher presented his PrD research on Conversational Storytelling. He told us: "We're transforming their approach, giving a keynote at their conference and I'm not even a scientist! I'm not an expert! We just saw something and within six months were showing results, transforming the entire industry. We turned it upside down, starting with story, not language.

"We also realized we need to apply PrD in therapy to design the treatment, a new product solution, for each client. There's innovation in the field, yes, but we need innovation for each particular client. The field is so preoccupied with evidence-based data. When I'm asked 'Where's the data to support that?' now I say, 'This is PrD. I'm being *presumptive*. This is the stage *before* evidence-based data.' I use the term 'PrD' quite a bit now. Its whole basis is working with your hunches. PrD allows one to get very far very fast."

Sometimes stakeholders are not keen on the notion of participating in PrD. In such circumstances it's typically up to the Facilitator to manage the situation. And, often, the best way to move people past their misgivings and hesitancies is to simply get the process moving. Once they experience it, the resistance tends to melt away.

The Art of Facilitation

355

Presumptive Design
DESIGN PROVOCATIONS FOR INNOVATION

We include this case, not to illustrate a particular artifact, but to underscore the need for mastery in running the Engagement Sessions.

The Case of the Reticent Respondent

Leo was on the road with a team doing early concept testing for a completely new product category. The challenge of researching new product categories is that there is only analogous information to go on. The thing is sort of like this and sort of like that, but in fact it is completely new and can't be described in terms of existing products. The product manager was having a tough time putting a case together because he couldn't find market data that really applied. So, he gathered a team: a hardware engineer, a software architect, himself, and Leo as the UX guy, and took it on the road.

The protocol was in two stages: The first asked users to tell the team about a recent experience using the related products by walking through a typical use case. The second stage asked them to "design" the new product using a prefixed set of elements that covered all of the related products' functionality. The hope was that users would naturally design the hybrid product representing the new category. There were several assumptions in this PrD:

- Users needed the new product category.

- Users would put the new product together based on component parts.

- Having users perform a walkthrough first would prime them for the design effort.

The team arrived at a computer components manufacturer, one of the company's best customers. The meeting had been set up with what the team hoped was a perfect candidate to test its assumptions. After the team took its seats in the conference room, the customer team came in: the team manager along with three of his team members, Mike, Ivan, and Josef.[5]

After getting the pleasantries out of the way, Leo turned to the manager and asked who on his team was going to help out that morning. He, in turn, turned to his team and asked them. It was clearly the first time any of them had heard Leo and his team were going to be there or what the session was going to be about. Seeing a catastrophe in the making, Leo jumped in and said, "Before you all raise your hands at once, let me explain a little about what we're hoping to do today." After hearing a quick description, the research team was heartened to see Mike shrug his shoulders and agree to be the sacrificial lamb. At that point, the research team expected the rest of the customer team to leave, allowing Mike to speak openly and directly.

Sadly, that wasn't going to be the case. Mike as it turned out was the junior guy on the team; he had the least domain knowledge and obviously had lowest status in the group. Add to that a strong dose of performance anxiety and the research team was beginning to sense the session was going to be nightmare. Because the warm-up exercise was both entertaining and something he could do, Mike loosened up a bit. Not so for Ivan. Ivan sat behind and off to the side of Mike, his arms crossed with his face in a permanent scowl. He gave the research team the warm feelings of a government intelligence handler, uttering single-syllable grunts if he said anything at all.

An hour later and Mike was through his ordeal. The research team knew it wasn't getting the best information from him, but it was good enough to not stop early. And then Leo turned to Ivan: "So, I noticed you seemed to have some opinions about what Mike was doing. We appreciate that you didn't interrupt him when he was trying to work with us, but I'm interested in hearing what you have to say."

Ivan's eyes narrowed slightly and then his arms unfolded and he sat a little straighter in the chair. "It's obvious," he said with a thick accent, only adding to the atmosphere, "vat you are trying to do." And with a small self-satisfied smile, for the next 30 minutes he laid out the team's entire strategy. Even more importantly, he endorsed it. "Eff you could make zhat happen, vell, I've never zeen anyting like it, and it vould be a uzeful device." Without the team's knowledge or prompting, a senior engineer, who would likely be the target candidate for the new concept, not only had understood what the team was doing but also saw great value in it.

So, you never know. Sometimes you just forge ahead and hope for the best, facilitating your way through a bad situation, and if you're lucky get pleasantly surprising results.

Appendix B: The Art of Box Breaking

Presumptive Design
DESIGN PROVOCATIONS FOR INNOVATION

Overview

Design thinking rests on *abductive reasoning*, or playing pretend. In highly analytic environments, such as high-tech engineering firms, pretending is an unfamiliar approach to problem solving. Organizations relying on deductive or inductive reasoning equate pretending with guessing. No one is going to bet their budget on a guess, because, well, it's a *guess*! It is based on intuition, gut feeling, and personal bias.

These organizations have a philosophical orientation towards error (pessimistic) diametrically opposed to that of organizations based on design thinking (optimistic). For manufacturing, engineering, finance, quality assurance, and any Six Sigma–focused process, error is a negative condition. It must be eliminated below or within a set of acceptable constraints. For designers, error is a source of inspiration and delight.

Abductive reasoning, as the starting position for design thinking, is the embrace of error.

In this appendix, we provide techniques to shift teams into a playful state of mind. With a sense of play, guessing and being wrong is not only okay but also the exact right thing to do. These techniques are not unique to PrD, but we have found them accessible, easy to facilitate, and effective. They are not the only such creative exercises, and they are not appropriate for every Creation Session. We offer them for consideration in larger/longer Creation Sessions. Larger sessions require formality to accommodate the diversity of team members and to address the organization's investment. *Ad hoc* sessions have just as much need for abductive reasoning, but getting team members into an abductive frame of mind is much easier. The exercises we describe can, with adjustments, be used for *ad hoc* sessions. The principles behind the exercises are important regardless of the scale of the Creation Session.

Remember the games we played in childhood? Think about the amazing worlds children imagine, their fresh viewpoints, and the sometimes puzzling, sometimes profound interpretations they offer. For most of us, childhood is a time of exploration and rationalization of the world, micro-acts of scientific discovery. And most of the time we get it all wrong.

The Art of Abductive Reasoning

Playing pretend is key to abductive reasoning. We don't have all the relevant data, so we make our best guess, pretend it's correct and see what happens. Kids do it constantly, building up a storehouse of knowledge by starting with their imaginings, then tempered by real-world events. Toddlers learn so much through trial and error, and who knows what imaginings lead them to try the things they do (Figure B.1)? Over time, with coaching from adults, peers, and the world itself, we spend less and less time imagining alternative worlds.[1]

That is, unless you're an artist or a designer. These individuals spend a considerable amount of time imagining the world as it could be—whether as

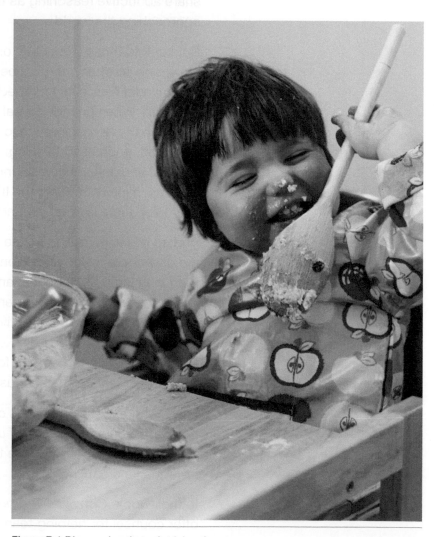

Figure B.1 Discovering through trial and error

361

an expression of a personal point of view or in service of a patron. Art, as Plato argued so vehemently, is so wrong, on so many levels, it is unfit for civil society.[2] Art, it turns out, is the expression of error; it is a purposeful effort to render a world, not as it *is* but as it is perceived or imagined to be.

Where art is pursued for personal expression, design is pursued in service of someone or something else. Regardless of their motivation, the two disciplines share abductive reasoning as their primary process for approaching the world.

But back to those kids. Early on, our theories about the world are wrong so often we must be protected from ourselves. What would happen if I jumped off this rock? These stairs? This cliff? When provided a safe environment to explore, however, these imaginary theories become the basis for extended, engrossed thinking: the endless playing with dolls, houses, and action figures. Unless the testing of the theories ends up in injury (running the tricycle into a brick wall, for example), there is great joy and delight in these engagements.

And so it is with PrD. In a safe environment in which adults are given permission to reason abductively, the room is filled with laughter, surprise, and delight. The PrD Creation Session is a designed experience, specifically focused on enhancing the team's abductive reasoning. Getting everyone to agree it's okay to be "silly" can be a challenge: Not all team members are prepared for silliness in an engagement ostensibly meant to be serious.

The Creation Session implies *creativity*. Abductive reasoning requires people to *make stuff up*. Therefore, for the Creation Session to be successful, the team needs to recognize and leverage its creativity.

In their book, *Convivial Toolbox*, Sanders and Stappers offer counsel for helping teams recognize their own creativity.[3] First, we must accept everyone is creative, but for some it is latent. Individuals reside in one of four levels of creativity: doing (getting something done), adapting (making things better), making (crafting with one's own hands), and creating (expressing one's ability). Depending on the context, each of us inhabits a particular level at any given time.

Some people move to higher levels because:

- They are motivated.

- They have an innate ability that fits with their chosen context.

- They have gained experience with creating things over time.

In any given group individuals will vary in their attainment of these levels.

The authors offer four principles they believe establish common ground for teams entering into a Creation Session:

1. All people are creative.

2. All people have dreams.

3. People will fill in what is unseen and unsaid based on their own experience and imagination.

4. People project their needs onto ambiguous stimuli because they are driven to make meaning.[4]

PrD embraces these same principles, notably, the two addressing ambiguity. As the early 20th century educationalist Graham Wallas suggested in his seminal book on creativity, *The Art of Thought*, creativity happens over time and emerges through five stages: preparation, incubation, intimation, illumination, and verification.[5]

We offer activities for these stages in the remainder of this appendix. We organize the activities in the order in which attendees experience them.

Creation Session Activities

The purpose of this appendix is not to provide an exhaustive set of exercises that build teams, break ice, inspire creativity, or improve prototyping skills. We offer examples to show how we structure the Creation Session. Naturally, which exercise we choose depends on the objectives of the effort—PrD always comes back to the objectives.

Prework

Prework is essential to priming Creation Session attendees' thinking, equivalent to Wallas's notion of preparation. In many workshops, brainstorming is used to get the ball rolling; attendees are asked to brainstorm about a problem, for example. We improve the Creation Session by asking attendees to consider a problem statement in advance. Making the problem statement a prework activity accomplishes several objectives:

1. It prepares the attendees for the Creation Session by focusing their attention on the problem(s) in advance.

2. It allows for a period of incubation between their consideration of the problems and the actual session.

3. It frees up time during the session to engage in more synthetic activities (as opposed to analyzing the problem).

4. It supports team building by revealing problem statements that are shared by multiple individuals.

This is not to suggest prework is limited to problem statements. We've requested several types of prework from Creation Session attendees:

- The assumptions the team holds dear

- The key markets they believe the company should pursue

- The most important objectives to achieve on the project

Any focus that ultimately moves *the goals of the session* forward is game. The key is to start attendees thinking about those goals in advance.

We use the prework as the participants' entry ticket to the workshop. We leverage it to prime internal stakeholders as discussed at the start of this section. We also use their responses during the Creation Session. In the session, we focus attendees' attention on their prework responses to identify the issues most important to the group as a whole.

Prework Logistics

We ask internal stakeholders to return their prework at least three days in advance of the session and make it a prerequisite of attending. In addition to signaling the high expectations and quality for the session, it raises the attendees' level of attention to the work itself.

We request the prework to be returned digitally—usually by email, but perhaps on a shared location—and we process the work to prepare it for the Creation Session.

Here's an example in which we ask participants to offer the top three challenges they perceive about the effort. We send out the following request to prospective attendees:

> Thank you for your interest in participating in the New Venture Visioning workshop. You've been invited because of your knowledge and expertise. To help make the workshop a success for you and the other attendees, please complete and return the prework described below by (one week) from today. We estimate the prework will take less than 30 minutes to complete.
>
> Prework is answering a maddeningly simple question: *What are the top three challenges New Venture must address within the next three years?*
>
> Please format your answers as follows:
>
> *Challenge Statement 1 (20 words or less)*
>
> (Brief paragraph explaining the challenge—100 words or less)
>
> *Challenge Statement 2 (20 words or less)*
>
> (Brief paragraph explaining the challenge—100 words or less)

Challenge Statement 3 (20 words or less)

(Brief paragraph explaining the challenge—100 words or less)

After collecting incoming statements, we print them on large sticky notes (5.5 × 8.5) in preparation for one of the first exercises in the Creation Session.

Arriving and Introductions

We exercise attendees' abductive reasoning to introduce each other and the workshop. Remember, the Creation Session is mostly theater. It's an Alice-Through-The-Looking-Glass environment in which abductive reasoning and silly make-believe are the norm. Every opportunity to shift participants' modes of thinking keeps them in an appropriate state of disorientation, at least disoriented from their usual day-to-day practice.

Figure B.2 Establish a theme for signage and badges

Arriving Off-Site

As mentioned in Chapter 15, hosting the Creation Session off-site reduces interruptions and distractions. But there's another benefit to hosting Creation Sessions in unfamiliar locations: enhancing the effect of separation from the "normal" way of doing things. As participants arrive, they see signage, carefully branded with the theme for the event. We position a table of name tags outside the door to the workshop room (Figure B.2); the tags are customized for the event.

(We discuss creating a theme and badging in more detail in the sections that follow.) These touches establish a sense of theater, signaling this meeting is out-of-the-ordinary before attendees pass through the door.

In many large organizations (where people are in meetings with others they've never met), meetings begin with introductions. Individuals offer their names, years of service, and what organizations they're in. For workshops, attendees are asked to embellish on the standard fare by offering what they hope to get out of the workshop. For Creation Sessions, we want the introduction to set the stage for abductive reasoning and creative delight. The name tags are the first of many props we use, telegraphing to internal stakeholders they are about to engage in something different from the usual all-day meeting.

Creating a Theme

We create name tags for larger Creation Sessions branded to the underlying theme of the PrD itself. For a sales-focused product, for example, we crafted a theme around famous salespeople through the ages. In addition to using the corporate brand, we embellished the name tags with a set of sales-oriented images. With each participant's name preprinted with whimsical imagery on the tag, we communicated a sense of both playfulness and seriousness.

We have created themes around collaboration, multinational projects, and explorers, to name a few. In each case, we brainstorm about the theme, identifying candidate images, exemplar individuals, or projects. The theme extends beyond the name tags, as we mentioned in Chapter 15. Signage, table tent cards (discussed further along), the program, imagery in presentations, posters, and the like all contribute and conform to the theme.

367

Introductions

We use the *imagery* on the name tags to serve a completely different purpose, an initially hidden but also playful intention. As we described in Chapters 10 and 15, we create teams based on a variety of attributes (role, personality, level of subject matter expertise, level of design expertise, e.g.). Getting attendees into their teams provides another opportunity for abductive reasoning. After arriving, name tags in place, coffee in hand, the internal stakeholders are called to attention by the Facilitator. The Facilitator welcomes them and lets them know the workshop will begin in a few minutes, after everyone has had a chance to meet each other and separate into their teams.

Finding Your Tribe

For introductions, we ask attendees to find other members of their team, based solely on the images on their name tags. Every attendee has a different image. While they may notice the image (because it is unusual to have a name tag at all, let alone one with a picture on it), rarely do attendees notice that everyone's image is different, until the Facilitator calls their attention to it.

We use a simple process to find appropriate imagery categories for each team and then appropriate images for each team member. Here is a small design problem in and of itself: identifying several *sets* of good images to enable clustering. For the "famous salespeople" theme, we first identified top salespeople through the ages. John Henry Patterson, the founder of NCR, for example, is considered one of the towering figures of sales. Without using anything specific to Patterson, we identified a variety of icons and images associated with Patterson. Selecting eight or so, we arbitrarily assigned an image to each member of team, placing it on each name tag.

Imagine the scene in which 30 people from four teams are mingling, trying to figure out whether the image on their badges are part of the same set as 29 other people. We don't inform them of the number of teams. We don't tell them how many people should be in their team. We don't give a clue about the nature of the images. What we do ask is for them to introduce themselves, as they usually do, to anyone they've never met before, and continue to try and solve the puzzle.

One of the key elements of this exercise (an element we return to in all of our Creation Session exercises) is multichannel or multimodal cognitive engagement. Rather than relying on a text-based way of solving the problem, we ask our participants to engage language *and* imagery to complete the exercise. For some this is a completely novel and disruptive exercise; for others it is merely delightful. This exercise, as with many others we employ, relies on "both sides of the brain." In doing so, we start people moving through the design thinking cycle by exercising their abductive reasoning.

Eventually, clusters appear in the crowd, and stragglers are left looking for help. The Facilitator asks each of the clusters to provide the overarching theme for their images, and the stragglers eventually find their way to their teams. In some cases, the Facilitator will have to offer the "decoder ring," to help get everyone properly situated.

In the end, the Facilitator asks if anyone sees another participant whom they've never met, and final introductions are completed before everyone is invited to sit at their team table.

Remember, the key point here is to set the stage for creativity and abductive reasoning, even during such prosaic activities as arrival and introductions.

With the group properly introduced and teams formed, we continue team building. Even if everyone already knows each other, they may not have had the opportunity to work together on a common problem. As discussed in Chapters 10

Team Building

and 15, we work hard to compose the teams in advance. We populate teams with individuals from all quadrants in the design thinking framework. Putting diverse people into a group is a good first step, but doesn't guarantee they'll cohere into a team. As in the "Introductions" exercise described earlier on, team building exercises are excellent opportunities to promote creativity and abductive reasoning.

Once again, we start with the theme. Just as we theme the session itself, we provide subthemes to help teams create their identity and brand. This isn't meant to drive competition (although a little bit of between-team competition can be useful in the Creation Sessions). It starts the cohesion process. Since these sessions are always short on time, we use whatever methods we can to move through the "forming"[6] stage. The attendees got a taste of their team theme during the introduction; their next touchpoint is at their table. As the Facilitator asks the teams to move to their table, members of the hosting team (marketing, UX, strategy) flip over a table card on each table.

For one Creation Session, in which the overarching theme was "working together," we chose monumental engineering projects as the team themes: the Eiffel Tower, Hoover Dam, International Space Station, etc. At each table, the table card provided the answer to the team's organizing theme. In addition to an image of the monument, the table card provided a brief paragraph relating the team's theme to the session. We take this opportunity to shape attendees' thinking, priming them for exercises to come.

Pictophone

We rely on several team building exercises, all of which share the common characteristic we mentioned previously: multimodal engagement by attendees. (At least two forms of mental processing are required to complete the exercise.) In one favorite of ours, a variation of a game popularly known as *Pictophone*, each table plays the familiar childhood game of "telephone," but with a twist (Figure B.3). As in the usual game, the Facilitator goes to each table, selects someone to start the game, and whispers a word or phrase in her ear. The prompt relates to the theme of the Creation Session or, more importantly, the focus of the PrD. Each team is usually, but not necessarily, offered a different phrase.

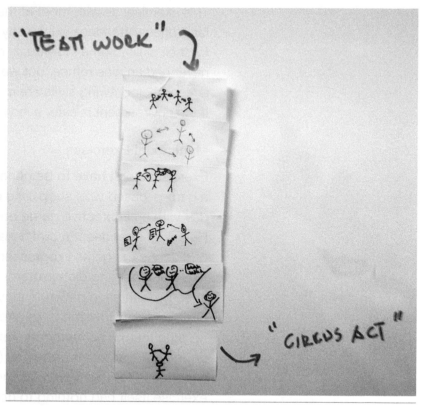

Figure B.3 A Pictophone example: "Team work" becomes "Circus Act"

In our variation of *Pictophone*, the first player must *draw an image* of the phrase she heard. She then passes the drawing to the next player, who must interpret it and whisper his interpretation to his neighbor next in line. (An alternative is to write a phrase and pass it to his neighbor.) And so it goes until the last player has drawn an image or announces his interpretation of the image provided to him. *Note*: All drawings must be kept guarded so downstream team members at the table don't get an advanced peek.

This particular exercise accomplishes several goals at once:

1. Of course, it builds teams by having everyone contribute to a common goal.

2. It continues the process of right-brain thinking for both the artist who's drawing what she's heard (or read) and the speaker who is interpreting what he sees.

Presumptive Design
DESIGN PROVOCATIONS FOR INNOVATION

This exercise, as with most of the Creation Session, requires facilitation. Attendees will be shy about drawing, or apologetic for their skills. Some individuals may protest or refuse (*we've* never had anyone refuse, but we *have* had to help individuals accept their drawing skills are more than adequate for the job). If the environment is safe, everyone actively engages.

Multimodal Exercises

Exercises don't have to be generic. To reinforce objectives of a games-based workshop, one of our associates started the day with an interactive game design exercise, a "metagame." He asked attendees to craft rules associated with the rolling of dice. As the game progressed, they needed to invent new rules for emerging dice patterns they hadn't encountered already. With each new rule they invented, they had to go back and consider the rules already in place, potentially revising them. The metagame experience was key to the attendees' purpose for the day (crafting a game-based experience for their own stakeholders), even though the exercise itself had nothing to do with the focus of the day.

Any exercise that drives multimodal interaction will work. Many of the exercises we use are culled from the discipline of improvisational comedy, again to establish an atmosphere of fun, spontaneity, and, yes, abductive reasoning. We start the morning session with an exercise, and we also use improv games later in the day, usually after lunch when energy is lagging.

One game we use to pump up the energy is a variation on *Monkey See, Monkey Do*. Teams are asked to stand up around the table or in a circle somewhere convenient in the room. The Facilitator usually demonstrates the exercise, since merely describing it can be difficult. In brief, participants are supposed to mime an action while describing a completely different action. For example, a team member might mime bouncing a ball, but say "I'm brushing my teeth." The next team member to the right must now mime brushing her teeth, and say "I'm petting a cat." And so it goes around the circle. The key to this exercise is the realization by everyone, almost immediately, how silly they and their teammates look. More important, individuals don't realize how challenging the activity is until it's their turn. We usually let the cycle go twice, to give people a practice round followed by mastery.

The room is usually very loud by the time that exercise is over, with a lot of laughing.

Whether in the morning or the afternoon, we use these exercises to put people in the right mood to tackle the more critical effort of the session: crafting an artifact that reveals their assumptions.

Affinitizing the Prework

An initial exercise in the Creation Session has attendees affinitize the prework statements we collected and printed (Figure B.4). Individuals take a stack of notes placing each one on a large open wall. Over the next 30 minutes, the statements begin to fall into clusters, and eventually somebody places a label above the clusters.

We do this exercise for several reasons:

- It demonstrates common themes across the group. Some individuals may think their challenge statements are unique, only to discover their concerns are shared by others.

Figure B.4 Affinitizing prework

373

- It allows everyone to see and "interact" with everyone else's statements, improving comprehension and possibly triggering other ideas.

- It gets people on their feet.

To the last point, going through the agenda, house rules, and other introductory material may take a half-hour of "downtime." We get people out of their seats and their blood moving to increase their creativity.

In a typical Creation Session, after the challenge statement affinitization, we ask teams to vote on the top three (five, 10, whatever makes sense) statements by marking the statements with a sticky dot or pen. One trick we've learned is to divide the total number of ideas by three; the result is the number of votes each individual has. Attendees can put all of their votes on one idea, or spread them around. Each team then selects one of the top scorers as their challenge statement. Using that statement as their focus, teams begin their first brainstorm exercise: "What will address this challenge?"

Ideation   Within every workshop is the need for generating ideas. Quantity over quality is the mantra. When we introduce brainstorming exercises, we also introduce ground rules to improve the teams' success.

Brainstorming Rules
- Defer Judgment.

- Encourage wild ideas!

- First thoughts first. Put down the first thing that comes to mind and don't over think your responses.

- Use the "yes and ..." rule, building on the ideas of others.

- Stay focused on the topic.

- Hold one conversation at a time.

- Be visual!

- Go for quantity over quality.

- Have fun!

All of these should sound familiar to anyone who's been in brainstorming sessions. Reminding attendees of the rules is essential, but it doesn't guarantee compliance. Be aware of seasoned veterans who have long since gotten over brainstorming and may be less cooperative or interested than their teammates.

We switch exercises up a little. Sometimes we use a process called "brainwriting."[7] Brainwriting expects individuals to silently write down as many ideas as they can think of in the first five minutes. After each person has a pile, the Facilitator prompts them to put their sticky notes up on a common board. With the ideas up, the team is asked to do the process again, but building on an idea they saw from someone else. A variation is to put ideas into a common "pool" in the center of the table. When individuals get stuck, they pull a card from the pool and use it for additional inspiration.

Another variation is to offer each team a "random" object (they may truly be arbitrary—things the hosting team has grabbed out of their desks, or perhaps from the junk prototyping materials) in the center of the table, and ask them to incorporate it into the ideas they're generating.

Of greatest importance, over anything else, is keeping the first brainstorm exercise short. Reducing the length of time in the first one, in particular, helps keep the pace, reduces the likelihood of overanalyzing, and gets those first ideas out on paper.

Innovation Games, Gamestorming, and the Convivial Toolbox

There exist entire books and businesses focused on creative exercises to engage stakeholders to generate ideas. The three books listed at the start of this section are just a few we have in our reference shelf.

Because PrD relies on crafting "an artifact from the future" for others to engage with, many of these exercises may not quite apply, or may need some adjustment.

For multiday workshops we don't attack the final artifact right at once, or all in a piece. We decompose the effort, ramping up the teams' creativity while simultaneously focusing them on the artifact.

News from the Future

This is a common exercise with several variations. It works well for teams with little graphical skills or who are highly verbal. The exercise is pure abductive reasoning: Teams are asked to write a newspaper article that has mysteriously and magically come from the future. The article is about the venture for which the Creation Session has been organized, written as if it has already been successful.

This exercise illuminates something odd about our brains. When we write something as if it is *going to occur*, we think about it completely differently from writing about something that has *already occurred*. By authoring the piece as if it has already happened, we suddenly need to consider all sorts of domino events that would have likely occurred as well. Those help shape or modify our original notions.

News from the future is one of the easiest, and most direct, expressions of PrD. The only reason it isn't PrD is stakeholders can't *use* the articles. We have offered such science fiction stories to stakeholders to gauge their reaction, solicit their input, and the like, but simply reading about something is not the same as engaging with it.

As a result, we consider this a powerful exercise to loosen up the teams' thinking and get them ready for the big event, but in and of itself "News from the Future" is not a suitable artifact as an outcome.

A Key Feature

We have attendees at PrD workshops who have very little design experience. We have attendees who've not attended a design-based workshop. At the other extreme, designers who attend the workshops bring a sense of perfectionism that is definitely not what PrD is about.

We offer teams a "practice run" before we have them jump into the main event. After the initial exercises described earlier on, we have them identify a single feature of the new venture that must be offered over any other: a *key* feature (Figure B.5).

Figure B.5 Crafting a key feature

The exercise gives people practice in crafting artifacts. It begins with brainstorming (or brainwriting), usually limited to 15 minutes, to identify the key feature. Whether teams land on *the right* feature is immaterial. With that said, teams do become attached to the ideas they've generated in this brainstorm. They may revisit and embellish on the feature later on in the workshop. In the end, it doesn't matter, because eventually their artifact will be in front of stakeholders. The stakeholders will quickly let the team know what is of value or irrelevant.

After identifying the key feature, the teams are challenged to create an artifact expressing the feature. For extra credit they build one that stakeholders can use. This last bit is often more than the teams can achieve because it requires a solid understanding of prototype "design patterns."[8] The point is to get familiar with the cadence, rhythm, and challenges of creating artifacts.

As with all exercises, the "singular feature" exercise is timeboxed (no more than 60 minutes allotted, including brainstorming/ideation) to force the team to go with their first thoughts—their "gut" reaction.

The exercise ends with a brief, five-minute report out so the entire group can learn and share.

Artifacts from the Future

The "main event" of the workshop is to craft an artifact addressing the key challenges the teams have identified. As with "News from the Future," it is an abductive approach: creating an artifact, not which stakeholders *will* use, but one they have already used. (Eventually, during the Engagement Session, stakeholders will use the artifact, but during the Creation Session, teams must believe they are simply reproducing an artifact that already exists and has conveniently traveled back in time.)

We allocate at least three hours for this exercise. Once again, it begins with an ideation session, perhaps revisiting the challenge statements, but equally likely focusing on the task or tasks the team expects stakeholders to perform. By focusing on a task, the team must consider how the artifact will be used, a key attribute of the Engagement Session.

We suggest teams rapidly create three different solutions. In design school, we're taught to identify three completely divergent solutions to the same problem—so, too, in this exercise. Teams are urged to complete not just one artifact, but at least three artifacts addressing the challenge statement(s) or problem they've selected. Faced with that prospect, three hours isn't very much time. We don't expect the teams to develop each idea fully, but they should be prepared to report out on the three ideas, and provide justification for the one they believe should be offered to external stakeholders.

The Facilitator must be on her toes during this exercise to help teams keep track of the time. Teams significantly underestimate the amount of time they need to produce an artifact. About halfway through, we usually announce teams should be on their way to building something. We announce the remaining time every 30 minutes thereafter. Teams will overinvest in their creations, whether to get every detail correct, or to add features. It's like a real product development cycle in miniature, replete with uncertainty, scope creep, and a desire to make it the best.

The Facilitator continues to reinforce the end goal: to build an artifact that provokes a conversation addressing the objectives. In many cases, less is more: The more ambiguous an artifact, the more open ended it is for interpretation by the stakeholders. Team members, Designers in particular, may not fully appreciate the need for ambiguity and push for more definition, but every element added to the artifact is an assumption. Before adding to the artifact, therefore, the team should quickly determine whether the addition would provoke the right kind of conversation.

Breaking Boxes

Three Solutions

As mentioned in the prior section, when the Facilitator requests teams to create three divergent solutions, she is forcing them to do several things at once:

1. Remain aloof from any one solution, a critical attitude teams must maintain as they move into the Engagement Sessions.

2. Question their initial solution to get fresh perspectives on the problem space and their assumptions.

3. Move through the design thinking cycle.

This approach will be familiar to the Designers on the team, but may not be to others.

Devil's Advocate

As discussed in Chapter 10, homogeneity in groups reduces their ability to find novel solutions. After the Bay of Pigs disaster, President Kennedy requested a postaction review of how things went wrong.[9] The review identified a key problem with the process Kennedy used: He didn't permit naysayers on his team to challenge his assumptions. Even if he wasn't conscious of it, his seniority in the group carried a tacit belief with the rest of the team his assumptions shouldn't be questioned.

Kennedy reconfigured his team process. In subsequent engagements, a specific individual was appointed as the "devil's advocate," to explicitly oppose the current approach the team was taking. The opposing view is designed to disrupt groupthink before it becomes counterproductive.

Consider offering this option to teams, especially if there is already a contrarian in the mix. By legitimatizing the role, the Facilitator defuses dysfunctional team dynamics. Assigning a devil's advocate increases the team's ability to devise divergent outcomes.

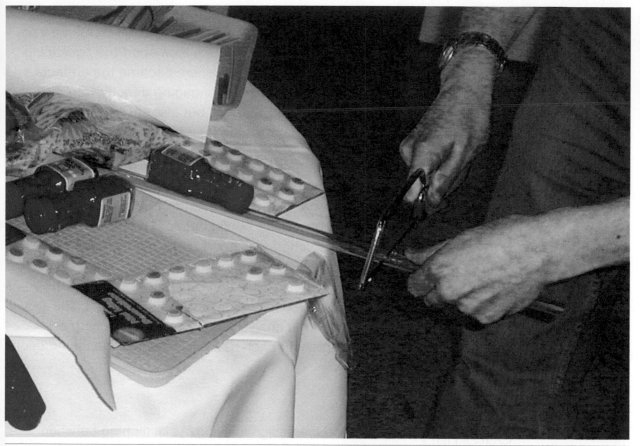

Figure B.6 Building artifacts by breaking boxes

All of the previous sections provide a lengthy discussion of how to break our participants' mental boxes. There comes a time in every Creation Session when participants literally break real boxes (Figure B.6).

In The Case of the Pushy Pillboxes, Leo learned firsthand the differences in approach designers and researchers took when creating an artifact from the future. Designers, and especially industrial designers, immediately began crafting solutions by sketching and imagining outcomes. The researchers spent their time analyzing the likely tasks, decomposing the steps, and charting key pieces of the experience on whiteboards.

Literally Breaking Boxes

Designers and researchers take very different paths in their approach to solving a problem.

See Appendix A: The Case of the Pushy Pillboxes

More intriguing were the materials designers used to craft their artifacts. Although a wide variety of stuff was offered, many of the industrial designers *took apart the packaging* and used it. The plastic containers became the artifacts. Not only were the designers engaging directly with the materials almost immediately, but also they were using "meta materials" to express their ideas.

That experience was extreme but not unique: Designers tear stuff apart. Even while a design is evolving, designers tear it apart, literally, and put the pieces back together in some other configuration. Through this physical destruction, designers make manifest the internal box breaking they are doing. This act of reconfiguration expresses the design thinking cycle more clearly than any other. As the designer reflects on the artifact, she crosses over from analysis to concept, envisioning a different approach. Each new cycle involves deconstruction of the prior.

Summary

PrD rests on the design thinking cycle: flipping between creating artifacts and evaluating them. The Creation Session is a journey through the design thinking cycle, from the moment attendees arrive until they have crafted an artifact. Many attendees will not be familiar with the design thinking cycle; others will not feel confident in their creativity. The objective of the session is to have everyone contribute to artifact creation with good humor and delight.

Although we mention a few of our favorite exercises and approaches, there are hundreds to choose from. We bias ours toward multimodal thinking because it facilitates moving people through the design thinking cycle. We design our Creation Sessions to be mildly disorientating. In their disorientation, attendees maintain a fresh perspective, both during the concept stage and during the analysis stage.

- Prepare attendees for the Creation Session by requiring prework.

- Consider hosting the session off-site, to disrupt the normal environment.

- Imbue every encounter with abductive reasoning, from the arrival, introductions, team building, and artifact creation.

- Get people on their feet, early and often. Creativity flourishes with an active mind and body.

- Pick activities and exercises to build up to the main event, allowing attendees to practice their design thinking skills.

- Keep up the pace. Purposely reduce the time for an exercise by 15%. Brainstorming isn't improved by letting time drag on.

- Help participants reduce their investment in their artifacts by having them create more than one, preferably three if time permits.

Contributor Biographies

S. Joy Mountford rebuilt the original Apple Human Interface Group to four times its size, building seminal products such as QTime, navigable movies. She is the founder of the university Design Expo, running for over 20 years. She originated interactive music projects over the Internet at Interval Research, alongside tangible musical products and books. She was Head of the Design Innovation Group at Yahoo and a VP of UXD, where she developed a showcase portfolio of data visualization projects helping explain large data sets. She speaks extensively on design thinking and how to use design effectively to innovate in corporations.

"Design to Engage" team members collaborated as graduate students at the IIT Institute of Design. Diego Bernardo (MDes, 2013) is now a design strategist at the University of Pittsburgh Medical Center. Maggee Bond (MDes, 2014) is a researcher at gravitytank, a design innovation firm based in Chicago, IL. Amanda Geppert (PhD candidate, 2016) is completing her doctoral degree exploring the democratization of codesign processes for civic capacity building. Alisa Weinstein (MDes, 2013) is senior design researcher at Uber Technologies in San Francisco, CA. Helen Wills (MDes, 2013) is a design research consultant working across product, service, and brand innovation in Atlanta, GA. Janice Wong (MDes and MBA, 2013) is a design and insights lead at Doblin in Toronto, ON.

Anne Schorr is the cofounder of Conifer Research, a Chicago-based ethnographic research firm that specializes in helping clients develop user-centered products, services, and business strategies. Anne has over 15 years of consulting experience helping clients gather and apply critical consumer insight. She has an enduring passion for research that has taken her around the globe to study topics as wide ranging as health practices in rural African villages to "smart" schools in Hong Kong.

Evan Hanover is the Director of Research at Conifer Research in Chicago, IL. There he is an anthropologist whose fascination with language drives a passion to understand the underlying meaning and value users impart to their lives and experiences. He also enthusiastically draws on his experience in improv theater to facilitate collaboration and bring user insights to life in client presentations and workshops. Outside the office, he plays the role of photographer for Chicago's robust theater community for which his work has appeared in such publications as the *Chicago Tribune*, *American Theater Magazine*, and the *New York Times.*

Jaime Rivera is a PhD student at the IIT Institute of Design, where he is exploring the intersections of cognitive science, technology, and experience design with the purpose to facilitate positive behavior change. His research proposes a structured participatory approach using provotypes (prototypes to provoke) to study how people react when an uncommon experience challenges their established assumptions about how technology influences behavior.

Steve Sato is the founder of Sato + Partners, a management and organization development consulting firm specializing in developing experience design and innovation strategies and organizational capabilities. He has cultivated and built design capability at a Fortune 20 tech firm and has an additional more than 20 years of management consulting experience working with Fortune 500 companies and nonprofits to develop customer-centered strategies, operationalize the plans, and build required experience design capability. Steve has a Master's in Design from the Institute of Design, Master of Engineering Management from Northwestern University, and a Bachelor's of Science in Mechanical Engineering from the University of Illinois.

Janna C. Kimel's 20 years in design and research has run the gamut from sitting at a sewing machine, sewing apparel and prototypes, to conducting qualitative research and strategizing the best way to integrate the voice of the customer. She has run her own consultancy, worked for Intel and Regence Blue Cross Blue Shield, and consulted with the likes of Ziba, IDEO, Microsoft, and Lunar. Motivation, behavior change, customer experience, and wearable technology are subjects she is passionate about, which means writing and presenting to share the gospel. She's a ramblin' wreck from Georgia Tech where she earned a Master's degree in Industrial Design.

Steve Portigal helps companies to plan strategically for user research and to unlock their team's research superpowers. He is principal of Portigal Consulting, author of *Interviewing Users: How to Uncover Compelling Insights*, and host of the *Dollars to Donuts* podcast. He makes his home in the San Francisco Bay Area where there's always a new ramen restaurant to check out.

Christopher Stapleton is the lead Creative Venture Catalyst at Simoisys Real World Laboratories, where he pursues the "art of innovation to enhance the human experience." He applies his work in experience design innovation to transforming lives with the next generation of entertainment, education, training, commerce, and health services. His background working in film, television, computer graphics, and on Broadway has translated into designing and producing mega-theme parks for Universal, Disney, and Nickelodeon. His pioneering work with Mixed Reality as the Founding Research Director of the UCF Media Convergence laboratory has transformed into starting his own design research firm, Simiosys.com.

David McKenzie is currently the Design Fellow at The Ohio State University, investigating prototyping in the front end of participatory design research to explore user needs and future concerns. He studied Product Design at the University of Edinburgh before practicing as a designer/maker. He also spent several years working in Korea as an educator while continuing his practice before returning to academia to explore and contribute to the field of design research.

List of Figure Credits

Except as noted, all figures are the authors' or in the public domain.

Part 1

Frontispiece: "You are here" by Joe Goldberg is licensed under CC BY 2.0

Chapter 1

Figure 1.2: "Emerging Landscape of design research methods" is adapted by permission from Convivial Toolbox, Sanders, L. & Stappers, P.J.

Figure 1.3: "Research approaches" is adapted by permission from Miki Konno

Figure 1.5: "What's on your iPhone home screen?" by Tony Buser is licensed under CC BY-SA 2.0

Chapter 2

Figure 2.1: "Differences: Discrimination among Fields" is adapted by permission from Charles Owen

Figure 2.2: "Hierarchy: Fields Decompose to" is adapted by permission from Charles Owen

Figure 2.3: "Differences: Design and Science are Complementary" is adapted by permission from Charles Owen

Figure 2.4: "Two-domain Creativity Model" is adapted by permission from Charles Owen

Figure 2.5: "Two-domain Creativity Model" is adapted by permission from Charles Owen

Figure 2.6: "Two-domain Creativity Model" is adapted by permission from Charles Owen

Figure 2.7: "Design Thinking" is adapted by permission from Steve Sato

Figure 2.8: "Design vs. Conventional Thinking" is adapted by permission from Steve Sato

Figure 2.9: "Design Thinking" is adapted by permission from Steve Sato

Figure 2.10: "Laseau's Funnel" is adapted by permission from Paul Laseau

Figure 2.11: "Design vs. Engineering Thinking" is adapted by permission from Bill Buxton

Figure 2.12: "Double Diamond Diagram" is adapted by permission from UK Design Council

Figure 2.13: "Design Thinking" is adapted by permission from Steve Sato

Figure 2.14: "Design Thinking" is adapted by permission from Steve Sato

Figure 2.15: "Design Thinking" is adapted by permission from Steve Sato

Part 2

Frontispiece: "Bascula9" by L. Miguel Bugallo Sánchez is licensed under CC BY-SA 3.0

Chapter 4

Figure 4.1: "Design Thinking" is adapted by permission from Steve Sato

Figure 4.2: "Windows Exchange Error Message" by Ivan Walsh is licensed under CC BY 2.0

Chapter 5

Figure 5.1: "Design Thinking" is adapted by permission from Steve Sato

Figure 5.3: "Laseau's Funnel" is adapted by permission from Paul Laseau

Figure 5.5: "Chocolate Hills overview" by P199 is licensed under CC BY-SA 3.0

Figure 5.6a: "193/365: Paper boat" by Magic Madzik is licensed under CC BY 2.0

Chapter 6

Figure 6.7: "Conventional Thinking" is adapted by permission from Steve Sato

Figure 6.9: "Three Cards" by ZioDave is licensed under CC BY-SA 2.0

Chapter 7

Frontispiece: "Sturbridgemill" by Keitei is licensed under CC BY-SA 3.0

Chapter 8

Figure 8.1: "Pokeravond" by Thomas van de Weerd is licensed under CC BY 2.0

Figure 8.2: "Double Diamond Diagram" is adapted by permission from UK Design Council

Chapter 9

Frontispiece: "Escaping the flood" is adapted by permission from Shutterstock

Chapter 10

Figure 10.3: "Asch experiment" by Fred the Oyster is licensed under CC BY-SA 3.0

Chapter 11

Figure 11.2a/b: "checkershadow images" is adapted by permission from Edward H. Adelson

Part 3

Frontispiece: "Interhotel 'Stadt Berlin', Auszubildende" by Bernd Settnik is licensed under CC BY-SA 3.0 DE

Chapter 14

Frontispiece: "Zan Zig performing with rabbit and roses" by Trialsanderrors is licensed under CC BY 2.0

Figure 14.10: "Path signage errors" is adapted by permission from Jon Meads

Figure 14.11: "Operational/Functional traps" is adapted by permission from Jon Meads

Chapter 16

Figure 16.1: "JellyBellyBeans" by Brandon Dilbeck is licensed under CC BY-SA 3.0

Figure 16.3: "Mobil Gas Station Rt.1" by Anthony92931 is licensed under CC BY-SA 3.0

Appendix A

Figure A.1: "Street chalkboard" is adapted by permission from Alisa Weinstein

Figure A.2: "Prompt book" is adapted by permission from Alisa Weinstein

Figure A.3: "Participatory games" is adapted by permission from Jaime Rivera

Figure A.4: "Skywords installation" is adapted by permission from Jaime Rivera

Figure A.12: "Smartwatch" is adapted by permission from Janna Kimmel

Figure A.13: "Pill bottle reminder" is adapted by permission from Janna Kimmel

Figure A.16: "iPhone Mirror" is adapted by permission from David McKenzie

References

Chapter 1

[1] IDEO. Human-centered design toolkit: an open-source toolkit to inspire new solutions in the developing world. 2nd ed. IDEO; 2011. Retrieved on July 24, 2014, from: http://www.ideo.com/images/uploads/hcd_toolkit/IDEO_HCD_ToolKit.pdf.

[2] Koskinen I, Zimmerman J, Binder T, Redstrom J. Design research through practice: from the lab, field, and showroom. Waltham, MA: Morgan Kaufmann Publishers; 2011.

[3] Owen C. Design thinking: notes on its nature and use. Des Res Q 2007;2(1):16–27.

[4] Brown T. Design thinking. Harvard Business Review; 2008. Retrieved on August 11, 2014, from: http://hbr.org/2008/06/design-thinking/.

[5] Schaffer RH. Four mistakes leaders keep making. Liberty Mutual Insurance; 2010. Retrieved on August 11, 2014, from: http://responsibility-project.libertymutual.com/articles/four-mistakes-leaders-keep-making.

[6] *Ibid.*

[7] Reeves M, Deimler M. Adaptability: the new competitive advantage. Harvard Business Review; 2011. Retrieved on March 16, 2015, from: https://hbr.org/2011/07/adaptability-the-new-competitive-advantage.

[8] Garvin DA, Roberto MA. What you don't know about making decisions. Harvard Business Review; 2001. Retrieved on July 9, 2014, from: https://hbr.org/2001/09/what-you-dont-know-about-making-decisions.

[9] Sanders EN, Stappers PJ. Convivial toolbox: generative research for the front end of design. Amsterdam, The Netherlands: BIS Publishers; 2013.

[10] Dunne A. Hertzian tales: electronic products, aesthetic experience, and critical design. Cambridge, MA: The MIT Press; 2005.

[11] Konno M, Fong B. Agile UX research practice in Android. San Francisco, CA: Google I/O; 2013.

[12] Nielsen J. Interviewing users. NN/g; 2010. Retrieved on July 21, 2014, from: http://www.nngroup.com/articles/interviewing-users/.

[13] Nielsen J. First rule of usability? Don't listen to users. NN/g; 2001. Retrieved on April 21, 2014, from: http://www.nngroup.com/articles/first-rule-of-usability-dont-listen-to-users/.

[14] Brooks FP. The mythical man-month: essays on software engineering. Anniversary ed. Boston, MA: Addison-Wesley Longman Publishing Co, Inc; 1995. p. 116.

[15] McGrath RG. Transient advantage. Harvard Business Review; 2013. Retrieved on August 13, 2014, from: http://hbr.org/2013/06/transient-advantage/ar/1.

[16] Gothelf J, Seiden J. Lean UX: applying Lean principles to improve UX. Sebastopol, CA: O'Reilly Media, Inc; 2013.

[17] Porter ME. What is strategy? Harvard Business Review 1996;74(6):61–78.
[18] Reeves and Deimler, *op. cit.*
[19] Edwards B. Drawing on the right side of the brain: a course in enhancing creativity and artistic confidence. New York: Penguin Group, Inc; 2012.

Chapter 2

[1] Rucker S. How good designers think. Harvard Business Review; 2011. Retrieved on August 11, 2014, from: http://blogs.hbr.org/2011/04/how-good-designers-think/.
[2] Owen C. Design thinking: notes on its nature and use. Des Res Q 2007;2(1):16–27.
[3] Kumar V. A process for practicing design innovation. J Business Strategy 2009;30(2/3):91–100.
[4] Kumar V. 101 design methods: a structured approach for driving innovation in your organization. Hoboken, NJ: John Wiley and Sons, Inc; 2012.
[5] Sato S. Using design thinking to measure design's impact: a systemic approach. CHIFOO; 2014. Retrieved on December 12, 2014, from: http://www.chifoo.org/filestorage/CHIFOO_DTMetricsFinal.pdf.
[6] Buxton B. Sketching user experiences: getting the design right and the right design. San Francisco, CA: Morgan Kaufmann Publishers; 2007.
[7] Design Council. Eleven lessons: managing design in eleven global brands. Designcouncil; 2007. Retrieved on March 7, 2015, from: http://www.designcouncil.org.uk/knowledge-resources/report/11-lessons-managing-design-global-brands.

Chapter 3

[1] Andreessen M. Why software is eating the world. The Wall Street Journal; 2011. Retrieved on March 12, 2015, from: http://www.wsj.com/articles/SB10001424053111903480904576512250915629460.
[2] McGrath RG. Transient advantage. Harvard Business Review; 2013. Retrieved on August 13, 2014, from: http://hbr.org/2013/06/transient-advantage/ar/1.
[3] Snowden DJ, Boone ME. A leader's framework for decision making. Harvard Business Review; 2007. Retrieved on March 6, 2015, from: https://hbr.org/2007/11/a-leaders-framework-for-decision-making/.
[4] Disruptive innovation. In: Wikipedia, the free encyclopedia; 2015. Retrieved on March 8, 2015, from: http://en.wikipedia.org/w/index.php?title=Disruptive_innovation&oldid=650169737.
[5] Christensen CM. The innovator's dilemma: when new technologies cause great firms to fail. Boston, MA: Harvard Business Review Press; 1997.

[6] Chesbrough H. Open innovation: the new imperative for creating and profiting from technology. Boston, MA: Harvard Business School Press; 2003.

[7] Ulwick A. What customers want: using outcome-driven innovation to create breakthrough products and services. New York: McGraw-Hill; 2005.

[8] Francis S. Phil Gilbert on IBM's design thinking. BP-3; 2013. Retrieved on August 14, 2014, from: http://www.bp-3.com/blogs/2013/05/phil-gilbert-on-ibms-design-thinking/.

[9] Weinzimmer LG, McConoughey J. The wisdom of failure. San Francisco, CA: Jossey-Bass; 2013.

[10] Schrage M. Serious play: how the world's best companies stimulate to innovate. Boston, MA: Harvard Business School Press; 2000.

[11] Frenken K. Innovation, evolution and complexity theory. Cheltenham, UK: Edward Elgar Publishing, Inc; 2006. p. 11.

[12] Randle W. Mutation driven innovation. TEDx talks; 2015. Retrieved on March 8, 2015, from: http://tedxtalks.ted.com/video/Mutation-Driven-Innovation-%7C-Dr.

[13] The key was to change the working relationship by dramatically slashing the time spent on requirements analysis. Rather than gathering requirements from dozens of users, and then prioritizing, circulating, and seeking approval before initiating prototype development, the team identified the top 20 or 30 requirements as quickly as possible and stopped. The goal was to present the client with a quick-and-dirty prototype within a fortnight. Why? Because it's far easier for clients to articulate what they want by playing with prototypes than by enumerating requirements. People don't order ingredients from a menu; they order a meal. The quick-and-dirty prototype is a medium of codevelopment with the client. Quick-and-dirty prototypes can turn clients into partners, enabling developers to manage expectations and deal with changing requirements more responsively. See Schrage, *op. cit.* p. 19.

Chapter 4

[1] PrD is very similar to IDEO's notion of "sacrificial concepts." See IDEO. Human-centered design toolkit: an open-source toolkit to inspire new solutions in the developing world. 2nd ed. IDEO; 2011. Retrieved on July 24, 2014, from: http://www.ideo.com/images/uploads/hcd_toolkit/IDEO_HCD_ToolKit.pdf. Their process is to frame an abstract question as a hypothetical scenario with two options the interviewee must choose between. PrD is similar in that the scenario doesn't need to be feasible; its only purpose is to gain understanding. As IDEO states, "A good sacrificial concept sparks a conversation, prompts a participant to be more specific in their stories, and helps check and challenge your assumptions" (p. 60). The difference here is the sacrificial concept itself is our design idea and the physical artifact built to represent it. These

are treated as provocations to stimulate stakeholder dialogue and participatory design.

[2] Spool calls this "hunkering," which describes the process of throwing artifacts out into the world to see how they work when they're no longer just our imagination. He notes that although it's important to throw design ideas away, we might not want to literally throw our physical artifacts out. They can become very useful in communicating the team's thinking process and journey. See Spool J. Design's fully-baked deliverables and half-baked artifacts. User Interface Engineering; 2014. Retrieved on July 31, 2014, from: http://www.uie.com/articles/artifacts_and_deliverables/.

[3] Beyer H. User-centered agile methods. San Rafael, CA: Morgan & Claypool; 2010.

[4] Brooks FP. The mythical man-month: essays on software engineering. Anniversary ed. Boston, MA: Addison-Wesley Longman Publishing Co, Inc; 1995.

[5] We use the term "artifacts" instead of "prototypes." Traditional user-centered design focuses on capturing user needs, which are then translated into requirements to guide later design generation. Typically, by the time the team is ready to even start user testing, prototypes already need to be conceptually "usable" in terms of a series of prespecified tasks. Thus, low-fidelity prototypes tend to only be "lo-fi" in terms of representation – not conceptualization. PrD, like usability, is task-based, but at the beginning of exploration the artifacts used in the Engagement Sessions have often not been designed to support specific tasks. They are often crude and confusing, which is one reason we prefer to not call them "prototypes." Another is that "prototype" sounds less exploratory; it sounds like a representation of the final product and not one of many possible ideas.

[6] Our thinking here is very much along the lines of Spool's. He has argued that what he calls "artifacts" and "deliverables" most meaningfully differ not in terms of fidelity but in terms of *time*, depending on whether they are crafted before or after the decision-made point, the point when the final design direction is decided upon. Before this time, a wireframe is just a proposition that helps us understand the problem, i.e., it's an "artifact." After this time, after the decision-made point, the same-fidelity wireframe is no longer a proposition but a representation of the intended final design. It's no longer an artifact but a "deliverable." See Spool, *op. cit.*

[7] Sitkin SB. Learning through failure: the strategy of small losses. In: Cohen MD, Sproull LS, editors. Organizational learning. Thousand Oaks, CA: SAGE Publications; 1996. p. 541–78.

[8] Schulz K. On being wrong: adventures in the margin of error. New York: HarperCollins Publishers; 2010. p. 27.

[9] Edmondson AC. Strategies for learning from failure. Harvard Business Review; 2011. Retrieved on November 25, 2014, from: https://hbr.org/2011/04/strategies-for-learning-from-failure.

[10] Snowden DJ, Boone ME. A leader's framework for decision making. Harvard Business Review; 2007. Retrieved on March 6, 2015, from: https://hbr.org/2007/11/a-leaders-framework-for-decision-making/.

[11] *Ibid.* The authors discuss what they call the "Cynefin framework," which is a way of categorizing and differentiating between such decision environments.

[12] McGrath R. Failing by design. Harvard Business Review; 2011. Retrieved on November 25, 2014, from: https://hbr.org/2011/04/failing-by-design.

[13] Sitkin, *op. cit.*

[14] McGrath R. Are you squandering your intelligent failures? Harvard Business Review; 2010. Retrieved on November 25, 2014, from: https://hbr.org/2010/03/are-you-squandering-your-intel/.

[15] Bazerman MH, Watkins MD. Predictable surprises: the disasters you should have seen coming and how to prevent them. Boston, MA: Harvard Business School Press; 2004.

[16] Kahneman D, Tversky A. Choices, values, and frames. Am Psychol 1980;39(4):341–50.

[17] Wason PC. On the failure to eliminate hypotheses in a conceptual task. Q J Exp Psychol 1960;12(3):129–40.

Chapter 5

[1] This is not as strange or foreign a concept as it sounds at first. In fact, it is a common process in fields as diverse as design, mathematics, and the sciences. It's possible that Carroll, being a preeminent mathematician, was referencing a common practice in solving problems. Consider the process required to solve calculus integration problems: The first step in solving for the original function in an integral is to "guess." That is, you assume you have a solution and you work backwards, or cut it into pieces afterwards.

[2] Satell G. Before you innovate, ask the right questions. Harvard Business Review; 2013. Retrieved on December 8, 2014, from: https://hbr.org/2013/02/before-you-innovate-ask-the-ri.

[3] Laseau P. Graphic thinking for architects and designers. New York: Van Nostrand Reinhold Company; 1980.

[4] Norman D. Human-centered design considered harmful. Interactions 2005;12(4):14–9.

[5] Buxton B. Sketching user experiences: getting the design right and the right design. San Francisco, CA: Morgan Kaufmann Publishers; 2007.

[6] Gothelf J, Seiden J. Lean UX: applying Lean principles to improve UX. Sebastopol, CA: O'Reilly Media, Inc; 2013.

[7] Bilalić M, McLeod P. Why your first idea can blind you to a better one. Sci Am 2014;310(3). Retrieved on February 25, 2015, from: http://www.scientificamerican.com/article/why-your-first-idea-can-blind-you-to-better-idea/.

Chapter 6

[1] Mayo-Smith J. Two ways to build a pyramid. Information Week; 2001. Retrieved on March 7, 2015, from: http://www.informationweek.com/two-ways-to-build-a-pyramid/d/d-id/1012280.

[2] Reinertsen D. Disagree and commit: the risk of conflict to teams. Electronic Design; 2000. Retrieved on March 14, 2015, from: http://electronicdesign.com/energy/disagree-and-commit-risk-conflict-teams.

[3] Dray S. Questioning assumptions: UX research that really matters. Interactions 2014;21(2):82–5. Retrieved on March 18, 2015, from: http://doi.acm.org/10.1145/2568485.

[4] Roberts P. FDA: software failures responsible for 24% of all medical device recalls. Threat Post; 2012. Retrieved on March 14, 2015, from: https://threatpost.com/fda-software-failures-responsible-24-all-medical-device-recalls-062012/76720.

Chapter 7

[1] Beyer H. Getting started with UX inside agile development. In: UX Immersion Conference, Portland, OR, 2012.

[2] Weinzimmer LG, McConoughey J. The wisdom of failure. San Francisco, CA: Jossey-Bass; 2013.

[3] Mayhew D. The usability engineering lifecycle: a practitioner's handbook for user interface design. San Francisco, CA: Morgan Kaufmann Publishers; 1999.

[4] Buxton B. Sketching user experiences: getting the design right and the right design. San Francisco, CA: Morgan Kaufmann Publishers; 2007.

[5] GE UX Center of Excellence. The business value of UX. geuxcentral; 2012. Retrieved on October 25, 2013, from: http://files.geuxcentral.com/wp-content/uploads/Business_Value_of_UX.pdf.

[6] Nielsen J. Why you only need to test with 5 users. NN/g; 2000. Retrieved on March 14, 2015, from: http://www.nngroup.com/articles/why-you-only-need-to-test-with-5-users/.

Chapter 8

[1] For an excellent analysis of this common meme, see Clarke R. Information wants to be free … Xamax Consultancy Pty Ltd; 2012. Retrieved on March 15, 2015, from: http://www.rogerclarke.com/II/IWtbF.html. Although Stewart Brand was the first to say the words, the notion stretches back to Thomas Paine and Thomas Jefferson.

[2] Karat C. Cost–benefit analysis of usability engineering techniques. In: Proceedings of the human factors and ergonomics society.

Orlando, Florida, 1990. p. 839–43; Karat C. Cost-justifying usability engineering in the software life cycle. In: Helander M, Landauer T, Prabhu P, editors. Handbook of human–computer interaction. Amsterdam: Elsevier Science; 1997; Pressman RS. Software engineering: a practitioner's approach. New York: McGraw-Hill; 1992.

[3] Spool J. Design's fully-baked deliverables and half-baked artifacts. User Interface Engineering; 2014. Retrieved on July 31, 2014, from: http://www.uie.com/articles/artifacts_and_deliverables/.

[4] Buxton B. Sketching user experiences: getting the design right and the right design. San Francisco, CA: Morgan Kaufmann Publishers; 2007.

[5] Boer L, Donovan J. Provotypes for participatory innovation. In: Proceedings of the designing interactive systems conference. New York: ACM; 2012. p. 388–97.

[6] Nielsen J. First rule of usability? Don't listen to users. NN/g; 2001. Retrieved on April 21, 2014, from: http://www.nngroup.com/articles/first-rule-of-usability-dont-listen-to-users/.

[7] Medlock MC, Wixon D, Terrano M, Romero R, Fulton B. Using the RITE method to improve products: a definition and a case study. Orlando, FL: Usability Professionals Association; 2002. Retrieved on March 17, 2015, from: http://www.microsoft.com/en-us/download/details.aspx?id=20940.

[8] Nielsen J. Interviewing users. NN/g; 2010. Retrieved on March 14, 2015, from: http://www.nngroup.com/articles/interviewing-users/.

[9] Buxton, *op. cit.*

Chapter 9

[1] Carey H, Howard SG. Tangible steps toward tomorrow: designing a vision for early childhood education. In: Ethnography praxis in industry conference proceedings. Chicago, IL: AAA; 2009. p. 268–83.

[2] Clarke AC. Profiles of the future. London: Pan Books; 1973.

Chapter 10

[1] Asch SE. Effects of group pressure upon the modification and distortion of judgment. In: Guetzkow H, editor. Groups, leadership and men. Pittsburgh, PA: Carnegie Press; 1951. p. 177–90.

[2] Asch SE. Opinions and social pressure. Sci Am 1955;193(5):31–5.

[3] Schulz K. On being wrong: adventures in the margin of error. New York: HarperCollins Publishers; 2010. p. 149.

[4] Owen C. Design thinking: notes on its nature and use. Des Res Q 2007;2(1):16–27.

Chapter 11

[1] Wason PC. On the failure to eliminate hypotheses in a conceptual task. Q J Exp Psychol 1960;12(3):129–40. Wason argued that people do not naturally seek to falsify their beliefs. Klayman and Ha took issue with Wason's argument, noting that a positive test can still produce disconfirming results. For example, if a greater proportion of students are predicted to succeed in a graduate program than really do, selecting students predicted to succeed (and thereby conducting a positive test) will likely produce disconfirming results. This led them to argue what Wason called a "confirmation bias" was really more of a "positive test strategy." Their point is it is the *result* of a test and not the type of test itself that determines whether it's confirming or disconfirming. See Klayman J, Ha YW. Confirmation, disconfirmation, and information in hypothesis testing. Psychol Rev 1987;94(2):211–28. For our purposes, though, as Koslowski points out, the positive test strategy is still a bias toward confirmation in that people are still seeking data expected to be congruent with their hypotheses. See Koslowski B. Theory and evidence: the development of scientific reasoning. Cambridge, MA: MIT Press; 1996.

[2] Lord CG, Ross L, Lepper MR. Biased assimilation and attitude polarization: the effects of prior theories on subsequently considered evidence. J Pers Soc Psychol 1979;37:2098–109.

[3] Lord CG, Lepper MR, Preston E. Considering the opposite: a corrective strategy for social judgment. J Pers Soc Psychol 1984;47(6):1231–43.

[4] See Brehmer B. In one word: not from experience. Acta Psychol 1980;45:223–41. Brehmer compares real-world learning with classroom learning, pointing out that in the latter, there is always a gold standard; the teacher provides a "right" answer. In the real world, however, there often is no such gold standard and, in some complex environments, when we think we're learning from experience, we may be fooling ourselves.

[5] Einhorn H, Hogarth R. Confidence in judgment: persistence of the illusion of validity. Psychol Rev 1978;85:395–416.

[6] *Ibid.* Following Einhorn and Hogarth, we can represent each variable with a symbol, allowing a closer look at how these variables interact with each other: x, our judgment (here our decision to go with a specific design solution); x_c, our criterion for deciding on x (here that it seems to fit our up-front research); y, our assessment of the outcome of x (here that it was a good design decision); y_c, our criterion used for making our assessment (y) of x (here that there were no showstoppers); Φ, our selection ratio (here how many design solutions we actually try out and assess); br, our base rate (here how many of our solutions are deemed "good"); r, our correlation (here the relationship between our design judgments and their assessments). If, after a series of projects, we're reinforced to think x and y are highly related, and that we're really good at predicting what design ideas will be successful, then our experiences will compel us to defend our design intuitions and ideas since, usually, $y \geq y_c$. What this ignores

is that y and y_c also apply to many of our ideas where $x < x_c$ – ideas we wouldn't have even considered. This means many of the ideas we didn't consider or build and assess would have also produced no showstoppers (or satisfied whatever metric we use to assess the outcome). Our gut feel of the correlation between x and y may therefore be misleading. The probability of an error is the probability of a false-negative plus the probability of a false-positive, which is equal to $P(y < y_c|x \geq x_c) + P(y \geq y_c|x < x_c)$. The whole second half of the equation here is missing, so how are we supposed to know how accurate we really are? Say we do some user research and then go with our first, best-guess solution and build it. That's a *really* low selection ratio. When $\Phi < br$, we'll seem to be right more often than not even when the relationship between x and y is low. The base rate (br) is the proportion of design ideas that perform greater than or equal to y_c. Whenever this is greater than the proportion of possible solutions actually tried, the positive hit rate can be high even when $x \geq x_c$ doesn't do a good job of differentiating between good and bad design solutions. In English, whenever the selection ratio of design solutions tried out and assessed is less than the base rate of how many solutions would have been good, we'll likely be convinced of the power of our design intuition *even if it's not that great*. And if y_c (the criterion we're using to assess the outcome of our design decisions) is just that there weren't any showstoppers, the resulting base rate is likely quite high.

Chapter 12

[1] Carlos T. Reasons why projects fail. Project Smart; 2015. Retrieved on February 26, 2015, from: http://www.projectsmart.co.uk/reasons-why-projects-fail.php.

[2] The "SMART" acronym was introduced by Doran GT. There's a S.M.A.R.T. way to write management's goals and objectives. Manage Rev 1981;70(11):35–6. Over the years, however, different authors have said the letters in the acronym stand for different things. Our presentation is more in line with Yemm G. Leading your team: how to set goals, measure performance and reward talent. New York: Pearson Education; 2012.

[3] Dozens of books are available for ideas on creating artifacts. We particularly like the following: *Sketching User Experiences, the Workbook*, by Bill Buxton; *Paper Prototyping*, by Carolyn Snyder; *The Convivial Toolbox*, by Liz Sanders and Pieter Jan Stappers. These three provide substantial techniques on creating interesting provocations.

Chapter 14

[1] Portigal S. Interviewing users: how to uncover compelling insights. Brooklyn, NY: Rosenfeld Media; 2013.

[2] Fischoff B. Hindsight ≠ foresight: the effect of outcome knowledge on judgment under uncertainty. J Exp Psychol Hum Percept Perform 1975;104:288–99.

[3] Snyder C. Paper prototyping: the fast and easy way to design and refine user interfaces. San Francisco, CA: Morgan Kaufmann Publishers; 2003.

[4] Peyrichoux I. When observing users is not enough: 10 guidelines for getting more out of users' verbal comments. UXmatters; 2007. Retrieved on July 21, 2014, from: http://www.uxmatters.com/mt/archives/2007/04/when-observing-users-is-not-enough-10-guidelines-for-getting-more-out-of-users-verbal-comments.php.

[5] Ibid.

[6] Ibid.

[7] Rubin HJ, Rubin IS. Qualitative interviewing: the art of hearing data. 3rd ed. Thousand Oaks, CA: SAGE Publications, Inc; 2012.

[8] Seidman I. Interviewing as qualitative research. 4th ed. New York: Teachers College Press; 2013.

[9] Ibid.

[10] Schütz A. The phenomenology of the social world [Walsh G, Lenhert F, Trans.]. Chicago, IL: Northwestern University Press; 1967.

[11] Seidman, op. cit.

[12] Hyman HH, Cobb WJ, Fledman JJ, Hart CW, Stember CH. Interviewing in social research. Chicago, IL: University of Chicago Press; 1954.

[13] Portigal, op. cit.

[14] Young I. Mental models: aligning design strategy with human behavior. Brooklyn, NY: Rosenfeld Media, LLC; 2008.

[15] Wilson NL. Substances without substrata. Rev Metaphys 1959;12(4):521–39.

[16] Alreck PL, Settle RB. The survey research handbook. Homewood, IL: Richard D. Irwin, Inc; 1985.

[17] Ibid.

[18] Heyn ET. Berlin's wonder horse: he can do almost everything but talk – how he was taught. The New York Times, September 4; 1904.

[19] Snyder, op. cit.

[20] Peyrichoux, op. cit.

[21] Portigal, op. cit.

[22] Stubbs D. Usability and product development tutorial. Usability Architects, Inc; 1991 [unpublished manuscript].

[23] Spool J. Three questions you shouldn't ask during user research. User Interface Engineering; 2010. Retrieved on June 10, 2013, from: http://www.uie.com/articles/three_questions_not_to_ask/.

[24] Young, op. cit.

[25] Portigal, op. cit.

[26] Ohno T. Toyota production system: beyond large-scale production. Portland, OR: Productivity, Inc; 1988.

[27] Hawley M. Laddering: a research interview technique for uncovering core values. UXmatters; 2009. Retrieved on December 30, 2014,

from: http://www.uxmatters.com/mt/archives/2009/07/laddering-a-research-interview-technique-for-uncovering-core-values.php.

[28] *Ibid.*

[29] Simon N. The participatory museum. Museum 2.0. Santa Cruz, CA; 2010.

[30] Engeström J. Why some social network services work and others don't – or: the case for object-centered sociality. Zengestrom; 2005. Retrieved on August 1, 2014, from: http://www.zengestrom.com/blog/2005/04/why-some-social-network-services-work-and-others-dont-or-the-case-for-object-centered-sociality.html.

[31] Simon, *op. cit.*

[32] Stubbs, *op. cit.*

[33] Grammarist. Subjunctive mood. Grammarist; 2009–14. Retrieved November 10, 2014, from: http://grammarist.com/grammar/subjunctive-mood/.

[34] Sanders EN, Stappers PJ. Convivial toolbox: generative research for the front end of design. Amsterdam, The Netherlands: BIS Publishers; 2013.

Chapter 15

[1] Reichheld FF. The one number you need to grow. Harvard Business Review; 2003. Retrieved on March 19, 2015, from: https://hbr.org/2003/12/the-one-number-you-need-to-grow/ar/1.

Chapter 16

[1] Nielsen has made famous the claim that running five users in a usability test uncovers 85% of the usability issues present. Molich, who cocreated heuristic evaluation with Nielsen, has conducted a series of studies where independent teams of usability experts evaluate the same interface. He has consistently found that the results of different usability evaluations typically have little overlap with each other, suggesting that the five-user assumption is misleading. Running five users does not uncover the majority of issues a solution has, although it might uncover the majority of issues a single moderator will find using a specific inspection method, task set, and so on. It should be further pointed out, however, that identifying the majority of usability issues a system has is not even a useful goal. What we should focus on is quickly identifying enough issues to drive a fruitful iteration. See Nielsen J. Why you only need to test with 5 users. Alertbox; 2000. Retrieved on November 15, 2011, from: http://www.useit.com/alertbox/20000319.html; Molich R. Usability testing myths. Net Magazine; 2013. Retrieved on April 10, 2013, from: http://www.netmagazine.com/features/usability-testing-myths#comment-11227;

Molich R, Dumas JS. Comparative usability evaluation (CUE-4). Behav Inf Technol 2008;27:263–81; Molich R, Ede MR, Kaasgaard K, Karyukin B. Comparative usability evaluation. Behav Inf Technol 2004;23(1):65–74; Molich R, Jeffries R, Dumas JS. Making usability recommendations useful and usable. J Usability Stud 2007;2(4):162–79.

[2] Creswell JW. Qualitative inquiry & research design: choosing among five approaches. 2nd ed. Thousand Oaks, CA: SAGE Publications, Inc; 2007.

[3] Wengraf T. Qualitative research interviewing. London: SAGE Publications Ltd; 2001.

[4] Patton MQ. Qualitative evaluation and research methods. 2nd ed. Newbury Park, CA: SAGE Publications; 1990.

[5] If we don't know enough about the variables of interest for maximum variation sampling, random sampling may be a worthwhile option. With samples too small for valid statistical inferences, many consider random selection a waste of time. The aim here, however, would be to use random selection (i.e., each stakeholder on the list has an equal chance of being selected) of our low-N sample to increase the odds of theoretical diversity, in light of our not being able to plan for purposive maximum variation in identified variables of interest. With PrD, however, our sample size will be so small that we shouldn't use this approach unless we really have no hypotheses to go off of. See Wengraf, *op. cit.*

[6] Holtzblatt K, Wendell JB, Wood S. Rapid contextual design: a how-to guide to key technique for user-centered design. San Francisco, CA: Morgan Kaufmann Publishers; 2005.

[7] Kelley, on his personal website, shares he originally intended "OZ" to be an acronym standing for "offline zero," which described the fact that the "wizard" must interpret the user's inputs in real time. See Kelley JF. Where did the usability term Wizard of Oz come from? Musicman; 1980. Retrieved on March 12, 2015, from: http://www.musicman.net/oz.html.

[8] Gaver WW, Boucher A, Pennington S, Walker B. Cultural probes and the value of uncertainty. Interact Funol 2004;11(5):53–6.

[9] United States Department of Defense Education Activity. Hot wash: clean up and cool down after an exercise. DoDEA, vol. XI, issue 7; 2011. Retrieved on March 16, 2015, from: http://www.dodea.edu/Offices/Safety/upload/11_7.pdf.

Appendix A

[1] Mathew AP, MacTavish T, Donovan J, Boer L. Materialities influencing the design process. In: DIS'10, Proceedings of the 8th ACM conference on designing interactive systems, 2010. p. 444–5.

[2] Chang C. Before I die. Candychang; 2011. Retrieved on March 14, 2015, from: http://candychang.com/before-i-die-in-nola/.

[3] An adjunct mini-conference to the CHI2004 conference. Retrieved on March 24, 2015, from: http://www.chi2004icsidforum.org/.

[4] Frishberg L. Presumptive design, or cutting the looking-glass cake. Interactions 2006;13(1):18–20.

[5] Names have been changed to maintain confidentiality.

Appendix B

[1] Schulz K. On being wrong: adventures in the margin of error. New York: HarperCollins Publishers; 2010. p. 291.

[2] *Ibid.*, p. 326.

[3] Sanders EN, Stappers PJ. Convivial toolbox: generative research for the front end of design. Amsterdam, The Netherlands: BIS Publishers; 2013.

[4] *Ibid*.

[5] Wallas G. The art of thought. New York: Harcourt, Brace and Company; 1926.

[6] Tuckman BW. Developmental sequence in small groups. Psychol Bull 1965;63(6):384–99.

[7] Mycoted. Brainwriting. Mycoted; 2010. Retrieved on October 9, 2013, from: http://www.mycoted.com/Brainwriting.

[8] Greenberg S, Carpendale S, Marquardt N, Buxton W. Sketching user experiences: the workbook. Waltham, MA: Elsevier, Inc; 2011.

[9] Janis IL. Victims of groupthink: a psychological study of foreign-policy decisions and fiascoes. Boston, MA: Houghton Mifflin Company; 1972.

Index

Presumptive Design
DESIGN PROVOCATIONS FOR INNOVATION

Index

Presumptive Design
DESIGN PROVOCATIONS FOR INNOVATION

Index

414

Printed and bound by CPI Group (UK) Ltd, Croydon, CR0 4YY

03/10/2024

01040325-0004